Irish sporting lives

Irish Sporting Lives

EDITED BY Terry Clavin AND Turlough O'Riordan

Acadamh Ríoga na hÉireann
Royal Irish Academy

Irish sporting lives
First published 2022
Royal Irish Academy, 19 Dawson Street, Dublin 2
www.ria.ie

The biographies in this book are selected from the Royal Irish Academy's *Dictionary of Irish Biography* (© Royal Irish Academy 2009, 2018; published by Cambridge University Press, reproduced with permission), a comprehensive, scholarly biographical reference work for Ireland, treating the lives of persons from the earliest times to the present day, and encompassing every sphere of human activity. Access to the online version of the *Dictionary* is freely available at www.dib.ie

ISBN 978-1- 911479-85-7 (PB)
ISBN 978-1- 911479-63-5 (pdf)
ISBN 978-1- 911479-64-2 (epub)

British Library Cataloguing in Publication Data. A CIP catalogue record for this book is available from the British Library.

Copyeditor and project manager: Helena King
Book design by Fidelma Slattery
Index: Lisa Scholey
Printed in the UK by Clays

Royal Irish Academy is a member of Publishing Ireland, the Irish book publishers' association

5 4 3 2 1

A NOTE FROM THE PUBLISHER

We want to try to offset the environmental impacts of carbon produced during the production of our books and journals. For the production of our books this year we will plant 45 trees with Easy Treesie. The Easy Treesie – Crann Project organises children to plant trees. Crann – 'Trees for Ireland' is a membership-based, non-profit, registered charity (CHY13698) uniting people with a love of trees. It was formed in 1986 by Jan Alexander, with the aim of 'Releafing Ireland'. Its mission is to enhance the environment of Ireland through planting, promoting, protecting and increasing awareness about trees and woodlands.

Contents

Editors' note

We have selected 60 sporting lives from the over 540 people active in the sporting realm who feature in the Royal Irish Academy's *Dictionary of Irish Biography* (*DIB*). Aside from household names such as George Best, Jack Kyle, Christy Ring, Lady Heath, Vincent O'Brien, Alex Higgins and Jack Charlton, the volume will also inform readers about less well-known but equally fascinating figures. These include the only Wimbledon tennis finalist ever convicted of murder, New Zealand's most revered rugby captain and an athlete who won nine Olympic medals for the USA.

Certain lives included here are abridged versions of those originally published in the *DIB*; in most cases this was to reduce the non-sporting aspects of the biography. Others have been expanded or rewritten to reflect both recently published research and the widespread digitisation of newspapers. Finally, six new entries have been prepared especially for this volume (Brede Arkless, Jack Charlton, 'Ma' Copley, Mollie Gill, Anne O'Brien and Molly Seaton) and two existing entries (Elizabeth Le Blond and Dave Gallaher) have been completely rewritten.

First and foremost, subjects eligible for inclusion in this volume must have died. As a result, some of Ireland's most famous sports names such as Roy Keane, Katie Taylor, Brian O'Driscoll and Sonia O'Sullivan do not feature here. That aside, persons eligible for inclusion also must be born in Ireland with careers in Ireland (like Christy Ring), born in Ireland with careers outside Ireland (like George Best) or born outside Ireland with careers in Ireland (like Jack Charlton). In the last case, the biography focuses on the Irish career, even though the non-Irish career may also be of significance. An exception to our general rule is made for Brede Arkless, who had a non-Irish career but was raised in Ireland and whose birth abroad was entirely fortuitous.

Our selection aims at capturing the different eras and range of sporting experience contained within the *DIB*. The earliest life dates from the early nineteenth century, with most being concentrated from the late nineteenth to the mid-twentieth century. There are relatively few from the late twentieth century onwards because most sports stars from this era are still alive. The main sports—Gaelic games, soccer, rugby, athletics, horse racing and boxing—are well represented, but so too are minority sports such as croquet, cricket, tennis and hockey. Formerly popular sports such as fox hunting, archery and handball feature, while the presence of Australian Rules Football and baseball highlights the importance of the Irish diaspora. The 'all-rounder', Kevin O'Flanagan, who was a soccer and rugby international, as well as an athlete of note, represents a type that was once common in Irish sporting life.

Thirty per cent of our subjects are women, which provides a positive gender balance bearing in mind how women were discouraged from participating in most sporting activities until relatively recently. With interest in women's sports now on the rise in Ireland, some of the women selected may in time attain a greater prominence as early trailblazers. Perhaps this volume can play a small part in this process. In the light of a surge in research into women's sports history, the editors commissioned five new entries (Brede Arkless, 'Ma' Copley, Mollie Gill, Anne O'Brien and Molly Seaton) on women subjects specifically for this volume. The entry on Molly Seaton was only made possible by the publication of new research on her as recently as September 2020. The women featured are referred to by the surname by which they are most commonly known.

We have included lives of organisers, promoters and trainers, such as the world-renowned racehorse trainer Vincent O'Brien, the Gaelic Athletic Association's founder Michael Cusack, the prolific golf course designer George Baillie and the much-loved boxing promoter 'Ma' Copley, none of whom engaged physically in sport at an elite level. The same is true for Henry Dunlop and John Fortune Lawrence, who both played pivotal roles in the establishment of sporting infrastructure and competition in Victorian Ireland. Others like Iris Kellett, Jack Charlton, Mollie Gill and Kevin Heffernan enjoyed considerable success as direct participants in sport but were as noteworthy for their careers as trainers or organisers.

Our featured sportswomen and sportsmen were not necessarily chosen for being the best or the most successful at their sport, though there are plenty of those: Jack Dempsey, Kay Mills, Christy Ring, Vincent O'Brien, Dave Gallaher, May Hezlet and Martin Sheridan to name but a few. In selecting entries, we aimed primarily to provide readers with material that is informative and engaging, hence the inclusion of colourful characters such as 'Ma' Copley, Moss Keane and Lady Heath, as well as those who have intrinsically interesting careers, for instance Mike McTigue, Mabel Cahill, Shay Elliott, Ken Goodall and Brede Arkless. There are also a handful of infamous figures, most notably the convicted murderer, Vere Goold.

Those who achieved sporting firsts feature prominently. Beatrice Hill-Lowe was the first Irish woman to win an Olympic medal, Pat O'Callaghan was the first athlete representing an independent Ireland to win an Olympic gold medal and Jack Kyle inspired the Irish rugby team to its first Grand Slam. Sporting innovators like William McCracken, who drove an important development in soccer's evolution, are also given their due, as are those who show the courage and fortitude exhibited by Teresa Mullen in winning a gold medal at the Paralympics while enduring cancer. Finally, the editors have sought to draw attention to unjustly forgotten or neglected figures such as Beauchamp Day, who was arguably Ireland's greatest runner, and Anne O'Brien, who was one of the best women soccer players in the world.

Although certain patterns, themes and developments can be detected across the sixty featured biographies, they are, above all, there to be dipped into and out of, to be savoured in and of themselves. The idiosyncrasies of a life, its protagonist's capacity for asserting their primacy over, or defiance of, impersonal historical forces, is nowhere better exemplified than in sport. As Professor Paul Rouse shows in his introductory essay, it is still an arena in which myth is more important than history.

POSTSCRIPT:

Measurements, such as height, weight, altitude or distance, are given as appropriate to the context, and converted from imperial to metric, or vice versa, where necessary.

Terry Clavin and Turlough O'Riordan, March 2022

'Almanacked, their names live':
Sporting greatness in historic context

I

There are people in this book who can lay claim to being among the greatest sports people in Irish history. By any measure, they have been, or remain, sporting heroes. These are names that carry national and international renown, names that transcend the generations, names that have passed into wider popular culture, recorded in song and monument and place. George Best (p. 12) has lent his name to an airport, Lady Heath (p. 156) was commemorated on an Irish postage stamp, Dan Donnelly (p. 85) has his name mapped onto Donnelly's Hollow in The Curragh, May Hezlet's (p. 172) portrait hangs in the Ladies' Clubhouse in Portrush, and Steve 'Crusher' Casey (p. 43) has a statue erected to his memory in his home village of Sneem. Others, like Christy Ring (p. 309) and Jack Doyle (p. 91), are immortalised in song.

Why, precisely, are certain sportspeople considered greater than others? What are the measures of greatness that define a sporting life? Successes obviously matter in any such reckoning, and the likes of Kay Mills (p. 238), Vincent O'Brien (p. 258) and Anne O'Brien (p. 251) ended their careers laden with the highest honours. Certainly, there is a dent in the legend of any man or woman who does not achieve the ultimate accolade in their sport. Yet the heroic loss should not be dismissed. Molly Seaton's (p. 326) reputation rests on how she nearly defeated an England football team, almost on her own, while Jack Kyle's (p. 204) superlative skills stood out in sharper relief when he toured New Zealand with an out-matched Lions side. Harry Bradshaw (p. 27) became renowned not for his many victories, but for the extraordinary circumstances in which he lost the British Open. Greatness, moreover, is often forged in the face of defeat and adversity. Jim Smith's (p. 338) biography shows that he spent much of his distinguished Gaelic football career being unfairly vilified for a freak accident that caused the death of an opponent.

Do we root greatness in brilliance, however fleeting, or in the length of time played at the highest level? How do we measure those who burned brightly (Dan Donnelly, George Best, Ken Goodall (p. 145)), versus the longevity shown by Mollie Gill ((p. 137) who won an all-Ireland camogie title in her mid-forties) or by the 'Methusaleh' of boxing, Mike McTigue (p. 232)? Or how do we compare greatness on a local scale with that on an international one? How do we weigh Kay Mills's fifteen all-Ireland medals against the two Olympic gold medals won by Pat O'Callaghan (p. 270)? There is an additional complicating factor when considering team sports. Did the player make the team look great, or did the team make the player look great? Sometimes it can be both: Nicky Rackard's (p. 303) greatness inspired his fellow teammates to apply themselves to their hurling, leading to the emergence of a Wexford team strong enough to win him two all-Ireland medals.

A key measure of sporting greatness lies not just in the sporting act itself, but in the timing of that act. The capacity of players to bend a game to their will, to forge a victory when it matters most, when all appears lost, or at least uncertain, is essential. Thus, Pat O'Callaghan snatches his second Olympic gold with his final hammer throw; Iris Kellett (p. 198), needing a fast final round in the Princess Elizabeth Cup, 'galloped Rusty around the course, vaulting him over fences early and from improbable angles'; and Alex Higgins (p. 177), facing defeat in a crucial world championship snooker match, retrieves his position 'by sinking a succession of daunting pots that few other players would have contemplated'. Terry Mullen (p. 248) won gold at the 1988 Paralympics in the most determined fashion, leaving her hospital bed to travel to Seoul.

In the making of a sporting hero, how you win can also be important. Most often this is a matter of aesthetics. The grace and skill of a brilliant sportsperson is singularly captivating. Christy Ring 'made the game of hurling a living art form' while George Best showcased 'a limitless repertoire of swerves, swivels and feints … he would dance through tackles … leaving defenders … with twisted blood'. Skill is only one aspect of the aesthetic; power, courage, persistence, resilience, passion and much else are also relevant. Nina Coote (p. 58) 'relied on dash and style, rather than accuracy'; John Doyle (p. 96) 'preferred to go through rather than around opponents, performing with an aggressive swagger'; and Pat Taaffe's (p. 350) ungainly but extremely effective riding style is likened to someone 'carrying out an indecent manoeuvre on a box of red-hot tin tacks'.

Then there is the greatest intangible of all—how a sportsperson makes you feel. This is something that draws on things so deeply subjective that they are impossible to fully force into words. Sport is a measure of dreams— dreams fulfilled and dreams dashed; you may not live them out yourself, but you can see them lived out by others and imagine how that feels. By virtue of his blistering pace and powerful shot, Kevin O'Flanagan (p. 281) lit up the dreary years of the 'Emergency' and so became a crowd favourite at soccer matches.

The idea that sporting ability is a way to demonstrate and explain heroism is something that reaches back across history and into myth. In Standish O'Grady's *Cuculain: an epic* (1882), Cú Chulainn was recast as a hero for the 1880s, his deeds as a hurler recreated for a new generation: when he played a match 'the clash of the metal hurles [sic] resounded in the evening air' and those who watch were awed into silence, as he rushed backwards and forwards 'urging the ball in any direction that he pleased, as if in mockery.' O'Grady's words are echoed in this volume by John A. Murphy who declares of Christy Ring: 'he has the folk status of a pre-historic hurling *gaiscíoch* (warrior, champion), typified by the many legendary occasions when, in heroic Cú Chulainn style, he would snatch victory in the face of defeat'.

This is a nod to the adulation heaped upon sporting heroes, to a sense that we can be more willing to forgive, overlook and even celebrate their personal flaws. Sometimes this is because it reflects an obsession with winning above all else. The Gaelic football coach, Kevin Heffernan (p. 164), treated his players with total ruthlessness, declaring 'I would drop my mother if I thought she was not worth her place'. Yet we revel also in our sports stars' self-destructively bad behaviour. Although this volume includes outstanding role models such as Jim Stynes (p. 344) and Brede Arkless (p. 2), some of the others featured are not always the most admirable or dedicated individuals. We learn that Jack Doyle remained a huge draw for boxing fans even as his 'spectacular victories, backed by his looks and a whirl of hype, allowed him to embark on a lifestyle that neutered his talent'. Elsewhere, Alex Higgins's 'flamboyant style and bad-boy image' were just what snooker needed as it gained popularity. Too often sports fans are complicit in their heroes' downfall; witness those devotees who curtailed Dan Donnelly's sparring exhibitions by plying him with drink.

If some of the lives featured can be politely described as 'colourful', there are a few that are outright notorious. And while Vere Goold ((p. 151) a murderer) and Fay Taylour ((p. 355) a Nazi supporter) incurred contemporary odium for their actions, Anthony Mullane's (p. 242) overt racism only tarnished his name long after his death. Mullane, who is described as 'A self-infatuated prima donna, overly enamoured by his own talent, charisma and celebrity …', shows how sporting fame can bring out our worst traits.

Two of our lives combined the roles of journalist and sports participant: through their writings on equestrianism and cricket respectively, Nannie Power O'Donoghue (p. 276) and Tom Horan (p. 186) played a crucial role in popularising their sports. The modern media—first through newspapers and magazines, and then on radio and television—in creating a market for organised sport, also turned its protagonists into celebrities. Unlike the 'shy and reticent' Christy Ring, many sports personalities have embraced their star billing: Steve 'Crusher' Casey proved so adept at hyping his own accomplishments in rowing and wrestling that it is now hard for historians to separate fact from fiction. Courting the media, however, can be a dangerous game, as Lady Heath discovered when the British press tired of her publicity-seeking flying stunts.

Certainly, for all the mutual benefits, the marriage of sport and the media was never without rancour: thus, Jack Charlton (p. 49) objected to aspects of RTÉ coverage of his Irish soccer team, even as that coverage made him into a national hero. Moreover, the televising of sporting events has drastically amplified the intensity and pressures of sporting fame. Television coverage catapulted George Best beyond mere sporting fame, fashioning him into a pop celebrity; sadly, he developed the lifestyle to match and 'though the name did not die before the man, … the gift did'.

There is also the transience of much sporting fame. While the media are instrumental in polishing the legend, the nature of these media—and of the protean world of sport—demands new glories. Most champions fade away into a nostalgia of yellowing newsprint, of sepia photographs, of old footage that sits out of shape and in blurred focus on modern screens. Their sporting deeds are a matter of record, yet they retreat in the public mind, shouldered to the margins by new stars, who will follow the same path. In this churn, only a select few survive beyond the immediacy of their triumphs. The still-flourishing Christy Ring legend probably benefits from the lack of footage of him, but more common is the fate of Dick Fitzgerald (p. 120), one of the earliest stars of Gaelic games, who failed to feature on the Gaelic football teams of the century or millennium 'because he played so long ago'. The many derelict handball alleys that still dot Ireland provide mute testimony to how sports can lose popularity, taking with them the fame of their greatest exponents—in this case that of Paddy Perry (p. 294).

II

This book is not a ranking of the greatest. Instead, it explores the evolution of the modern Irish sporting world through the lives of the diverse people who have made it. This world was created in the nineteenth century out of the sporting traditions of the past, its evolving structures moulded by social, economic, political and cultural change.

Technology also played a role, particularly through new media (as we have seen) and the development of railways. Henry Dunlop (p. 102) sited his athletics complex beside the Lansdowne Road railway station, allowing his various sports clubs to draw upon Dublin's wealthy suburbs for their memberships. Similarly, the prolific golf course designer George Baillie (p. 7) worked hand in glove with the railway companies, which altered their timetables to suit recreational golfers.

The proliferation of such sporting clubs was essential to the emergence of the modern sports world. Previously the preserve of the few, access to formally organised modern sport was democratised at the end of the nineteenth century and on through the twentieth. Michael Cusack (p. 65), for instance, founded the Gaelic Athletic Association (GAA) to be 'open to Irishmen of all classes, creeds and political persuasions, committed to cultivating and promoting indigenous games'. But the gendered formulation and qualifying clause points to certain gaps and inconsistencies in this process.

When considering the range of forces that have shaped the modern Irish sporting world, we cannot avoid dealing first with the fraught relationship between sport and national identity. The divides of Ireland are evident across the lives in this book. The pages of *The Irish Sportsman*, Ireland's first dedicated sporting newspaper, reflected the views of people who saw themselves as Irish—but Irish within the context of the British empire. In 1877, on the fortieth anniversary of Queen Victoria's accession to the throne, an obsequious editorial entitled 'Long to reign over us', extolled the new sporting world created during her reign, 'the barbarous Pastimes of other days have given place among our people to the graceful amusement of cricket'. Indeed, by the 1870s cricket was a thirty-two-county sport, played by a cross-section of Irish society. The biography of the Victorian sports entrepreneur John Fortune Lawrence (p. 211) highlights how his success in marketing cricket owed much to aristocratic and viceregal backing; that of his contemporary Henry Dunlop notes that the development of his sports club at Lansdowne Road benefitted from the fact that 'many civil servants, professionals and military officers resided locally'. Dunlop and another early sports organiser Vere Goold were both public officials. Even more striking is the number of our subjects who either served in the British military (John Ryan (p. 316), Elisha Scott (p. 322), Johnny Carey (p. 37), Jack Doyle, Lady Heath, Beauchamp Day (p. 73) and Dave Gallaher (p. 125)) or had close personal or family associations with it (Elizabeth Le Blond (p. 216), May Hezlet and Beatrice Hill-Lowe (p. 223)).

The modern sporting world (with its clubs and governing bodies and dedicated sporting grounds) that was created in nineteenth-century Ireland bore all the trappings of empire: the Union Jack blowing out on Irish winds, the strains of regimental music played by army bands, the patronage of the lord lieutenant and the local gentry. And this sporting world was associated with notions of modernity, sophistication and social prestige. Beatrice Hill-Lowe was drawn into sport as part of a social life that revolved around 'attending hunt balls, acting in summer fêtes, and competing in and judging arts-and-crafts fairs'.

Sports offered the opportunity to identify with empire. Emigrants Dave Gallaher (as a New Zealand rugby player) and Tom Horan (as an Australian cricketer) both participated in highly successful tours to the British 'motherland' that cemented the loyalty of their respective self-governing dominions to the empire. Likewise, Lady Heath expressed the hope that her South Africa to England solo flight would have the same effect. Conversely, the biography of Nannie Power O'Donoghue shows that in Ireland these 'Imperial' pastimes aroused nationalistic opposition, such as that coming from tenant farmers who condemned hunting because they associated it with landlordism. (Fox hunting was certainly one of the most popular sports in nineteenth century Ireland, but, like all blood sports, it arouses fierce opposition today from animal-rights activists.)

The reaction of late nineteenth and early-twentieth century Irish nationalists against British sporting culture turned the Irish sporting experience on its head. This was true even for the lives of individual people. Michael Cusack, a man who loved rugby and cricket, changed course radically in the 1880s to found the GAA. This association promoted sports which it described as 'Irish native games', bathed them in ideas of Irishness and sought from the beginning to make Irish people choose between 'Irish laws' and 'English laws', between 'native' and 'foreigner'.

Between 1901 and 1905 the GAA at national level introduced a set of rules that decreed that anyone who played, promoted or attended 'foreign games' (the listed 'foreign games' were cricket, hockey, rugby and soccer) could not participate in the GAA. Later, it was added that anyone who was a member of the police or the British army was prohibited from membership of the GAA. These rules were clearly part of a wider resurgence of ideas of an Irish-Ireland, also extending across language, music and theatre. When the Camogie Association developed a national structure in the 1930s, the 'ban' was successfully installed there too, despite the fierce resistance of many members.

Three of the GAA luminaries featured in this volume (Mollie Gill, Dick Fitzgerald and Sim Walton (p. 361)) participated in the struggle for Irish independence, yet

Gill and Fitzgerald combined their fervent Irish nationalism with a stance of opposition to the GAA's ban. Here, we can see the love of play contending with dogma; so, too, with the Tipperary hurler John Doyle, who 'opposed opening up Croke Park to rugby and soccer, though he enjoyed watching both'. Moreover, there were always GAA members, such as the handballer Paddy Perry and the rugby international Moss Keane (p. 192), who played 'foreign games' under an assumed name. In the end the ban was swept away in 1971 thanks to the efforts of some of the GAA's most famous names, the outstanding Galway footballer Sean Purcell (p. 297) foremost amongst them.

As Liam O'Callaghan has written, the divide between 'native games' and 'foreign games' can be understood as 'a conflict between two modes of thought: those who saw as imperative the expression of nationality through sport and those who were swayed by personal conviction and social context'. Many Irish men and women did not consider their Irishness in any way compromised by their sporting preferences; neither should a preference for 'foreign' games be taken per se as a rejection of Irishness or of Irish nationalism. Johnny Carey found fame as a Manchester United soccer player, but he nurtured a lifelong love of the Irish language and had played Gaelic football to a high standard in his youth. The hammer thrower Pat O'Callaghan played senior rugby, yet he was nationalistic enough to boycott the Olympics in 1936 because the Olympic authorities had acknowledged the partition of Ireland. Likewise, the golfer Philomena Garvey (p. 132) refused to play in the prestigious Curtis Cup because the emblem of the British and Irish team she was selected for incorporated only the Union Jack.

On top of that, within the 'British' world of sport, international competition offered a significant opportunity for expressions of Irishness. Martin Sheridan (p. 332) was a radical Irish nationalist who revelled in defeating British athletes at the 1908 London Olympics, albeit while competing for the USA. On his ensuing visit to Ireland, he was greeted as a hero because sporting victories over England were more deeply cherished than those over any other country. Witness how Jack Charlton's Irish soccer team sparked communal celebrations across the country by merely drawing with England in the 1990 world cup! And success in international sport offered the opportunity to promote 'the nation'. When he returned from winning gold in the 1928 Olympic Games, Pat O'Callaghan said: 'I am glad of my victory ... for the fact that the world has been shown that Ireland has a flag, that Ireland has a national anthem, and in fact that we have a nationality.'

Some sports provided a means of transcending Ireland's political divisions with rugby being the most successful. The Belfast Presbyterian Jack Kyle took pride in the all-Ireland composition of the Irish rugby team and condemned Ian Paisley for melding unionism with religious bigotry. But sport can only do so much. When Ulsterman Ken Goodall made his rugby debut for Ireland in 1967, his unionist grandmother draped a cloth over her television as the Irish national anthem was played. Soccer has in practice served to highlight Ireland's divisions. Elisha Scott's achievements as the Protestant manager of Belfast Celtic, the city's Catholic team, were put to naught when his club was pushed into oblivion by the infamous riot at the Belfast Celtic–Linfield derby in 1948.

Gender was the second factor that shaped modern sport. In the propaganda of the Victorian sporting revolution, boys were made men in the crucible of sport. It was on the playing field that they were said to learn the qualities of courage, vigour, strength and stamina. Science fuelled a belief that men and women were complementary opposites, and it was widely held that excessive sporting activity could diminish a woman's capacity to procreate. Thus, newspaper accounts referred disapprovingly to tennis champion Mabel Cahill's (p. 32) manly (for which read energetic) playing style. Mollie Gill recalled how camogie players were regarded as 'unsexed young women'.

All the major sporting organisations to emerge during this period were dominated by men. There was no question of women being invited to play soccer, rugby, or cricket, or of them sharing organisations—let alone pitches—with men. Of our selected sportswomen, May Hezlet, Elizabeth LeBlond, Mabel Cahill, Lady Heath and Mollie Gill found themselves having to act as public advocates for the right of women to engage in sport. The most eloquent way of doing so was by holding their own in sporting competition with men, something accomplished by Lady Heath, Iris Kellett, Nina Coote and Fay Taylour. Elizabeth Le Blond and Nannie Power O'Donoghue demonstrated women could climb mountains and ride horses and through their writing both did much to encourage women's sporting endeavour. Furthermore, 'Ma' Copley (p. 61) became a successful boxing promoter in the most macho sporting environment imaginable.

Our earliest women subjects came from well-to-do backgrounds and engaged in suitable ladylike pursuits, such as archery, croquet, equestrianism, golf and tennis. The mountaineer Elizabeth Le Blond was the exception that proved the rule because she was an independently wealthy aristocrat. Even she observed certain proprieties, such as only changing out of a conventional skirt and into climbing attire once out of public sight. This volume shows how societal expectations obliged the first generation of

Irish sportswomen to compete in impractical and un-wieldy forms of dress, most notably Mabel Cahill who played tennis in a girdle, corset, petticoat, ankle-length dress and headdress, even in intense heat. Nannie Power O'Donoghue endorsed these expectations by steeple chasing side-saddle and also by insisting women should not ride astride a horse. Conversely, May Hezlet advocated shorter skirts, while, under Mollie Gill's leadership, the Camogie Association adopted less constrictive playing attire. Later, the careers of Molly Seaton and Joan O'Reilly (p. 288) indicate that the sight of women baring parts of their flesh in public remained controversial well into the twentieth century. Because of this O'Reilly, an international class sprinter, was denied the opportunity to compete at the Olympics and abandoned athletics for hockey.

In time the sporting boundaries began to shift. The horse trainer and showjumper, Iris Kellet, enjoyed a multi-faceted career through the second half of the twentieth century in a manner that would not have been possible earlier. But for all that, she too was not permitted to compete in the Olympics during her prime. In other sports little progress was made. Although Anne O'Brien was one of the best women soccer players in the world, so few resources were put into women's soccer in Ireland that the national team could not afford to fly her home for matches. This proud patriot played for her country just four times.

Wealth and class were another major influence on sporting engagement. The first sporting clubs based in Ireland were the preserve of the ascendancy and middle class. Later, as the Irish middle classes grew, an alliance of blood, land and commerce was forged in rugby, tennis and golf clubs in the growing suburbs where money found money. The importance of disposable income to engagement with sport was manifest in the education system. As rugby became the game of the middle classes across Ireland, fee-paying schools—particularly along the east coast—produced generations of Irish rugby players.

The cult of amateurism was an important function of the class basis of sport. Professionalism in sport was seen as a mark of corruption, of disreputability. Henry Dunlop framed the rules of his athletics club to exclude 'professional athletes, mechanics, artisans and labourers'. Indeed, Michael Cusack founded the GAA partly out of disgust at what he saw as the exclusionary nature of Dublin athletics, and his creation gave renewed impetus to amateurism in Ireland by showing that it could be compatible with a more socially diverse membership. The enduring influence of the amateur ideal across a variety of sports was borne out in the late 1940s when the golf authorities investigated Philomena Garvey's amateur status because her job involved selling golf clubs. Later still, Ken Goodall's 'defection' from rugby union to professional rugby (rugby league) led to his being ostracised by Ireland's rugby union authorities for two decades.

Even openly professional sports like soccer remained heavily influenced by Corinthianism. William McCracken's (p. 227) cleverness in exploiting a loophole in the offside rule was condemned for being against the spirit of the game. Another Irish soccer international Kevin O'Flanagan took his amateur status so seriously that when he played for Arsenal 'he would only accept his train fare to attend training, refusing match day meal vouchers—noting he had to eat anyway'.

Professionalism allowed those of humble means to devote themselves to, and thereby excel at, their chosen sport. But there was another side to this too. For long professional boxers such as the middleweight champion Jack Dempsey (p. 80) operated on the fringes of legality and fought for stake money supplied by their financial backers and by gamblers; his fights were often broken up by police raids. Beauchamp Day, once Ireland's greatest runner, 'was contracted for much of this time to gambling syndicates, and participated in many exhibition and handicap events running under the instructions of his employers, which often meant strategically losing races'. Some like Day and Vincent O'Brien, who established himself as a major horse trainer by landing a string of betting coups, proved adept at navigating the pitfalls of professional sport. Against that the cyclist Shay Elliott (p. 115) was sucked into a dark abyss of race fixing and drug taking, so prevalent in his sport. His life ended in depression and apparent suicide.

Finally, there is a fourth factor to be considered and one particularly important in an Irish context—emigration. Well over one-third of the men and women featured in this volume had to go abroad to pursue their sports career. Most of them never came back. Happily, towards the end of the period under consideration, the diaspora did make a notable contribution to Irish sporting life: of the fifty-six players who played for the Republic of Ireland soccer team during the Jack Charlton era, thirty-three were born outside Ireland.

III

There is only one certainty in every sporting career—it will end. When that end comes, the story of sport moves on so quickly that even the immediate past can seem more like ancient history. It is with horses, rather than with humans, that the poet Philip Larkin revealed this truth. In his poem, 'At Grass', Larkin wrote of two horses in a meadow, sheltering in the shade, one wandering about eating grass, the other looking on. The ageing horses were anonymous by then, but about fifteen years previously, some two dozen races had brought them fame: 'To fable them: faint afternoons, Of Cups and Stakes and Handicaps.' They mattered so much in their day that thousands came to see them run—and win. Their names would live on forever in almanacs. But their (sporting) day was done. There is a question in the middle of Larkin's 'At Grass' that sits right at the heart of the life of those who finish up in sport. It reads: 'Do memories plague their ears like flies?'

That notion of the plague of memories filling a head, crowding out the present, is what does the most damage to a sporting afterlife. How do you live forwards when your life pulls you backwards into its past? Do you think, looking back, that it was really worth it? Were all the sacrifices justifiable? Crucially, was enough joy found in the journey, or was the obsession with the result overpowering of all else?

The nub of the issue comes down to a matter of identity. For many competitors, sport is such an obsession, so central to everything that they have sought and thought throughout their days, that it comes to colonise their self-image. How do you then learn to live without the thing that has become so much a part of what you are, the thing that you love doing more than anything else? It is claimed that the vista created by Larkin was one of contentment at the end of a well-lived life. Yet its deep melancholy is inescapable; like Philip Larkin's horses, for every sportsperson there is no happy alternative to living out years (even decades) 'at grass', however contented they may be. Nothing beats playing. As Larkin concluded: 'Only the groom, and the groom's boy, With bridles in the evening come.'

This reminds us that a sporting life is not a normal thing. A single feat, or series of feats, that a woman or man achieves, usually before they turn thirty, becomes the prism through which all else is viewed. Lives are summarised in the *DIB* as 'hurler', 'rock climber', 'boxer', 'golfer'. But that is not all and cannot be all. Sometimes, little is known of a sportsperson's life outside their play. Once one of the fastest runners in the world, Beauchamp Day faded from top-class professional athletics around 1910. We glimpse him in 1916, being invalided away from the western front, suffering from shellshock. We also know that he married twice, that he had a daughter and that the certificates relevant to those events describe him as being of 'independent means'. He lived on until 1972, and much of what might have happened through those sixty years remains obscured.

As the memory of their glory years receded, many of our cast of characters succumbed to regret, poverty or alcoholism (Mike McTigue, Alex Higgins, George Best, Shay Elliott, Lady Heath, Nina Coote). Others such as Steve 'Crusher' Casey, Anne O'Brien, Ken Goodall and Nicky Rackard experienced setbacks post-retirement, and came through them, finding a way to live outside the limelight. Then there are those who did not get to experience the long, commonly anti-climactic afterlife of the sports star. The deaths suffered by Dave Gallaher (killed in action in the first world war) and Joey Dunlop ((p. 109) perishing in a motorcycle racing crash) served to burnish their legends; Gallaher's grave is a place of pilgrimage for touring New Zealand sides, while over 50,000 people attended Dunlop's funeral. The tragedy of their loss remained undiminished for friends and family—but the sports world found a way to honour their memory.

Perhaps the best that can be hoped for is to remain involved in sport in either a coaching or organisational capacity. Iris Kellett trained generations of showjumping stars while Kevin Heffernan accomplished as a coach what he could not achieve as a player—a victory over Kerry in an all-Ireland final. More prosaically, Bill McCracken was still enthusiastically scouting for young football talent into his eighties. Conversely, after following a stellar playing career with moderate success in football management, Johnny Carey was happy to see out his working life as a local authority official.

For others, their sporting career is a launching pad for new endeavours, such as the work Jim Stynes engaged in on behalf of disadvantaged youth. Or it is just one act in a much bigger story. Jack Kyle spent thirty-five years pursuing his medical career in Zambia because of the anonymity it allowed: 'I wanted to be seen as a surgeon first and foremost … it was very important to me that life was not defined by my rugby career'.

The story of any one person's relationship with sport is unique unto themselves. But, in sport, the personal is also intimately connected with the universal; most sport is lived as a shared experience even if not shared in precisely the same way. What is most striking in this book is the diversity of experience contained within; these lives illustrate the sheer variety of Irish sport. And they are a reminder, too, of how the wheel never stops turning.

Paul Rouse
March 2022

Brede Arkless

1939–2006

ROCK CLIMBER AND MOUNTAIN GUIDE

Brede Arkless (née Boyle) was born 10 August 1939 in Moston, Manchester, England, the daughter of James Boyle, a fitter, and his wife Mary (née Harrison). Born prematurely while her Dublin-resident parents were visiting family in Manchester, she had a working-class upbringing in Sandymount, Dublin. A highly active child with a love for hiking, cycling and swimming, Brede left school aged fourteen to do clerical work. In her mid-teens she started rock climbing in Dalkey, Co. Dublin, without initially showing any great aptitude for it. She emigrated to the USA with her mother in 1957, then returned briefly to Ireland before moving to London, where she worked in an office and went rock climbing at weekends in the Lake District and in north Wales. Eventually, she left London to go waitressing by night and climbing by day in the Lake District.

While living and working in Manchester in the early 1960s, she became a part-time climbing instructor for the Mountaineering Association (MA). In January 1964 she married Geoff Arkless, a full-time instructor, and moved into his hut outside Llanberis, Wales, at the foot of Mount Snowdon. Around 1966 she became the second woman to qualify as a British Mountain Guide. As the MA wound down in the late 1960s, she and Geoff did guide work for the Association of British Mountain Guides (ABMG). A 1960s contemporary recalled her 'as a performer with great competence and composure in all branches of mountain activity; as a genial character with a sharp, sidelong, and deflating wit who could hold her own in company; as a singularly attractive woman, blonde-curled, blue-eyed, lively and of enormous strength' (*Guardian*, 18 April 2006). She enjoyed beating male guides in arm wrestling contests.

In the late 1960s Brede and Geoff established their own climbing school at Deinolen, Wales. They had six children by the mid-1970s, taking turns climbing and childminding. Every summer the growing Arkless family moved from Snowdonia to the Chamonix Valley, beneath Mont Blanc, France, where they camped in the woods. Brede and Geoff offered climbing lessons and acted as guides on popular routes. Brede often shepherded clients up Mont Blanc (4,809m; 15,774ft) while heavily pregnant. The children were brought mountaineering as soon as possible; one of her sons climbed Mont Blanc aged thirteen.

Most ABMG guides had other jobs, but Brede worked full time on the mountains, dividing each year between Wales, Scotland and the Alps. Into the late 1980s she was Britain's only woman mountain guide. She and her husband drifted apart, separating in the mid- to late 1970s. She began a relationship with another Llanberis-based climber Mick Pointon; they would have two children together by 1980, though they never married. A practicing Catholic in other respects, she attended Mass whenever possible; her Irish upbringing was also evident in her accent.

In 1979, much to the consternation of the Alpine mountain guide fraternity, she became the first woman to receive a carnet from the Union International des Associations de Guides des Montagne (UIAGM), the gold standard for international mountain guides. Around this time, her growing disenchantment with the sexism pervading climbing led her to offer courses for women, the first of their kind. She saw that women beginners tended to get discouraged in mixed gender classes because, unlike men, they could not haul themselves up a rock face, irrespective of technique, through sheer physical strength. Furthermore, she contended that women needed to be taught differently because they had weaker arms than men but stronger legs and better balance.

Her parental responsibilities, a lack of funds and the reluctance of men to include women in their expeditions precluded regular forays to the great mountain ranges; there were some, however, usually as part of all-woman groups. In the Himalayas she got to 5,600m (18,372ft) in the Padar region in Kashmir (1970) and again on the Bakhor Das in Pakistan (1978), where a giant boulder tumbled just past her. As her children grew up, she went on about a dozen or so expeditions from 1980. In 1989 she was part of a high-profile British women's expedition to the Himalayan summit of Gasherbrum II, where two other members of the group reached the 8,034m-peak (26,358ft). Back in the Himalayas ten years later, she was in the first expedition to retrace the route taken in 1934 by Eric Shipton and Bill Tilman across the Chaukhamba range between the Hindu shrines of Badrinath and Kedarnath. She also climbed in Mexico, Borneo and Bolivia.

Wearying of the male chauvinism and overcrowding of European mountaineering, she moved in 1990 to New Zealand, finding there a more welcoming and egalitarian climbing community. By then a single mother, she brought her four youngest children with her, settling in Twizel, a small town in the Southern Alps. She acted as a guide for various companies, trained mountain guides and ran her own climbing courses, feeding clients from her vegetable garden. She migrated to Europe each year for the summer mountaineering season.

In 2000 she attempted to become the oldest woman to climb Mount Everest after being invited to join a Swiss expedition at a cost of US$12,500, about one-third the going rate. She was disillusioned by the experience declaring 'Everest is full of non-climbers and rich people ... people who shouldn't be where they are' (*Press* (Christchurch), 24 February 2001). Stricken by a stomach bug, she abandoned her ascent at 7,000m (22,965ft) and vowed never to return, pointing out that the Himalayas boasted many great summits untainted by the commercialism and egotism rampant on Everest.

Financial constraints meant she scaled only one peak of over 8,000m (26,246ft), but she was a source of inspiration for women climbers and admired by all aficionados. Whereas most mountaineers quit in their forties and most women lost interest once they started a family, she remained a full-time climber into her mid-sixties while raising eight children. This was despite an injury sustained in her early twenties that caused her ankle to be gradually destroyed by arthritis. She preserved her mobility by cycling as much as possible. Latterly she shaved years off her age—presumably to reassure clients astounded to find themselves roped to a grandmother. No other woman climber approached her longevity.

Still going strong upon being diagnosed with pancreatic cancer in 2005, she cycled the 285km (177 miles) from Twizel to Christchurch for exploratory surgery, which revealed an inoperable tumour. Over the next year, she travelled the world bidding farewell to family and friends while climbing in the Dolomites, New Zealand and Australia. She died in Cromwell, New Zealand, on 18 March 2006, following which her remains were buried in Twizel cemetery. The attendant media tributes hailed her for leading the rise in women's participation in rock climbing and mountaineering. In 2011 an outdoor activity centre in Newham, London, was named after her in recognition of her work with disadvantaged children. Two of her sons and one of her daughters became rock climbing instructors.

Terry Clavin

Sources

General Register Office UK (birth certificate, marriage certificate); *North Wales Weekly News*, 22 June 1978; *The Times* (London), 1 April 1981, 22 June 1985; 18 March 2006; *The Irish Times*, 11 August 1988; *San Diego Union-Tribune*, 26 March 1995; *Independent* (London), 2 September 1995; 10 April 2006; *Sunday Star-Times* (Auckland), 3 November 1996; *Dominion* (Wellington), 22 April, 3 May 2000; *Press* (Christchurch), 24 February 2001; *Daily Telegraph*, 15 April 2006; *Guardian*, 18 April 2006; *New Zealand Alpine Journal*, vol. 58 (2006), 144–5; *Newham Recorder*, 11 May 2011; 'Some historical data about the IFMGA', ifmga.info/sites/default/files/13_geschichte_ivbv_e.pdf; 'About Brede Arkless', web.archive.org/web/20120423052334/http://www.outdoorsinthecity.co.uk/about/about-brede-arkless/ (all internet material accessed September 2020)

George Baillie

*c.*1848–1922

George Lockhart Baillie was born around 1848 in Inveresk, Scotland, the son of Lockhart Baillie, an Inland Revenue official of Inveresk, and his wife Margaret (née Telfer). From the age of ten George played golf at the nearby Royal Musselburgh Golf Club. By 1868 he was a teacher in Dundee, and he was still teaching there in 1871 when he married Christina Archibald from Musselburgh. They would have seven surviving children. During the 1870s he also taught at Park School, Glasgow, and at High School, Carlisle.

In 1880 he arrived in Belfast to become head of the commercial department of the Belfast Academy (renamed 'Belfast Royal Academy', 1887), where a member of the board of governors, Thomas Sinclair, requested his help in founding a golf course. Captain John Harrison, the 'laird' of Holywood, Co. Down, gave them permission to use his land at Kinnegar, free of rent, which became the first home of the Belfast Club (later the Royal Belfast Club), founded 9 November 1881, with Baillie as the honorary secretary. Baillie laid out the course with the assistance of Walter Day, a golfer from Musselburgh. Comprising nine holes on eighty acres of low-lying, marshy ground, the design was unavoidably primitive, with the hazards including whin bushes and a quarry.

The Royal Belfast is the oldest existing and first organised golf club in Ireland, and its inaugural competition, played on St Stephen's Day 1881, marked the beginning of the modern era of Irish golf. It was an inauspicious start: the prize winners over two nine-hole circuits shot rounds of 121, 130 and 131. Locals, the younger ones especially, would visit Kinnegar to mock what they saw as a bizarre sport for old men. Through Baillie's unstinting efforts as organiser and golf instructor the membership grew while the scoring improved. Initially the club's best golfer, he was considered a steady rather than a brilliant player. He won club competitions and developed a rivalry with Ireland's premier golfer, the Scottish-born Thomas Gilroy. In 1885 he was part of the Royal Belfast selection which partook in Ireland's first inter-club match when they travelled to play the Dublin Club on its Phoenix Park course. The same year the reclamation of land from Belfast Lough allowed

Baillie to extend the Belfast course, following which most of the holes were over 200 yards long.

In 1888 when the flourishing club boasted over 100 members, Baillie resigned as its secretary so he could develop other, less cramped golf venues. Travelling by train with Gilroy to Portrush, Co. Antrim, in 1888, he was impressed by the possibilities of designing a course in the sand dunes, and one, moreover, which was in the vicinity of a railway station. He became a founding member and was elected joint honorary secretary and treasurer of the County Club (Portrush), renamed in 1895 the Royal Portrush Golf Club. He laid out the links, comprising forty acres and nine holes; the course was extended to eighteen in 1889. The *Belfast News Letter* (2 April 1888) reported that it 'abounds in hazards of the bunker type. The greens are clear and springy and completely free from brackens and from whins ... there is now no necessity for our local players to cross the channel for the thorough enjoyment of the game'. On the opening of the links (12 May 1888), Baillie competed with more than forty others for a scratch prize and won the silver cup, which became known as the George Baillie Cup.

Attracted by the beautiful landscape at the terminus of the Belfast & County Down Railway at Newcastle, Co. Down, he laid out a nine-hole course and was a founding member and elected joint honorary secretary and joint honorary treasurer at the inaugural meeting (23 March 1889) of the (Royal) County Down Club at Newcastle. Baillie thus played a major role in the foundation and organisation of two world-famous golf links (Portrush and County Down). When the great professional Scottish golfer Old Tom Morris (1821–1908) was invited to extend the links at Newcastle in 1890, he wondered 'why they send for me, this Mr Baillie kens mair about laying golf links than I dae. They had nae need to send for me' (*Early Irish golf*, 73).

Elsewhere, Baillie helped in founding golf courses in Ireland at Leopardstown (1891), Lisburn (1891), Rostrevor (1892), Ballynafeigh (1893), Bundoran (1894), Larne (1894), Knock (1895), Massereene (1895), MacGilligan (1896), Greenore (1896), Garron Point (1899), Ardara (1899), Castlerock (1900), Kirkistown (1902), Magilligan (1906), Scrabo (1907), Whitehead (1909), Toome (1909), Omagh (1910), Balmoral (1914) and perhaps elsewhere. Nearly all were in Ulster, particularly on its north-east. In some cases, he was merely consulted on the feasibility of the project; in others he designed the course and oversaw the club's establishment as its secretary before moving on. By 1909 he had been involved in the creation of twenty-two golf clubs, always with a view to working with nature rather than conquering it. In Scotland he designed the course for the New Galloway Golf Club. Arriving there on 1 April 1902, he inspected the relevant fields and marked out the course that day, drawing up the design in the evening; he also advised on the likely cost and on the level of subscriptions and fees. He charged £4 for his services while the expense of making the course, which opened on 17 May, came to £17.

The first to identify the opportunities provided by railways in the development of golf, he may have been paid a retainer by railway companies; these companies altered their timetables to suit the golfing public and agreed with golf clubs on reduced fares. Baillie promoted golf at home and abroad, advertised in the *Golfing Annual* and the *Belfast News Letter*, and organised golf tours through his relationships with the railway companies and the hotels they owned.

These initiatives were performed alongside his duties at the Belfast School of Commerce, which he had founded after he left the Belfast Royal Academy in 1890. The commerce school offered courses in book-keeping and secretarial work; he wound down this operation in 1915. By 1901 he and his wife were members of the Church of Ireland, though they had been married in a Presbyterian church. Playing golf into old age, he died 21 July 1922 at his home, 75 Fitzroy Avenue, Belfast, and was buried at Carnmoney cemetery, Belfast.

Helen Andrews

Sources

National Records of Scotland, 1861 Scotland Census 'George Baillie, resident of 4 High Street, Inveresk', 1871 Scotland Census 'Lockhart Baillie, resident of 4 High Street, Inveresk'; General Register Office Scotland (marriage certificate); General Register Office Belfast (death certificate); National Archives of Ireland, Census of Ireland, 1901, 1911; *Belfast News Letter, passim*; *Dundee Courier*, 25 June 1868; *Northern Whig*, 26 September 1887; 14 December 1903; 21 August 1922; *Derry Journal*, 7 April 1899; *Tyrone Constitution*, 22 October 1909; 'Golf clubs of Ireland', *Irish Field*, 14 May 1910; Joseph Tatlow, *Fifty years of railway life in England, Scotland and Ireland* (1920); 'Reminiscences of Robert Young', *Irish Booklore*, vol. 1, no. 1 (January 1971), 17; *'The Owl' bicentenary edition. Belfast Royal Academy 1785–1985* (1985), 151; W. H. Gibson, *Early Irish golf* (1988); J. L. (Ian) Bamford, *Royal Portrush Golf Club 1888–1988* (1988); Harry McCaw and Brum Henderson, *Royal County Down Golf Club* (1988); William A. Menton, *The golfing union of Ireland 1891–1991* (1991); Sean Breen, *The Greenore centenary* (1996); 'Baillie, George L. (*c.*1848–1922)', irishgolfarchive.com/baillie-george-l-c-1848-1922/, (internet material accessed September 2020); private information

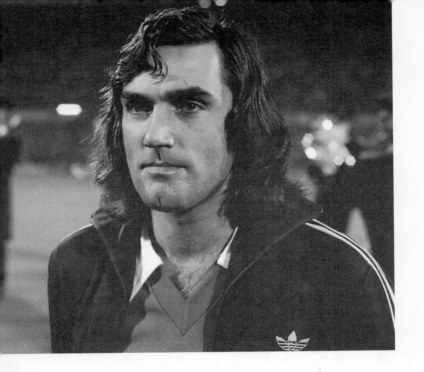

George Best

1946–2005

SOCCER PLAYER

George Best was born 22 May 1946 in the Royal Maternity Hospital, Belfast, eldest child among four daughters and two sons of Richard 'Dickie' Best (1919–2008), a shipyard iron turner, and his wife Ann Mary 'Annie' Best (née Withers), a factory worker. When George was aged three, they moved to 16 Burren Way in the newly built Cregagh council estate in east Belfast. The family was Free

Presbyterian in religion; Best's father and grandfather each served as master of the local Orange lodge, which Best joined in his teens. (In adulthood he deplored the sectarianism and political violence afflicting Belfast and described Orange marches as 'provocation' (*Blessed*, (2001), 28).) Attending Nettlefield primary school, Best was a bright and attentive student. After passing the eleven-plus examination (the only pupil in his class to do so), he won a scholarship to Grosvenor High School, a grammar school which he disliked, owing to its social elitism and preference for rugby over soccer. Frequently truant, he transferred after one year to Lisnasharragh intermediate school (a secondary modern), where he remained till age fifteen, taking a printing course in his last year.

THE PRODIGY

Though his father was a keen amateur footballer, Best's athletic talent derived primarily from his mother, who was an excellent hockey player. From early childhood, Best demonstrated an exceptional natural ability, especially for ball-control skills. He played for the Lisnasharragh school team and for Cregagh Boys' Club but was rejected for the Northern Ireland schoolboys' squad because of his small and slight build. The Cregagh coach, Bud McFarlane, recommended him to Bob Bishop (chief Northern Ireland scout for Manchester United), who after seeing him in action telegrammed Matt Busby, United's manager, with the words: 'I think I have found a genius' (*Hamlyn illustrated history of Manchester United*, 55).

In July 1961, one week after qualifying as a printer's apprentice, Best crossed the Irish Sea for a two-week trial with Manchester United but left, homesick, after one night. He returned a fortnight later, passed the trial and remained with United informally as a putative amateur (1961–3), playing first on the B and then on the youth teams. A diligent and enthusiastic trainer, he often worked alone to perfect his skills. Although he stood a shade over 5ft (1.5m) and weighed a mere 8st. (51kg) at age fifteen, his ability and potential were evident. Busby allowed his talent to blossom by making sure that he was not overly coached.

On his seventeenth birthday (22 May 1963), Best signed a professional contract for wages of £17 per week. Throughout autumn 1963 he played on the youth and A sides, but Busby unexpectedly blooded him on 14 September 1963 in a home Division One game versus West Bromwich Albion; switching between left and right wings, Best evaded repeated efforts at intimidating tackles, helping United to a 1–0 win. In his next first-team appearance, against Burnley at Old Trafford (28 December), he enthralled the home crowd with a dazzling display and scored the first goal in United's 5–1 victory. He was deployed regularly for the remainder of the 1963/4 season, making 17 league (scoring 4 goals) and 7 FA Cup (2 goals) appearances, and playing in both legs of the European Cup-winners' Cup quarter-finals. United were league runners-up. On 15 April 1964 Best made his international debut for Northern Ireland in a 3–2 away victory versus Wales. In 1964 he also won the FA Youth Cup with the Manchester United youth team.

THE COMPLETE FOOTBALLER

Over the next four seasons, he emerged as the best all-round player in a United team that won two Football League championships (1964/5 and 1966/7) and one European Cup (1967/8). Along with Bobby Charlton and

Denis Law, he formed United's 'golden trinity'. Best's cardinal physical traits were an extraordinary sense of balance and an elastic flexibility of movement, combined with speed and acceleration. Boasting sudden spurts of pace and a limitless repertoire of swerves, swivels and feints, he would dance through tackles and snake through a defence, leaving defenders, in the words of teammate Pat Crerand, with 'twisted blood' (*Manchester United*, 151). He could ride a challenge and disdained diving to gain a free kick. Notwithstanding his slender frame, Best's was a perfectly proportioned physique (by his maturity he had grown to 5ft 7in. (1.75m) and 10st. 3lb. (65kg)). Despite his short stature, he routinely beat taller players in the air with the timing and power of his leaps. An excellent ball winner, he avoided contact with his opponent with the quickness and timing of his tackles. He usually lined out as a winger but roved at will into the middle. Busby allowed him to play naturally and stood by the traditional football verities of spontaneity, creativity and virtuosity. In Best, Busby had found the player he most wanted, and in Busby, Best had the manager he most needed. For several illustrious seasons they were in a near-perfect fit.

THE GLORY YEARS

In Best's first full season (1964/5) United won their first football league championship in eight years. Best played 41 league matches, scoring 10 goals, with 55 total matches and 14 goals, answering lingering doubts about his capacity to withstand the physical rigours of senior football. With Best off form, Manchester United's first eight matches in 1965/6 yielded only two wins. Busby confronted him about his late-night socialising and dropped him for three matches. After a brilliant performance for Northern

Ireland in a 3–2 victory over Scotland (2 October 1965), he was recalled for a European Cup match versus HJK Helsinki; running the Finnish side ragged, he scored twice in a 6–0 romp and then scored in his return to league football in a 2–0 victory over Liverpool.

In the European Cup quarter-final second leg against Benfica, at Lisbon's Estadio de Luz (9 March 1966), Best gave a superlative individual display, scoring twice within twelve minutes, as United won 5–1: for the second goal, he beat two defenders before rounding the goalkeeper and slipping the ball across the line. The performance catapulted him from brilliant young footballer to pop celebrity. A Portuguese newspaper christened him 'El Beatle', and British newspapers carried a photo of him disembarking from the team airplane at Heathrow sporting a giant sombrero, the first occasion that he was featured on newspaper front pages. Two weeks later Best suffered a knee injury and missed most of the remaining season. United fizzled out in all competitions, eliminated from both the European and FA cups at semi-final stage, and finishing fourth in the league. Best played 31 league matches in 1965/6, scoring 9 goals; in 42 matches overall, he notched 16 goals.

In 1966/7 United won their second league championship in three seasons. Best appeared in all 45 league and cup matches, scoring 10 goals (all in the league). The 1967/8 season marked the apotheosis of his greatness. With Law injured, Best became United's chief goal scorer. He scored 28 goals in 41 league appearances, 32 goals in all matches; both totals were personal bests. Although he scored in eight of the last ten league games, United could not retain the championship, finishing second.

United did win the European Cup, the club's holy grail since the 1958 Munich air disaster. Best was prominent in the semi-final tie versus Real Madrid, scoring the lone goal in the home leg, then setting up the decisive goal late in the away leg with a precisely directed cross. The final against Benfica was contested at London's Wembley Stadium on 29 May 1968. With the score 1–1 after ninety minutes, Best was moved to centre-forward for extra time; three minutes in he received a headed pass, beat his marker, out-foxed the keeper and kicked into the open net. United won 4–1, becoming the first English club to win the European Cup. Best was named Footballer of the Year in England for the 1967/8 season and European Footballer of the Year for 1968. He was the youngest winner of either award.

THE POP STAR

With an attacking style and outstanding players, Manchester United was the most popular side in England. The club's prowess coincided with the launch by the BBC in 1964 of *Match of the day*, the first regular weekly television broadcast of English league football, and with England's World Cup win in 1966, which increased public interest in the sport. Football broke out of its male working-class ghetto and appealed to a broader social mixture, including women.

As United's most gifted and charismatic player, Best became the first modern superstar of British football, if not of British sport. An icon of the new Britain of the swinging 1960s, he was hyped as the 'fifth Beatle', linked to the musical group by his youth, social class, long hair and image of playfully exuberant rebellion. Remarkably handsome, with dark brown hair and large, bright and alert blue eyes, Best exerted a great appeal on women. Clean-cut, well-groomed and fashionably attired, he was well-spoken, with refined and gentle manners, and an air of shy vulnerability. Best had a long string of sexual dalliances, dating fashion models, beauty queens (including two Miss Worlds) and actresses.

The Manchester United management had no idea how to handle Best's celebrity and left him to his own devices. Employing a commercial agent and three secretaries to handle his fan mail, he modelled clothes, advertised products and opened a chain of men's fashion boutiques; his by-line appeared above ghost-written newspaper and magazine columns. His income from such activities dwarfed his footballing wages (which by contemporary standards were considerable: £1,000 per week including bonuses in 1966). Intellectually curious, he socialised with writers, journalists and broadcasters; the chat show host Michael Parkinson (his first biographer) was a friend.

THE PROBLEM YEARS

During the glory years Best's indiscretions were largely overlooked by Busby, but after the 1967/8 season, the hard partying became a problem and coincided with the decline of the United team. In the second leg of the unruly Intercontinental Cup tie against Estudiantes of Argentina at Old Trafford in October 1968, Best was sent off for the first time in his career. Thereafter, he often incurred repercussions for infractions of discipline, both from the club (for missed training sessions, curfew violations and the like) and from the Football Association for offences on the pitch (especially outbursts of temper directed at referees for failing to penalise aggressive challenges against him). He became a divisive figure within the club; many teammates thought him indulged by management.

Best's decline as a footballer was not as precipitous as folk memory would have it; until the end of 1971 he remained United's best player. For five straight seasons he led United in league goals scored (1967/8 to 1971/2). During the 1968/9 season Best was drinking heavily but playing marvellous football. Now carrying the team, he felt excruciating pressure to produce in every match. United dropped to an eleventh-place league finish and the defence of the European Cup ended in semi-final elimination. Best appeared in 41 league matches, with 19 goals, and scored 22 goals in 53 matches in all competitions.

Busby retired as manager at the end of the season, and Wilf McGuinness, formerly reserve team trainer, became the new 'chief coach', but his authority was ill defined. Although Best began the 1969/70 season in brilliant form, his drinking was out of control, and he was increasingly disenchanted with the club and with the caution and negativity of British football. He began to miss training sessions before unravelling mid-season. After flipping the ball out of the referee's hands at the end of a match, he was fined and suspended for four weeks. In the first match back, he scored six goals in an 8–2 thrashing of Northampton Town in the FA Cup fifth round (7 February 1970). Soon after he was sent off in a Northern Ireland versus Scotland match for spitting and throwing mud at the referee (18 April 1970). United finished eighth in the league; Best scored 15 league goals in 37 matches, with 23 goals in all competitions.

Best's indiscipline continued through the first half of the 1970/71 season. He arrived three hours late to an FA disciplinary hearing (4 January 1971) and received a suspended six-week ban and a £250 fine. Four days later, he failed to report to Stamford Bridge for a tie versus Chelsea (receiving a two-week club suspension) but kept a weekend date with actress Sinéad Cusack, in whose London flat he was besieged by media for the next three days. Busby's return as United manager later that month shook Best into applying himself. He scored 12 league goals over the second half of the season, for a season's total of 18; the club finished eighth in the league.

Frank O'Farrell, who became United's manager in June 1971, handled Best with a kindly indulgence. Best continued his fabulous form of spring into the autumn; the calendar year 1971 would be the last great period of his career. United topped the league table at year's end, inspired by a sober and hardworking Best, who scored 14 league goals, including two hat-tricks. He came third in voting for the European Footballer of the Year in 1971, scoring 26 league goals in the calendar year. By January 1972, however, Best had fallen off the wagon. He played poorly for the remainder of the season (scoring only four league goals) and United finished eighth for the third straight season. For all his problems, Best played forty league matches in both 1970/71 and 1971/2.

In May 1972 Best failed to report to the Northern Ireland team for the home championships. Discovered by media in a hotel in Marbella, he announced his retirement from football. By summer's end, bored by the pointless hedonism of his daily routine, he had reconciled with United. In the early months of the 1972/3 season, he laboured through nineteen league appearances, scoring four goals, playing every match until the end of November (and none thereafter). Frustrated by his and the team's poor form, Best drifted back into bad behaviour. On 18 October he was sent off in a Northern Ireland versus Bulgaria match for kicking an opponent. Dropped by United in November for missing training, he was placed on the transfer list in December. On 19 December 1972 Best submitted his resignation to the club's board.

In summer 1973 he was persuaded by Busby and the new United manager, Tommy Docherty, to return to the club. He played twelve matches in the 1973/4 season (all in the league), scoring two goals. Drinking heavily, he was off pace and bloated. His last match, both for United and in top-flight English football, was 1 January 1974, a 0–3 away defeat to Queen's Park Rangers. After a row with Docherty on 5 January, Best vowed never again to play for the club. Playing in all or part of eleven seasons for Manchester United, Best appeared in 361 league matches, scoring 137 goals; in all competitions with the club, he made 470 appearances, with 179 goals.

After leaving United, Best did not appear for Northern Ireland for three years but returned for five matches in 1976–7. Capped 37 times, scoring 9 goals, he described playing for his country as 'recreational football'. Best's greatest international performance was in a 1–0 home victory versus Scotland (21 October 1967); though he failed to score, he mesmerised with a dazzling virtuoso display. He achieved his only international hat-trick in a 5–0 home victory over Cyprus (21 April 1971).

THE BURN-OUT

George Best's life after 1971 was that of a man dominated by his addiction to alcohol and marked by the attendant consequences: episodes of erratic, outrageous, irrational and sometimes violent behaviour; problems with his finances (including periods of near destitution); instances of trickery or outright theft to access drink; motoring offences and accidents; brushes with the law; sporadic efforts at rehabilitation always ending in renewed heavy drinking; at least one period of suicidal depression; and finally, serious alcohol-related illness and premature death. Best opened two Manchester nightclubs in 1973–4; both were initially successful, his presence drawing the crowds. But he became a compulsive high-stakes gambler, betting on horses by day and hitting the casinos by night.

For the next decade he appeared for some fourteen clubs on five continents, often signing short-term contracts to earn quick money. He played five matches for £11,000 with Jewish Guild of Johannesburg, South Africa (May–June 1974). In August 1974 and October 1975, he played three friendlies for Dunstable Town of the Southern League. The 1975/6 season saw him in the English League Division Four for three matches with Stockport County (November–December 1975), and in the League of Ireland with Cork Celtic (December 1975–January 1976), where he played three matches before being sacked for lacking enthusiasm.

The most sustained football of Best's latter career was in the North American Soccer League (NASL), where he competed for six summer seasons (1976–81), playing for the Los Angeles Aztecs (1976–8), the Fort Lauderdale Strikers (1978–9), and the San Jose Earthquakes (1980–81), and with San Jose in the NASL winter indoor season of 1980/81. Removed from the goldfish bowl of his life in Britain, Best flourished initially, both personally and athletically, playing well in his first two seasons with the Los Angeles Aztecs. Then, after three erratic, drink-sodden seasons, he performed decently on a poor San Jose team in his last NASL season (1981), scoring one of the finest goals of his career against Fort Lauderdale (22 July 1981). In six NASL seasons, he played 150 matches, scoring 57 goals.

Best combined his NASL career with several winter seasons with British clubs. His arrival would produce good gates before the novelty soon wore off both for Best and the supporters. During the 1976/7 season he made thirty-seven appearances for Fulham in the English second division, scoring after seventy-one seconds in his debut versus Bristol Rovers in front of a home crowd of 20,000. He had a desultory tenure over portions of two seasons (1979–80) with Hibernian in the Scottish League premier and first divisions (22 games and 3 goals). After playing five matches for AFC Bournemouth of the English third division (March–May 1983), he briefly appeared for two clubs in Hong Kong, and for Brisbane Lions and Osborne Park Galeb in Australia (July 1983). His last competitive match was in the Irish Cup for Irish League B Division side Tobermore United against Ballymena United (28 January 1984; his only appearance with a Northern Ireland club). He later described such appearances as a 'freak show'.

PERSONAL LIFE; LAST YEARS

Best married first (January 1978) in Las Vegas, Nevada, Angela MacDonald ('Angie') Janes (b. 1952), from Essex, England, a fashion model, fitness trainer and sometime personal assistant to pop singer Cher. Upon meeting two years previously, they had begun a chaotic, on-again, off-again relationship. They had one son, Calum Best (b. 1981), a fashion model and minor celebrity. (Best also fathered a daughter in 1969 but never met her.) In March 1981 Best checked into a rehabilitation clinic and stayed sober for nine months, the first of many stays in rehab clinics and health farms. After he began a year-long relationship with Mary Stavin, an actress and former Miss World, Best and his wife separated definitively in 1982 (they divorced in 1986).

Best hit rock bottom in the mid-1980s, engaging in lengthy periods of binge drinking, accompanied by desperate behaviour. He had the first of several operations in which anti-alcohol pellets were sewn into his stomach and served eight weeks of a three-month prison sentence (November 1984–February 1985) for assaulting a policeman.

Having spent a decade flitting between London and southern California, from the mid-1980s Best lived in Chelsea, London, apart from a year in Portavogie, Co. Down (2001). For eight years (1987–95), Best's partner was Mary Shatila; she sorted out his business affairs and personal finances (he had been declared bankrupt in November 1982) and acted as his agent for personal appearances. He worked as an after-dinner speaker, in stage and pub shows, and as a television football pundit, and made the round of television talk shows; when sober, he could be an engaging guest, but a drunken appearance on BBC's *Wogan* in September 1990 was deeply embarrassing. He produced several ghost-written autobiographies and memoirs. Too often, however, the income from such sources merely funded his drinking and gambling. He married (July 1995) Alexandra Jane ('Alex') Pursey (b. 1972), an airline cabin attendant less than half his age; they divorced in 2004.

After spending five weeks in hospital with a severe liver condition (March–April 2000), Best had a liver transplant in July 2002. Hospitalised with a kidney infection, after seven weeks in intensive care, he died 25 November 2005 in Cromwell hospital, London. His funeral service in the Grand Hall at Stormont castle was relayed to 25,000 mourners in the castle grounds, and broadcast live on television; some 100,000 persons lined the route of the funeral cortège to Belfast's Roselawn cemetery.

HONOURS; LEGACY; ASSESSMENT

Best received an honorary degree from Queen's University Belfast (2001). His life and career were depicted in the feature film *Best* (2000), starring John Lynch. He was the subject of a documentary film, *Fußall wie noch nie* (*Football as never before*; 1971; rereleased 2015) by German director Hellmuth Costard, and a stage musical, 'Dancing shoes: the George Best story' (2011) by Marie Johns and Martin Lynch, directed by Peter Sheridan. The Belfast harbour airport was renamed the George Best Belfast City Airport in 2006. A group statue of Best, Law and Charlton was unveiled outside Old Trafford in 2008. Best has been depicted widely in mural art in Belfast and elsewhere in Northern Ireland. The depth of affection he attracted throughout Ireland represents a confluence of two archetypes that allure the Irish psyche: the warm-hearted rogue and the blighted genius.

With his precocity, his virtuosity, his creative attacking style; his disdain for systems, for the careful, conservative and cautious; Best was the great romantic of British football. Akin to many of the great romantics of literature and the arts, the productivity of his genius was fleeting. To paraphrase the poet A. E. Housman, Best was an athlete declining young: the name died not before the man (the harpies of modern celebrity saw to that), but the lad's rare gift slipped betimes away. Many have bewailed the wasted years, the unrealised potential, the failure to achieve full athletic maturity. Yet for several glorious seasons, Best was the greatest, most rounded talent ever to grace British football and one of the greatest ever in the world. In adjudging his legacy, posterity would be well guided by the assessment of Matt Busby: 'We had our problems with the wee fella, but I prefer to remember his genius' (*Hamlyn illustrated history of Manchester United*, 58).

Lawrence William White

Sources

Michael Parkinson, *Best: an intimate biography* (1975); George Best (with Ross Benson), *The good, the bad and the bubbly* (1990); Tom Tyrrell and David Meek, *Hamlyn illustrated history of Manchester United 1878–1996* (1996); *The Irish Times*, 30 May 1998; 3 August 2002; 5 December 2005; George Best (with Roy Collins), *Blessed: the autobiography* (2001 and 2002 editions); *Guardian*, 25 November 2005; *Daily Telegraph*, 25 November 2005; *Independent* (London), 26 November 2005; David Meek, *George Best: tribute to a legend* (2005); Eamon Dunphy, *A strange kind of glory: Sir Matt Busby and Manchester United* (2007 edition); Andrew Endlar, *Manchester United: the complete record* (2007); Darren Phillips, *The complete George Best: every game, every goal* (2008); Jim White, *Manchester United: the biography* (2009 edition); *Observer*, 19 April 2009; 'Manchester United: the official statistics website', www.stretfordend.co.uk; 'Northern Ireland's Footballing Greats', nifootball.blogspot.com; 'Soccer Ireland: an Irish football encyclopaedia', www.soccer-ireland.com (all internet material accessed June 2012)

This entry has been abridged for publication. The full version is available at www.dib.ie.

Harry Bradshaw

1913–90

PROFESSIONAL GOLFER

Harry Bradshaw was born 9 October 1913 in Killincarrig, Co. Wicklow, eldest among four sons and two daughters of Edward 'Ned' Bradshaw, golf caddie and later golf professional, and Elizabeth Bradshaw (née Walsh) of Killincarrig. He was educated locally. A golf prodigy, he had a hole-in-one at the age of ten on an eighty-yard par three at Delgany Golf Club, Co. Wicklow. He joined Delgany Golf Club, where he progressed from caddie to assisting his father, who was the club's professional. As a teenager, he tended to hook the ball wildly, before he developed a grip that allowed him to hit with great accuracy. Thereafter, he concentrated on honing his peerless approach play from within 100 yards of the hole. Another feature of his game was what was called his 'hit and hark' approach to putting: he never lifted his head to follow the ball until he heard it drop.

He played in his first tournament as a professional in 1932, the same year he shot a course record 68 at Delgany. In 1938 he won his first professional tournament, the Bromford-Adgey Cup at Skerries Golf Club, Co. Dublin. In 1941 he was appointed golf professional at Kilcroney, Co. Wicklow, and in 1950 he began his long association with Portmarnock Golf Club, Co. Dublin, when he was appointed golf professional there. By then he had already made his mark on domestic Irish golf, having won the Irish Open in 1947 and 1949. In Ireland he won the Irish Dunlop Trophy three times, the Willie Nolan Trophy eleven times, the Moran Cup twelve times and the Irish Professional Championship ten times, the last a record later equalled by Christy O'Connor Snr (1924–2016).

He was not well known outside of Ireland prior to the famous 'bottle' incident at the 1949 British Open at Sandwich. Having headed the qualifiers and shot an opening 68, he had continued his good form into the second round when his drive at the par-four fifth hole just missed the fairway and landed in a beer bottle that was standing upright with the neck and shoulder broken off. The rules were unclear on whether the bottle constituted a hazard and he elected to play the ball where it lay, judging (correctly) that he was not entitled to a free drop. Closing his eyes and turning his head away, he swung, shattering the bottle and advancing the ball about twenty-five yards. He was shaken and recorded a lacklustre round of 77. Back to his best in the next two rounds, he would have won the title had his putt on the last not stopped just short. Instead, he tied with the South African Bobby Locke who defeated him by twelve strokes in the thirty-six-hole play-off with superlative rounds of 67 and 68. As a result of his experience with the broken bottle, the rules were changed to cater for the possibility of such an incident recurring. It was the closest a golfer from the Republic of Ireland would come to winning the British Open until Padraig Harrington's victory in 2007.

Bradshaw subsequently revenged himself on Locke by narrowly beating him to the Irish Open title the following month. He was then one of four British and Irish golfers to participate in a sixteen-week tour of South Africa from December 1950 to March 1951 during which he engaged in further jousts with Locke, deepening their new-found friendship.

Establishing himself on the international golf circuit, he went on to win the Dunlop British Masters on two occasions (1953, 1955), and in 1958 he became the first Irishman to win the PGA Close Championship. He had also won the Dunbar Open in Scotland in 1953 and the Gleneagles Pro-Am with Joe Carr in 1955. The highlight of his career came in Mexico City in 1958, when, in partnership with Christy O'Connor Sr, he won the Canada Cup (later the World Cup) for Ireland, also losing a play-off for the individual title. His performance was particularly impressive, given that he was forty-five and carrying weight while competing at altitude in oppressive heat. He and O'Connor were fêted upon their return home, and their victory is considered to have played the determining role in popularising golf in Ireland. He capped a memorable year by receiving the Association of Golf Writers' Trophy for 1958.

He appeared in three Ryder Cup teams. At Wentworth in 1953, he won his foursomes match partnering Fred Daly and his singles match against Fred Haas, but in 1955 he lost both his matches (foursomes and singles) at the Thunderbird Golf and Country Club in California. In 1957 he was a member of the side that defeated the American team 7–4 at Lindrick in Yorkshire, only the third victory by the Britain and Ireland side in the twelve matches played up to that time. He holed a five-footer to tie his match with US Open champion Dick Mayer after a classic encounter. In 1963 he also took on Bill Casper, one of America's top golfers, in a match at Portmarnock televised as part of the prestigious *Shell's wonderful world of golf* series. Bradshaw's three-stroke victory earned him $3,000, which was then considered a bonanza in golfing terms.

He remained the golf professional at Portmarnock until 1983, latterly spending most of his day in the club shop. Even after his formal retirement, he remained on the payroll at Portmarnock as an informal ambassador for the club. Nicknamed 'the Brad', he was extremely popular with amateur and professional alike, was a great raconteur and tremendous company, and was noted for his lack of rancour towards, or criticism of, other players. He died 22 December 1990 in St Vincent's hospital, Co. Dublin, and was buried in St Fintan's cemetery, Sutton, Co. Dublin.

He married (1944) Elizabeth Foley from Carlow; they had four children. His three brothers, Eddie, Hughie and Jimmy, were all professional golfers.

Jim Shanahan

Sources

Irish Independent, 7 September 1943; 11 July 1949; 24 December 1990; *The Irish Times*, 3 October 1953; 7 October 1957; 13 August 1981; 22 November 1988; 24 December 1990; *Sunday Independent*, 23 December 1990; John Gleeson (ed.), *Fyffes dictionary of Irish sporting greats* (1993); Louis McRedmond (ed.), *Modern Irish lives: dictionary of 20th-century Irish biography* (1996); William A. Menton, *The golfing union of Ireland 1891–1991* (1993); Brendan G. Cashell, 'Harry Bradshaw of Portmarnock', *Through the green* (December 2013), 40–42; information from Breda Mullally (daughter), 4 July 2006

Mabel Cahill

1863–1905

TENNIS PLAYER

Mabel Cahill was born 2 April 1863 in Ballyragget, Co. Kilkenny, twelfth of thirteen children of Michael Cahill, gentleman landowner and barrister-at-law, of Ballyconra House, Ballyragget, and his first wife, Margaret (née Magan), Ballymore, Co. Westmeath (1823–c.1875). Born into a Catholic gentry family, she attended school in Roscrea, Co. Tipperary, probably the Sacred Heart Convent School.

Mabel and her siblings were drawn into lawn tennis parties and tournaments, the craze for lawn tennis having swept through Ireland from the late 1870s. In 1884 she appears in her first recorded tennis competition, the Kilkenny County and City Tournament held in Archersfield, which she won playing off a handicap. (Unlike 'open' events, handicaps gave lesser players scoring advantages.) During 1884–6 she participated regularly in other lawn tennis tournaments held across Ireland, including Dublin's prestigious Fitzwilliam Square tournament in 1886, where she lost 6–0, 6–1 in the first round of the open event. For the rest of the 1886 season, she focused mainly on handicap singles events, winning this event at the Lansdowne Lawn Tennis Club Tournament in Dublin; playing off 'scratch', she also claimed the handicap event at the Kilkenny County and City Tournament in Archersfield. She does not seem to have participated in tennis tournaments in Ireland during 1887–9.

Emigrating to New York City, most likely first arriving there on 7 October 1889, she lived in Manhattan—alongside Central Park—and began playing tennis on the new courts built there. Her brother Louis, who was also living in New York, became a regular tennis partner. Entering the Annual Invitation Ladies' Tournament at the Staten Island Cricket Club in autumn 1889, she won the ladies' singles and mixed doubles events. While she had been outmatched in first class open events in Ireland, she found the standard of tennis to be lower in America. Her tennis also improved after she came to America, something she credited to practising regularly against men.

She became a member of the New York Tennis Club in 1890, the year she travelled to Philadelphia for the United States Championship, being the only non-American of the eight women to compete in the singles event. The format of the singles championship saw the defending champion progress automatically to the final, where she would play the winner of a knockout competition played between all other entrants. Cahill reached the final of the knockout competition, but a foot cramp in the deciding set forced her out of her match against the eventual champion Ellen Roosevelt, a first cousin of future US President Franklin D. Roosevelt. Believing herself wronged by the match officials, who refused her more time to recover, the fiery Cahill bore a grudge against Roosevelt over this incident.

She returned to the US Championship in 1891 to defeat both Ellen Roosevelt and her sister Grace in claiming the singles honours. The final victory over Ellen Roosevelt was 6–4, 6–1, 4–6, 6–3, the best of five sets format having been introduced that year for the US Championship, which reverted to best of three sets after 1901. She then added the women's doubles (with Emma Fellowes-Morgan), defeating the Roosevelt sisters in a close, best-of-three-sets final, along with the mixed doubles (with Marion Wright), though this event did not have championship status. In the 1892 United States Championship she claimed the ladies' singles, ladies' doubles and mixed doubles, the last now a championship event, becoming the first person to record a treble at a major tennis tournament. The ladies' doubles and mixed doubles were won easily in partnership respectively with Adeline McKinley and Clarence Hobart, but she had to fight hard in the singles final against Bessie Moore, eventually prevailing 5–7, 6–3, 6–4, 4–6, 6–2. Moore, who had looked the likely winner going into the final set, tired after staying outside during the interval while Cahill cooled indoors for longer than was stipulated. Women were then obliged to play tennis in suffocating attire comprising heeled boots, long sleeves, headgear, a necktie or scarf and an ankle-length dress over a petticoat and corset, all supported by a girdle.

Mabel Cahill was now a sporting star and a syndicated article about her appeared in the American press in 1892. It described her as 'a petite, attractive brunette, with short black hair, and the brightest of grey eyes, full of life and spirits' ('Mabel Cahill—Lawn Tennis Champion'). Newspaper reports refer to her 'manliness', describe her preparation as more like that of a professional than of an amateur, and pay tribute to her energy around the court and to the ferocity of her groundstrokes. Few opponents could cope with her serve, which she almost invariably delivered overhand, a tactic considered unusual enough to be noteworthy. In 1891 she observed that women who played the tennis ball gracefully from the wrist rather than from the shoulder were putting themselves at a competitive disadvantage.

She also competed in various American tennis tournaments during 1890–93, never losing a completed singles match in the USA. She was not a popular champion and had to withstand the hostility of both spectators and match opponents. It is unclear whether this was on account of her playing style or of her foreign birth. For all that, her American rivals were soon emulating her dedication, energy and power. Her final appearance in open events in first class lawn tennis came in July 1893 at the New York State Championships. Tennis was an amateur sport, and it is likely that the income she inherited from her father's estate had run out.

From the early 1890s she tried to become a professional writer, publishing a novel in New York entitled *Her playthings, men* (1891). It was not a success; neither were her shorter works—*Carved in marble* (1892) and *Purple sparkling* (1892). She dabbled in journalism and published articles on tennis in journals, wherein she denied the frequently expressed view that the exertions of tennis were bad for women's health. By 1896 at the latest, when she was described as a professional rider, she was participating in equestrian events. She also hunted as a member of the Ocean County Hunt and Country Club in Lakewood, New Jersey.

Moving to London, she stayed briefly in a workhouse in April 1897, probably upon her arrival. She struggled to earn enough money writing articles for magazines and performing on stage in music halls where she sang and acted, often as a chorus girl, in variety shows and burlesques. She was still in London in January 1900 but living in Ormskirk, Lancashire, by the start of 1905, drawn presumably by the work going in the seaside music halls of nearby Blackpool and Southport. Stricken with tuberculosis, Mabel Cahill died in the Union Workhouse, Ormskirk, on 2 February 1905. Three days later she was buried in a pauper's grave in the graveyard of the church of Saint Peter and Saint Paul. Her death went unnoticed, and her last years were for long a mystery. In 1976 she was inducted into the International Tennis Hall of Fame.

Paul Rouse

Sources

Frank Leslie's Illustrated Newspaper, 16 August 1890; *Illustrated American*, 23 May 1891; Mabel Cahill, 'The English and Irish girl champions', Valentine G. Hall (ed.), *Wright & Ditson officially adopted lawn tennis guide* (1891), 137–41; *Town topics, the Journal of society*, 22 June 1893; Case #1020, Probate Register (Michael Netterville Cahill [*sic*]), *Early California wills* (1952), vol. 1, 78, transcribed at Cal Data Nook, SF Genealogy, www.sfgenealogy.com (internet material accessed August 2011); John Gleeson (ed.), *Fyffes dictionary of Irish sporting greats* (1993); Ralph Hickok, *A who's who of sports champions: their stories and records* (1995); Joan N. Burstyn (ed.), *Past and promise: lives of New Jersey women* (1997), 173–4; Tom Higgins, *The history of Irish tennis* (2006); Mark Ryan, 'Mabel Cahill—Lawn Tennis champion, writer, stage actress', www.tennisforum.com (internet material accessed August 2020)

Johnny Carey

1919–95

SOCCER PLAYER

John ('Johnny', 'Jackie') Carey was born 23 February 1919 at 4 Adelaide Place, Lower Baggot Street, Dublin, the son of John Carey, a van driver, and Sarah Carey (née Byrne). Educated at Westland Row Christian Brothers School, he played soccer for Home Farm. Keen on all sports, he was a strong swimmer. He also played Gaelic football and, aged sixteen, was selected for the Dublin Gaelic football junior team, but the invitation was withdrawn when it was discovered he played soccer. After joining St James's Gate in

Dublin in August 1936, he was spotted by a Manchester United scout and, two months later, joined United (then in the second division of the Football League) for a fee of £250. He made his first-team debut against Southampton in September 1937 at inside-left and performed well despite his side losing 2–1. United were promoted in his first season with the club, and in his first season in Division One (1938/9) Carey consolidated his position, making 34 league appearances and scoring 6 goals.

With the Football League suspended upon the outbreak of war in September 1939, Carey played for United in wartime regional leagues and guested for other teams such as Liverpool, Manchester City and Middlesbrough until 1943. On 17 May 1941 he scored the winner for United in a 1–0 victory over Burnley to win the Lancashire Cup. He also guested occasionally in League of Ireland games with Shamrock Rovers and played in a 3–2 defeat for a League of Ireland XI against a Scottish League XI at Dalymount Park, Dublin, on 28 April 1940. After joining the Queen's Royal Hussars, Carey served in the Middle East and Italy from 1943, coaching army football teams and playing part time for some Italian clubs. Known as 'Cario', he became a great favourite with local fans and was offered professional terms to stay in Italy, but after the war he returned to England and was made captain of Manchester United in October 1945 by their new manager, Matt Busby.

Under Busby's tutelage, he helped transform United into one of England's top clubs, leading them in a thrilling 4–2 FA Cup final victory over Blackpool in 1948 and to their first league championship in forty-one years in 1952 (the team had been runners-up in four of the previous five seasons). He was the first Irishman to captain his club to wins in both the league championship and FA

Cup. After the war he usually played at right-full-back and brought his inside-forward's footballing skills to the position. Although strongly built and a good tackler, he used brain rather than brawn: he was a master of the well-timed interception and set up counter-attacks with his passing skills. Busby regarded him as one of the greatest United players, on a par with Bobby Charlton or George Best. Like Busby, Carey was a thoughtful, quiet-spoken man and a pipe smoker, with a passion for skilful football, but he had great presence on the pitch and was a natural leader. Sporting and dignified, he was popularly known as 'Gentleman Johnny'. He never lost his love of the Irish language and always prefaced any speeches in Ireland with a few words in Irish.

Carey first played for Ireland (Football Association of Ireland (FAI)) in a 3–3 draw against Norway in a World Cup qualifier (7 November 1937) and was capped 29 times (1937–53), 19 as captain, scoring 3 international goals. He also played nine times for Northern Ireland (1946–9) and was one of seven southerners on the team that finished runners-up in the British home championship of 1947. During the 1948/9 season he captained both Irish international teams. On 10 May 1947 he captained a Rest of Europe team to a 6–1 defeat against Great Britain in front of 135,000 spectators at Hampden Park, Glasgow. Within the space of three days (28, 30 September 1946), he played for the two Irish national teams against England. In the second game (the first ever between England and an FAI team) Ireland were beaten 1–0 in Dublin despite Carey's best efforts. The English goalkeeper Frank Swift recalled that 'Johnny Carey was ... the man of the match. He almost started the game at centre-forward, played at right-half in the first half and then went to right-back …. But no matter where he played, he just seemed to get better and better' (*Football Association of Ireland*, 47). Carey was instrumental in Ireland's greatest footballing triumph in this period, captaining the team in a 2–0 win over England at Goodison Park, Liverpool (21 September 1949), when he effectively marked England's star player Tom Finney out of the game. This was the first time a team from outside the UK had beaten England at home. In 1949 Carey became the first Irish player to win the English football writers' Footballer of the Year award, and in 1950 he was voted Britain's sportsman of the year. Until his retirement from international football in 1953, he was Ireland's most influential player; at times he was effectively the team coach.

Although primarily a right-full-back, Carey was a great all-round footballer: he played in every outfield position for United except outside-left, once even playing in goal against Sunderland in February 1953 when the regular goalkeeper had fallen ill; he also played in seven different positions for Ireland. When some of the 'Busby babes' began to break through into the United first team, he decided to retire from playing in May 1953. Despite the war, he had played 344 games and scored 18 goals for Manchester United, and his long and successful career at Old Trafford did much to make United a favourite club with Irish supporters.

Although offered a coaching position at Old Trafford, he decided to become manager of second-division Blackburn Rovers (1953–8) and guided them to the first division in 1958. He brought the same relaxed, courteous manner to managing that he had to playing; like Busby, he dispensed much fatherly advice to young players and encouraged his teams to play constructive, attacking football. He managed

Everton (1958–61) and, despite reaching fifth place in 1961 (their best post-war position to that date), he was infamously sacked in the back of a taxi. As manager of Leyton Orient (1961–3), Carey gained the club promotion to Division One for the first time in 1962, but it was relegated the following season. He moved to Nottingham Forest (1963–8) and put together an impressive team. In 1967 Forest were runners-up to Manchester United in Division One, and also reached the semi-final of the FA Cup, going down 2–1 to Tottenham Hotspur, the eventual winners.

Carey also coached Ireland (FAI) (1955–67), becoming the team's first recognised manager. (He had already taken charge of the Ireland team at the 1948 Olympic games in England, when they lost 3–1 to the Netherlands in a first-round match at Fratton Park, Portsmouth.) On 27 November 1955 he began his reign with a 2–2 draw at home to Spain and then won his next three games, including a 3–0 victory over world champions Germany in a home friendly (25 November 1956). Other notable results were a 2–0 win against a highly fancied Czechoslovakia team in a European Nations' Cup qualifier (5 April 1959), and a 3–2 victory over Austria (13 October 1963) to take Ireland to the quarter-finals of the same competition. Carey managed Ireland for 45 games, winning 17, drawing 7, and losing 21. Among his greatest disappointments were elimination from a World Cup qualifying group when Ireland conceded a last-minute goal to draw 1–1 with England at Dalymount Park (19 May 1957) and going down 1–0 to Spain in Paris (10 November 1965) in a play-off for a place in the 1966 World Cup (the nearest Ireland came to qualifying for the finals of a major tournament under Carey). His job was not an easy one: the team was chosen by a five-man FAI committee, known for its inconsistent and occasionally bizarre selections. Players often arrived on the day of the match, leaving time for only the simplest tactical instructions. Carey was a popular and respected figure among Irish players, but some believed that he should have done more to challenge the FAI's amateurish ways. Towards the end of his reign senior players increasingly took on the managerial role. Carey stepped down as Ireland manager in February 1967.

He returned to Blackburn as general manager (1969–71) but was dismissed when the club was relegated to Division Three. By then he had had enough of football management and worked in the treasurer's office of Trafford Borough Council until his retirement in 1984. He visited Old Trafford regularly, acting during the 1970s as a scout for Manchester United. He died 23 August 1995 at Macclesfield District General Hospital, Cheshire; he was survived by his wife Margaret.

James Quinn

Sources

General Register Office Dublin (birth certificate); Stephen McGarrigle, *Manchester United: the Irish connection* (1990), 28–30; John Gleeson (ed.), *Fyffes dictionary of Irish sporting greats* (1993); *The Irish Times*, 24 August 1995; *The Times* (London), 26 August 1995; Louis McRedmond (ed.), *Modern Irish lives: dictionary of 20th-century Irish biography* (1996); Peter Byrne, *Football Association of Ireland: 75 years* (1996), 43–7; Stephen McGarrigle, *The complete who's who of Irish international football 1945–96* (1996); Sean Ryan, *The boys in green: the FAI international story* (1997); John Scally, *Simply red and green* (1998), 52–3; Jack Rollin, *Soccer at war, 1939–45* (2005), 102, 104, 330; Trevor Keane, *Gaffers: 50 years of Irish football managers* (2010), 24–44

This entry has been abridged for publication. The full version is available at www.dib.ie.

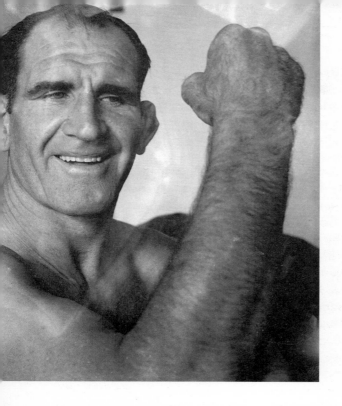

Steve 'Crusher' Casey

1908–87

Steve ('Crusher') Casey was born 4 December 1908 in Loughane, near Sneem, Co. Kerry, eldest among seven sons and three daughters of Michael Casey, stonemason, and Bridget Casey (née Sullivan) of Ballaugh, Sneem, Co. Kerry. His father, who had returned to Ireland after twenty years in the USA, had reputedly been a sparring partner of the legendary world heavyweight boxing champion, John L. Sullivan, and had been a champion rower in a team of Sneem men in the US funded by the Vanderbilt family. His mother was the daughter of another prominent local athlete, Johnny 'Mountain' Sullivan.

The Caseys supplemented their farm income with fishing, and, living in Ballaugh, a townland most easily accessible by boat, all the family were expert rowers. The brothers specialised in four- and six-oar racing and were virtually unbeatable at local regattas. Steve and his brothers Pat (1910–2002), Jim (1912–2000) and Mick (1913–99) got to keep the Salter Challenge Cup after winning this prestigious race at the Killarney regatta three times (1930, 1932 and 1933). The brothers were also serial victors at various tug-of-war competitions, including the 1932 Munster championship.

Steve emigrated to London c.1933, working first as a labourer on a building site. He was followed by his brothers. In London, either Steve, Pat, Jim and Tom Casey (1914–c.1985) or Steve, Pat, Tom and Mick were unbeatable in the four-oar sweep with Ace Rowing Club. Reports that the Caseys could have represented Britain at the 1936 Olympics are incorrect, however, as the strict definition of amateurism adopted by the Amateur Rowing Association precluded the selection of 'artisans' like the Caseys. In addition, they never rowed in the showpiece rowing events, such as the Henley regatta, and competed in heavier, fixed-seat craft, not the lightweight racing boats favoured by Olympic competitors.

In 1933 or 1934, while working as a hotel porter on the Tottenham Court Road, Steve was spotted by Mike Hawley, a wrestler turned owner of a local gym. Casey began attending the gym where he wrestled under Hawley's tuition. By 1935 he had quit his job to become a professional wrestler on the British circuit. When the Irish wrestling champion Dan O'Mahony returned from America to engage in a series of bouts in Ireland during August–October 1936, Casey impressed each time on the undercard.

In October 1936 Casey left for Boston, USA, to come under the wing of the dominant local promoter, Paul Bowser. Wrestling was then a mix of theatre and sport. The fights were fixed, but professional jealousies often undermined these arrangements. A similar lack of cooperation between the various regional promoters was producing a proliferation of 'world' titles. O'Mahony had been a spectacular box office success for Bowser in the mid 1930s before being undone by his evident lack of wrestling skills. Still eager to tap into the large Irish market in America's north-east, Bowser drafted Casey to be a more credible alternative.

Although advanced by Bowser primarily for commercial reasons, Casey, who was touted in America as 'Crusher Casey', was sufficiently accomplished at wrestling to pass muster while being hardy and canny enough to cope with any attempted 'double-cross'. At well over 6ft tall (reports vary between 6ft 2in. to 6ft 4in. (1.88m–1.93m)) and weighing 17st. (107.95kg), he was considered to have the most powerful hands of any wrestler. His signature move was an over-the-shoulder toss called the 'Killarney flip'.

Casey gradually developed his ringcraft on the gruelling wrestling circuit. Most of his fights were in the Boston region, which was the most important wrestling market, with occasional forays beyond. After 316 victories in sixteen months, he defeated Louis Thesz for the Bowser-controlled American Wrestling Association (AWA) title on 11 February 1938 in Boston. As champion, Casey proved a reasonable draw, without having anything like O'Mahony's former pulling power. Partly as a result, the National

Wrestling Association, which had briefly recognised him as champion, stripped him of its title in September 1938.

Casey and O'Mahony sought to exploit the interest their American successes had generated in Ireland by staging a fight in the soccer ground at Milltown, Dublin. Some 16,000 fans watched them fight each other to a draw on 26 August 1938. The rematch (18 September 1938), which was won by Casey in the twentieth round, attracted less than 3,000 spectators to Mallow racetrack, Co. Cork. The bishop of Ross had instructed Catholics not to attend, as the contest was on a Sunday, but for Irish audiences the novelty was wearing thin in any case.

Back in America, Casey was part of a roster of big names who took turns as the AWA champion, depending on Bowser's reading of the market. After losing the title in March 1939, he regained and lost it five more times over the next six years, developing a productive rivalry with Maurice Tillet ('the French Angel'). Casey was Bowser's most reliable earner during a lean period for wrestling.

Rowing, his true sporting love, was fitted in around his wrestling. He was a member, along with his brothers, Jim and Tom, of the Riverside Boat Club in Boston. In 1940 Steve, Jim and Tom Casey competed in a singles race against the 45-year-old Boston sculler Russell S. Codman for a cup donated by Leverett Saltonstall, governor of Massachusetts. The *Boston Herald* put up $1,000 in prize money while the protagonists raised another $2,000 in stakes. The race caught the imagination of the Boston public and a crowd of at least 40,000 saw the three Caseys each finish ahead of the 1925 US single sculls champion.

In early 1941 Steve volunteered for the US army and was stationed in Portsmouth, New Hampshire, where he acted as a fitness instructor. He was discharged in October, as he wanted to concentrate more on wrestling, only to be called up in January 1942 when the US entered the second world war. Based again in Portsmouth, he continued in competitive wrestling until he damaged his back in an exhibition bout in August 1942. This injury forced him out of wrestling before he made an impressive comeback in 1944. After losing the AWA title for the last time in June 1945, he was dogged by recurring back problems, yet he kept wrestling until 1951.

His brothers Jim, Pat and Mick followed him into wrestling, with Jim being the most successful of the three: Jim won Texas, Canadian, Southern US and Pacific Coast heavyweight wrestling titles. Steve and Jim refused to fight each other. Tom Casey became a promising professional boxer in America until a hand injury finished his career.

From the late 1940s Steve Casey owned and ran a sports bar and restaurant in Boston, devoting his free time to coaching rowers. On New Year's Eve 1967 he was shot three times in an armed robbery and spent almost a year in hospital; one of the bullets could not be removed. He lived near Boston in Cohasset, Massachusetts, where he had a 150-acre farm. Dying there on 10 January 1987, he left a wife, Mary (née Neiter), a daughter and two sons. In 2000 a statue was erected to his memory in Sneem.

In Ireland Steve Casey was most famous for being a member of a celebrated sporting family dubbed 'the toughest family on earth' by the *Daily Mirror* (9 September 1937). Much embellished by the Caseys themselves, the 'Legend of the Caseys from Sneem' has over the years become exactly that, making it hard to separate fact from fiction. The Caseys were inducted into the Irish Sports Hall of Fame (1982) and the Kerry Sports Stars Hall of Fame (2001).

Jim Shanahan

Sources

Cork Examiner, 22 August 1934; 24 May 1935; 27 August, 17, 19 September 1938; 3 October 1946; *Irish Independent*, 20 August 1935; 3 August 1977; 17 May 2000; *The Times* (London), 2 June 1936; 27 July 1981; *Irish Press*, 20 November 1936; 25 August 1938; 23 April 1956; *Kerryman*, 17, 24 September 1938; 26 October 1946; 13 January 1968; 16 January 1987; *Boston Globe*, 12 January 1987; Jim Hudson, *The legendary Casey brothers* (1991); John Gleeson (ed.), *Fyffes dictionary of Irish sporting greats* (1993); *Galveston County Daily News*, 28 July 1997; *Houston Chronicle*, 6 January 2000; *The Irish Times*, 2 March 2002; Steven Johnson, Greg Oliver and Mike Mooneyham, *The pro wrestling hall of fame: heroes and icons* (2012); Tim Hornbaker, *Legends of pro wrestling* (2016); John W. Pollard, *Danno Mahony: Irish world wrestling champion* (n.d.); www.wrestlingtitles.com/us/newengland/awa/ma-awa-h.html; 'Views from the turnbuckle—wrestling's greatest comet', www.wrestlinginc.com/news/2014/09/views-from-the-turnbuckle-wrestling-greatest-comet-580911/; 'A study of Danno O'Mahoney', www.1wrestlinglegends.com/column/yohe/yohe-02.htm; 'Paul Bowser wrestling biography', legacyofwrestling.com/Bowser.html; 'Riverside history: Crusher Casey and the famous Caseys', www.riversideboatclub.com/news/2016/3/31/riverside-history-crusher-casey-the-famous-caseys (all internet material accessed July 2021)

Jack Charlton

1935–2020

SOCCER PLAYER AND MANAGER

Jack Charlton was born 8 May 1935 in Ashington, a colliery village in Northumberland, near Newcastle, the eldest of four boys of Bob, a miner, and his wife Cissie (née Milburn), a housewife. He attended Hirst North Primary School and then Hirst Park school, a secondary modern. At a young age, he started playing soccer, partly inspired by his older cousin, Jackie Milburn, one of the greatest centre-forwards in the history of Newcastle United, and by four uncles, all of whom were professional football-ers. He played for local boys' teams, first with Ashington YMCA and then with Ashington Welfare.

In 1950, aged fifteen—having flirted with becoming a miner or a policeman—he joined Leeds United. He made 773 appearances (629 in the league) for Leeds, scoring 96 goals, before retiring just before his thirty-eighth birthday. With Leeds he won the first division title (1968/9), the second division title (1963/4), the FA Cup (1972), the League Cup (1968) and the Inter-Cities Fairs Cup (1968 and 1971). In 1967 he was named the Football Writers' Association Footballer of the Year.

Making his England debut when he was twenty-nine years old in 1965, he won 35 caps (scoring 6 goals) and played in the World Cup final on 30 July 1966 when England defeated West Germany 4–2 at Wembley Stadium. His brother Bobbie was also in the England team. While Bobbie was celebrated as a stylish and technically gifted footballer, Jack was a 6ft 3in. (1.9m) central defend-er who was robust, pragmatic and ferociously competitive. One of the iconic images from the aftermath of England's World Cup victory is of Jack and Bobby embracing on their knees on the pitch. Nonetheless, the brothers had a difficult relationship and were estranged for many years.

Following his retirement from playing, Jack was ap-pointed manager of Middlesbrough in May 1973. He led his team to the Division Two title for 1973/4, becoming the 1974 English Manager of the Year. In 1977 he resigned and applied to take charge of the England team but re-ceived no reply. Instead, he managed Sheffield Wednesday for the next six years taking the club from the third di-vision to the second division in 1980. Following a brief return to Middlesbrough in 1984, he endured an unhappy spell managing Newcastle United in 1984–5.

Although he had a respectable career in club management, his appointment as Ireland manager in 1986 came as a surprise. It was, moreover, shrouded in controversy as the former Liverpool manager, Bob Paisley, was believed to have been the preferred choice of the senior executives within the Football Association of Ireland (FAI). Initially considered an outsider for the job, Charlton emerged as a compromise candidate and narrowly prevailed after five ballots of a bitterly divided FAI Council.

Charlton's first game in charge of Ireland was a friendly against Wales in Lansdowne Road, Dublin, on 26 March 1986—a 1–0 defeat before fewer than 15,000 supporters. But he quickly made progress. As the sportswriter, James Lawton, wrote of Charlton: 'In a highly-strung, quick-fire personality, there was a most powerful streak of natural-born leadership' (*Irish Independent*, 12 June 2018). Charlton moulded a strategy that was clear and pragmatic. This meant playing long balls to turn opposing defenders towards their own goal and then harrying them into mistakes. His evocation of this style as 'Put 'em under pressure' became the catch-cry of 'the Charlton Era'.

For all that his detractors considered the approach unpleasant on the eye—and ill-fitted to the quality of players at his disposal—there was no denying its success. Charlton demonstrated tactical innovation and a willingness to evolve that belied the views of critics who saw no sophistication in his methods. His deployment of first Mark Lawrenson and then Paul McGrath—both accomplished central defenders—as holding midfield players was inspired. That he had neither strikers nor wingers with exceptional pace further led Charlton to concentrate on pinning teams in their own half, rather than hitting them on the break.

Initial signs of progress came when Ireland went to a three-team tournament in Iceland and beat the hosts and Czechoslovakia. Then, as part of the European championship qualifying campaign (1986–7), Ireland travelled to play recent World Cup semi-finalists, Belgium, and drew 2–2. Vital wins against Scotland (away) and Bulgaria (at home) followed as Ireland topped its qualifying group for the 1988 European championships in Germany. It was the first time that Ireland had qualified for the finals of a major international soccer tournament.

The highlight of the European championships came in the first game at the Neckarstadion in Stuttgart (12 June 1988), when Ireland defeated England, courtesy of a Ray Houghton header and a superb goalkeeping display by Packie Bonner. After then playing brilliantly in a draw with the USSR (in Hanover), the Irish were unlucky to depart the competition by losing the final group game in Gelsenkirchen against the Netherlands to a freakish late goal. Thousands of Irish fans travelled to Germany for the tournament bringing a new dimension to the Irish sporting experience. This was captured in Christy Moore's ballad 'Joxer goes to Stuttgart' (1989).

Interest in the national soccer team grew further during the qualifying campaign (1988–9) for the 1990 World Cup. The campaign started with three difficult away games, which resulted in draws against Northern Ireland and Hungary, and a loss to Spain. Then, however, a run of four home wins over Spain, Malta, Hungary and Northern Ireland left Ireland needing to defeat Malta away. Two John Aldridge goals brought a comfortable victory.

The first Irish team to qualify for the World Cup contained many British-born players who were the sons or grandsons of Irish emigrants. Charlton mined the Irish diaspora, adding players such as Ray Houghton from

Glasgow and the Liverpudlian John Aldridge to home-grown players such as Ronnie Whelan. Of the fifty-six players who played for the Republic of Ireland during the Charlton era, thirty-three were born outside Ireland. Against a historic and contemporary backdrop of mass emigration and contested ideas about Irish identity, the national soccer team expressed a broad, inclusive vision of Irishness that celebrated the diaspora.

The World Cup was held in Italy with Ireland in a difficult group alongside the Netherlands, England and Egypt. The first match was a 1–1 draw with England in Cagliari, Sardinia, where Kevin Sheedy equalised for Ireland seventeen minutes from time. It was greeted in Ireland like a victory. Crowds poured onto the streets across the country. There was also relief that the game had passed off without great incident, given the reputation of England's supporters. Italy's leading sports daily, *Gazzetta Dello Sport*, noted that the sterility of the football had even put the hooligans to sleep.

Ireland followed this with a disappointing scoreless draw against Egypt in Palermo, Sicily. There was a major national controversy when RTÉ television pundit Eamon Dunphy outraged public opinion by declaring himself 'embarrassed and ashamed at that performance'. Dunphy was Charlton's most vocal critic, and the controversy intensified when he travelled to Italy but was prevented from asking a question at an Irish team press conference. RTÉ's saturation coverage fuelled a public interest that extended beyond traditional sporting audiences, turning the World Cup into a shared national experience—it also confirmed Charlton's status as the most popular figure in Irish public life.

In the final group match in Palermo against the reigning European champions, the Netherlands, the Irish trailed to an early goal until the seventy-first minute when

Ireland's long-ball tactics pressured the Dutch goalkeeper into fumbling the ball into the path of Niall Quinn, who scored, securing yet another draw. This qualified Ireland for the second round where the match with Romania in Genoa ended scoreless after extra time. In Ireland's first ever penalty shoot-out in international competition, a Packie Bonner save from Daniel Timofte was followed by a clinching penalty from David O'Leary.

Three days before the Irish team played Italy in the quarter-finals in Rome, they were granted an audience with Pope John Paul II. Charlton recorded in his World Cup diary: 'As a non-Catholic, I found it a very moving experience' (*Jack Charlton's world cup diary*, 161). Ireland saved its best World Cup performance for the Italian match—but lost. Before 73,000 spectators at the Stadio Olimpico, Italy's Salvatore 'Toto' Schillaci scored the decisive goal in Ireland's 1–0 defeat. An estimated half a million people welcomed the Irish team home to Dublin—50,000 of them waiting at the airport to greet them as they stepped off the plane.

There was disappointment (and, indeed, surprise, such were the changed level of expectations) when the Irish team narrowly failed to qualify for the 1992 European championships. A rejuvenation of the team during the qualifying campaign for the World Cup in the USA in 1994 saw the emergence of Roy Keane, one of the best midfielders in the English Premier League, along with promising young players such as Gary Kelly, Phil Babb and Jason McAteer. The qualifying campaign reached its endgame with Charlton's team needing at least a draw against Northern Ireland at Windsor Park, Belfast. Amid a dramatic worsening of violence in Northern Ireland, the match was played on 17 November 1993 in an exceptionally hostile atmosphere. The Republic of Ireland scored a late equaliser to snatch a draw and with that, World Cup qualification.

Ireland's opening game at the 1994 World Cup was against Italy in Giants Stadium, New Jersey, on 18 June 1994. A huge proportion of the 75,000 fans present were Irish— those who had travelled to America and those who were based there—and they saw a remarkable 1–0 victory (again courtesy of a Ray Houghton goal) over an Italian side who went on to reach the World Cup final. Thereafter, however, Charlton's players failed to cope with the heat, particularly in a schedule that had Ireland's remaining games kicking off in the midday sun. The next match was a 2–1 defeat to Mexico in Orlando, before a draw against Norway back at Giants Stadium secured Ireland's place in the last sixteen for the second World Cup running. But in the second-round match in Orlando, Ireland succumbed 2–0 to the Netherlands, ending their World Cup in a damp squib.

Charlton's unsuccessful last qualifying campaign with Ireland—for the 1996 European championships—ended with two losses to Austria, home and away, and an embarrassing away draw with Liechtenstein. Pitted in a play-off against the Netherlands, Ireland lost 2–0 on 13 December 1995 at Anfield, Liverpool. Days later and before he could be formally sacked by the FAI, Jack Charlton resigned as manager of Ireland. He said: 'In my heart of hearts, I knew I'd wrung as much as I could out of the squad I'd got— that some of my older players had given me all they had to give' (*Jack Charlton: autobiography*, 298). He had been merciless in his removal of ageing players (Liam Brady) or those who did not do exactly as he said (David O'Leary), but by 1995 he did not have the same quality to allow for such ruthlessness.

By the time of his departure, he had presided over an era of unprecedented Irish achievement in international soccer. Charlton had boosted soccer's popularity, but the sport remained beset by problems of weak organisation, poor infrastructure, and an inadequately funded and supported domestic professional league. This did nothing to diminish the magnificence of the social and cultural moment in Ireland, and Charlton's role in providing many memorable occasions for communal celebration.

Charlton's personality endeared him to many, as did his fishing trips and pub appearances throughout the country. He was as relatable as he was likeable, the earthiness of his character finding expression in an international team whose play was grounded in unending commitment. That he was English in Ireland during some of the worst years of the 'Troubles' in Northern Ireland inspired a diversity of sentiments. At his first match in Lansdowne Road a banner was displayed which read 'Go Home Union Jack'. Later, his unique personality allowed for the consideration that he was not a typical Englishman. If nothing else, his presence demanded that a different aspect of Englishness be accommodated within the popular discourse. By contrast, English soccer supporters taunted him as a traitor and booed him during a match between Ireland and England at Wembley in 1992. He was visibly dismayed when English supporters rioted during Ireland's 'friendly' with England at Lansdowne Road in 1995.

Subsequently Charlton was offered numerous managerial positions but declined them all. Instead, he traversed Britain and Ireland delivering up to five after-dinner speeches a week. He was involved in numerous football-themed publications, most notably his diaries for the 1990 and 1994 World Cups, while his autobiography came out in 1996. He also published books on hunting and fishing, and made more than twenty-five documentary films, on subjects ranging from salmon fishing and the Duke of Buccleuch (referred to as 'His Dukiness' by Charlton) to his national service in the cavalry and holidaying in Blackpool. All of this was in keeping with a childhood in which he was endlessly resourceful in developing new ways to make money—from selling newspapers, chopped wood and fish, to making pig swill.

Awarded an OBE in 1974, he was also appointed a deputy lieutenant of Northumberland, inducted into the English Football Hall of Fame (2005) and made a freeman of Leeds (2009). In Ireland he was made a freeman of Dublin (1994) and given honorary Irish citizenship (1995). He returned regularly to Ireland, keeping a holiday home in Ballina, Co. Mayo, from 1991 to 2014, using it as a base from which to fish. Diagnosed latterly with lymphoma and with dementia, he died in his home in Northumberland on 10 July 2020. He was survived by his wife Pat (née Kemp), whom he had married in 1958, and by their three children, John, Deborah and Peter. There is a life-size statue of him at Cork Airport and a mural on a wall in Ballina.

Paul Rouse

Sources

Jack Charlton (with Peter Byrne), *Jack Charlton's world cup diary* (1990); Tom Humphries, *The legend of Jack Charlton* (1994); Stanley Liversedge, *Big Jack: the life and times of Jack Charlton* (1994); Jack Charlton (with Peter Byrne), *Jack Charlton: autobiography* (1996); Declan Lynch, *Days of heaven: Italia '90 and the Charlton years* (2010); Leo McKinstry, *Jack and Bobby: a story of brothers in conflict* (2011); Peter Byrne, *Green is the colour* (2012); Colin Young, *Jack Charlton: the authorised biography* (2016); *Irish Independent*, 12 June 2018; Rob Bagchi, *The biography of Leeds United* (2019); *Daily Telegraph*, 11 July 2020; *The Times* (London), 11 July 2020; *New York Times*, 11 July 2020; *The Irish Times*, 11, 18 July 2020; *Sunday Independent*, 12 July 2020; *Guardian*, 12 July 2020; *Yorkshire Post*, 14 July 2020; Jonathan Wilson, *Two brothers: the life and times of Bobby and Jackie Charlton* (2022)

Nina Coote

1883–1945

CROQUET PLAYER

Nina Edith Coote was born 23 September 1883 in Tunbridge Wells, Kent, England, only child of Orlando Robert Coote (1855–1927), land agent, and his wife Edith Mary (née Hume) (1858/9–1920). Hailing from a landed family based in the Irish midlands, Orlando Coote was an avid sportsman and sports administrator. He was the principal founder and first captain (1887), and subsequently president, of Athlone Association Football Club (forerunner of League of Ireland club Athlone Town); earlier in the 1880s he had founded a soccer club in Castlerea, Co. Roscommon. A founding officer (1896) of Athlone Garden Vale Hockey Club, he was involved in hockey administration in Connaught and Ireland, and was associated with tennis, rowing, yachting, cycling and coursing. By 1901 the family, who were adherents of the Church of Ireland, were residing at Bunnavally, Co. Westmeath, near Athlone.

Regarded by contemporaries as a beautiful young woman, Nina Coote began playing croquet at an early age and discovered a natural affinity for the sport. A member of Garden Vale Tennis and Croquet Club in Athlone, she won the South of Ireland croquet championship in both 1901 and 1902. After losing in the semi-final of the 1903 croquet championship of Ireland to the eventual winner, her Garden Vale clubmate Mrs Edith Preston, Coote contested the 1903 English ladies' open championship in Wimbledon, which she won in a remarkable upset, defeating Preston in the final. In 1905 Coote again won the English ladies' open championship and also won the mixed doubles, partnering Cyril Corbally, one of the 'Irish terrors' who had made a huge impression on the sport. The same year she won the Irish gold medals for croquet and the English Croquet Association's gold caskets, the prestigious mixed doubles championship. Twice in 1904 she defeated in competition Lily Gower, considered the greatest croquet player (man or woman) of the time. In 1905 she tied with Gower in seventh place in the champions' cup (latterly the president's cup), which was open to men and women, and came ninth the following two years. In 1908 she repeated Gower's earlier success in winning the English Croquet Association's men's gold medal, and after this triumph the rules were changed to prevent women entering the competition. The ladies' champion cup began in 1911, and in the inaugural year Gower (now married to R. C. J. Beaton) triumphed, with Coote third.

Coote's playing relied on dash and style, rather than accuracy. She played a fast-paced game, completing her games in record times, with a golf-style side-swing. Her form, although occasionally brilliant, was erratic, allowing the more consistent, if less elegant, Gower to dominate the competitions. Off court Coote had a lively personality, with a sharp tongue, and spared no one with her caustic barbs and comments.

After the first world war, her playing ability faded and she retired from active participation, becoming a successful manager of croquet teams, doing so with a firm and dictatorial style. In 1936, after a failed love affair, she became gradually withdrawn and reclusive. She turned to spiritualism and became convinced she would die in her sixty-first year. Increasingly eccentric, she helped make the prophecy come true by deliberately delaying a minor operation that would not otherwise have been dangerous. She died 6 January 1945 in Roehampton, Greater London, from complications resulting from the operation.

Patrick M. Geoghegan

Sources

General Register Office England and Wales (birth certificate); National Archives of Ireland, Census of Ireland, 1901; *The Times* (London), 9 January 1945; D. M. C. Prichard, *The history of croquet* (1981); Nicky Smith, *Queen of games* (1991); Frank Lynch, *A history of Athlone Town F.C.* (1991), 3–9, 21; John Gleeson (ed.), *Fyffes dictionary of Irish sporting greats* (1993); John Bernard Burke, *A general and heraldic history of the peerage and baronetage* (1999 edition), 657; Tom Hunt, *Sport and society in Victorian Ireland: the case of Westmeath* (2007); 'The Croquet Association: History and Archives: croquet records', www.croquet.org.uk/history/index (internet material accessed September 2010)

Clara ('Ma') Copley

1865–1949

BOXING PROMOTER

Clara ('Ma') Copley was born 14 May 1865 at Masbrough, Rotherham, England, to Jonas Roddis, fishmonger, and his wife Mary Roddis. Clara was the sixth of their nine children. She married Joseph Copley of Leeds on 22 November 1886 at Darfield, Yorkshire. They had two sons, James Henry, born 1887, and Percy, born 1889. In 1891 the family was living in Rotherham, where Joseph had become a fishmonger. By 1895 the couple was operating a fish and chip stall in the fairground at Rotherham, and from this beginning took an interest in fairground entertainment. They moved to Liverpool where they operated an amusement arcade and owned a commercial waxwork museum.

Moving to Belfast, by 1901 the couple was operating a novelty stall at the Chapel Fields fairground, a large area of open land opposite St Malachy's church, Alfred Street, in the city centre. Clara and Joseph were to live at the Chapel Fields for the next forty years. In 1908 she opened the Theatre Royal, a 'fit-up theatre' housed in a wooden building, in Bangor, Co. Down. During the next four years her theatre company, in which she also regularly performed herself, often staged three or four different productions each week.

Copley continued to develop her fairground interests at Chapel Fields, and by the 1920s she had become the proprietor of the site, with the entertainments advertised in the press as 'Copley's Amusements'. She had been interested in boxing since her early years and had allowed Jim Lagan, a local ex-professional boxer, to operate a boxing booth as part of the fair. Each booth would have a handful of professional boxers associated with it, and members of the public would be invited to attempt to last three rounds with a boxer of their choice; those few who did received a prize of around £1.

In 1934 Copley and Lagan started to use the booth to stage regular unlicensed boxing tournaments. Lagan died within a few months, and Copley took over the booth, relocated it within a large tent and continued to stage these tournaments as sole promoter. As they became increasingly popular, she constructed a wooden arena to replace the tent and also applied to the British Boxing Board of Control (BBBC) to take out a boxing promoter's licence.

The BBBC had introduced licensing in 1929 to improve the way in which the sport was administered and controlled. When Copley was granted her promoter's licence in April 1936, she became, at the age of seventy, the UK's first licensed woman boxing promoter and also the first woman boxing promoter to operate on the island of Ireland. What she had constructed became known as the 'Chapel Fields Arena', sometimes also known as the 'Belfast Arena', and it proved to be the breeding ground for many of Belfast's top-line boxing professionals during the bleak 1930s. The first tournament was held there on 30 May 1934, and her first licensed tournament took place on 4 April 1936. Rinty Monaghan, later to become the world flyweight champion, fought for Copley many times as an aspiring young professional and learnt his trade at the arena. She nurtured the careers of many notable Ulster boxers, including Jim 'Spider' Kelly junior, Bunty Doran, Tommy Armour and Jackie Quinn.

Copley fought hard to establish herself as a promoter in Belfast during the 1930s. A leading rival, Jim Rice, tended to promote shows of greater quality using larger and more prestigious venues, such as St George's Market, the Ulster Hall, St Mary's Hall and Grosvenor Park. Copley provided the quantity, staging nearly 600 boxing tournaments (averaging between two and three a week) in the four years her arena operated, greatly exceeding any of her rivals. She was ably assisted by her matchmaker, Mick Ross, who also acted as her general manager. Ross paired the fighters to provide competitive and entertaining contests. She kept a close eye on the financial side and rarely missed a tournament for she genuinely appreciated the sport. Copley took a maternal interest in many of her boxers, most of whom were young lads from tough backgrounds; they all knew her as 'Ma'. The support she provided to her boxers was long remembered by many.

The city council had become concerned about the safety of the arena, packed with spectators when her boxing tournaments took place, and ordered its closure. Her last show there took place on 24 September 1938. Within eleven days she had relocated her operation to the nearby Ulster Hall, where she promoted another two hundred tournaments until 1942, when, aged seventy-seven, she finally retired from the sport. She had purchased some land and property at Donegall Pass, not far from Chapel Fields, and she lived out her years at 56 Donegall Pass, where she died on 14 March 1949, after being bedridden during her final months. She was survived by her husband James, then aged eighty-nine, and by her son James Henry.

In her later years she enjoyed regaling a constant stream of visitors with reminiscences of her colourful and eventful life. In March 2012 the Ulster Historical Circle erected a plaque in Copley's memory (with an incorrect year of birth) at her former residence in Donegall Pass.

Miles Templeton

Sources

General Register Office England and Wales (birth certificate, marriage certificate); National Archives UK, England and Wales census, 1891; National Archives of Ireland, Census of Ireland, 1901; British Boxing Board of Control archives, (application for license); *Sheffield Independent* 16 February 1895; *Belfast Telegraph,* 16 December 1901; 27 March 1926; *County Down Spectator and Ulster Standard,* 2 October 1908; *Boxing,* 5 June 1935; *Irish News,* 26 September 1938; *Belfast Morning News,* 26 September 1938; information from Brian Madden (Irish boxing historian); information from Doreen Dedenney (granddaughter)

Michael Cusack

1847–1906

Gaelic Athletic Association
founder and sportsman

Michael Cusack was born 20 September 1847 in Carron, on the eastern edge of the Burren, Co. Clare, third of five children of Matthew Cusack, herdsman, and Bridget Cusack (née Fleming), both native Irish speakers. Educated at Carron national school, he completed his teacher training at Enniscorthy's District Model School (1864–5) and the Central Model School in Marlborough

Street, Dublin (1866). After he qualified, he taught at St Colman's College, Newry, Co. Down (1871–4); Blackrock College, Co. Dublin (1874–5); and Clongowes Wood, Co. Kildare (1876–7). In October 1877 he set up an academy in Dublin to prepare students taking civil service and other public examinations; it prospered, moving from premises in Nelson Street to 4 Gardiner Place, and at its height Cusack was earning £1,500 a year. In June 1876 he married Margaret Woods, sister of a Dublin barrister; they had seven children.

Cusack was a strongly built man and a good all-round athlete who played hurling, football and cricket, and excelled at the high jump and weight-throwing events. In May 1875 he entered the Dublin Amateur Athletic Club sports meeting, and his excellent performances in the 16-lb (7.25kg) and 42-lb (19kg) weight-throwing events were praised by the *Irish Sportsman*. He competed in further events during the year, including the O'Connell centenary games at Lansdowne Road, Dublin, in August. He was also a keen cricketer and a member of the French College Cricket Club from 1875. His academy promoted athletic spirit as well as academic achievement; in 1879 he fielded and captained a Cusack's Academy rugby XV, and he continued to play rugby occasionally until about 1882 (he is pictured above in a rugby jersey). He returned to athletics as a competitor and became Irish 16-lb shot champion in 1881. He regularly attended athletics meetings as an official and a participant, but soon became disillusioned with the poor organisation, social exclusivity and increasing professionalism of Dublin athletics; he was also appalled by the association of gambling and sport. At first, he attempted to reform Irish athletics by working through established clubs and organising open meetings.

In 1879 he became a member of the council of the ailing Irish Champion Athletic Club and a founding member of the City and Suburban Harriers (although he had a poor opinion of cross-country running); in 1882 he helped to found the Dublin Athletic Club. But he soon concluded that the sporting establishment was unwilling to welcome working people or include traditional Irish sports in their programmes.

Cusack had strong cultural as well as sporting interests. A native Irish speaker, he was a member of the Society for the Preservation of the Irish Language, founded in 1876, and became treasurer of the breakaway Aontacht na Gaeilge (the Gaelic Union) in January 1882. He also helped found Aontacht na Gaeilge's *Gaelic Journal,* which first appeared in November 1882 and was an important milestone in the language revival movement. By 1882 he had linked his desire to reform Irish athletics with a plan to revive hurling, his interest in traditional Irish sports possibly reinforced by his involvement with Aontacht na Gaeilge. In 1879 he had discussed his intention to revive Irish games with the athlete and Fenian P. W. Nally, who had established the National Athletic Sports Meeting in Mayo in September 1879 to counter the elitism of the controlling body in Dublin (Cusack later singled out Nally as the key influence in persuading him to found the GAA). In February 1883 Cusack helped to found the short-lived Dublin Hurling Club, of which he was vice-president and team captain. Although it attracted little interest and dissolved within a year, it managed to formulate and publish new rules for the game, and in his column in the *Shamrock* he advised young people to take up hurling and gave useful hints on how it should be played. In October 1883 he made another effort to revive hurling by founding Cusack's Academy Hurling Club and in December the Metropolitan Hurling Club. His club had only about forty players, but he soon established contacts with like-minded enthusiasts throughout Ireland in Galway and Munster, and on Easter Monday 1884 his Metropolitan club played a game in Ballinasloe against a local team.

By now he had turned sharply against games of English origin, denouncing rugby and cricket as corrupting alien influences, and he regularly used his columns in various publications—*United Ireland*, *Irishman*, *Shamrock* and *Irish Sportsman*—to criticise the anti-national and socially exclusive character of existing sporting bodies. When in summer 1884 the Dublin weekly sports journals *Irish Sportsman* and *Sport* advocated bringing all athletics meetings in Ireland under the control of English rules, Cusack saw this as a challenge to the growing spirit of national self-reliance, and it spurred him to take his own initiative. In an article, 'A word about Irish athletics' published in the Parnellite *United Ireland* (11 October 1884), he claimed that sports in Ireland were organised by those 'hostile to the dearest aspirations of the Irish people'. As a result, traditional Irish games had declined and the strength and endurance of the Irish people were gradually being sapped; the influences that had corrupted the towns and cities were now spreading to the countryside, and most athletics meetings consisted of little other than 'foot-races, betting and flagrant cheating'. It was imperative, therefore, that Irish people should found their own sporting organisation 'to encourage and promote in every way every form of athletics which is peculiarly Irish, and to remove with one sweep everything foreign and iniquitous in the present system'. His article elicited an enthusiastic response from Maurice Davin, a well-known athlete from Carrick-on-Suir, Co. Tipperary, who like Cusack had often served as a judge at athletics events. They called a meeting in Hayes's Commercial Hotel, Thurles, Co. Tipperary, on 1 November 1884. Thurles was chosen because of its convenience for many of the best athletes in the country and its proximity to the residence of Archbishop T. W. Croke, an ardent supporter of traditional Irish sports. Only eight men attended the meeting, but Cusack read about sixty messages of support, and they founded the Gaelic Athletic Association (GAA), a national sporting body, open to Irishmen of all classes, creeds and political persuasions, committed to cultivating and promoting indigenous games. Davin was elected president and Cusack one of three honorary secretaries. Croke, C. S. Parnell and Michael Davitt were invited to become the association's patrons. At a second meeting in Thurles on 17 January 1885, Cusack was involved in drawing up new procedural rules for the association and sporting rules for traditional games.

The GAA spread rapidly, and over the next few months Davin and Cusack regularly organised and attended games to explain the rules of hurling and football and see that they were enforced; by December 1886 nearly 600 clubs were affiliated to the association. Cusack travelled extensively throughout the country promoting the new body, and its growth owed much to his organisational skills and dynamic personality. In its early days the association came under attack from other athletics organisations and from unionist newspapers for its openly nationalist political leanings; but, as Gaelic games correspondent of *United Ireland*, Cusack defended it spiritedly throughout 1885–6. In the bitter battle with the largely Dublin-based Irish Amateur Athletic Association (IAAA; founded in February

1885) over the control of Irish athletics, Cusack proved an uncompromising defender of the GAA, denouncing the IAAA as a 'ranting, impotent West British abortion' ('The IRB and the beginnings of the Gaelic Athletic Association …', 426). His conduct as secretary, however, was controversial: he had great difficulty in working within a committee system, rarely consulted anyone, neglected routine administration and was abusive towards both opponents and colleagues. In March 1886 Croke wrote to Cusack advising him to adopt a more conciliatory attitude, but Cusack responded with an insulting letter. When Croke stated that he could not continue as a patron if Cusack carried on with his dictatorial and insolent ways, there were numerous calls for Cusack's resignation, and he reluctantly apologised. Criticism of Cusack's administrative neglect continued, however, and at a stormy meeting in Thurles on 4 July 1886 a majority voted for his removal as secretary, which marked his demise as a genuinely influential force within the GAA.

At the GAA's request he was denied access to *United Ireland* to attack his former colleagues, and in January 1887 he founded a weekly Gaelic games magazine, the *Celtic Times*. He used this to promote Irish language, culture, industry and trade unionism, and to denounce the leadership and administration of the GAA, including criticising the growing influence of the IRB in the association; and to attack rival newspapers, especially the *Freeman's Journal*. His language was as vitriolic as ever: he described the GAA executive as a 'junta of knaves and fools' and a 'miserable, mischievous and traitorous gang' (*Celtic Times*, 15 October 1887). The circulation of the *Celtic Times* declined from 20,000 in May 1887 to 10,000 in December, and the last number was published on 14 January 1888. Even without the paper, he kept up his feud with the association and in September 1888 denounced Davin and Davitt for their part in organising a GAA tour of America. From the late 1880s his fortunes and his health declined: his academy had closed in 1887, his wife died in 1890 and several of his children were placed in orphanages. He earned a precarious living through occasional journalism and private tutoring. In March 1893 he regained a role of some importance when elected Dublin county secretary, though his election caused considerable dissension and many resignations from the GAA. From a position of bitter hostility in the late 1880s and most of the 1890s, Cusack's relationship with the GAA's leadership mellowed in his final years, and the contribution he had made to the association was acknowledged, although he was defeated in the election for GAA secretary in September 1901.

In his youth he may have been a Fenian, and he sometimes gave the impression of being an advocate of physical-force nationalism, particularly when attempting to regain his position in the GAA in the 1890s. This, however, stemmed more from his blustering personality than any real commitment to revolutionary republicanism. Pugnacious, boastful and a heavy drinker, he styled himself 'Citizen Cusack' and with his bushy beard, frock coat, broad-brimmed hat and blackthorn stick, was a conspicuous Dublin character. His irascibility and outspoken nationalism led to him being caricatured as the aggressive and xenophobic 'Citizen' in the 'Cyclops' episode of James Joyce's *Ulysses*. He died penniless in Dublin on 27 November 1906 and was buried in Glasnevin cemetery; his funeral was attended by many leading members of the GAA and Sinn Féin.

James Quinn

Sources

Celtic Times, 19 February–31 December 1887; T. F. O'Sullivan, *Story of the GAA* (1916), 3–21; David Greene, 'Michael Cusack and the rise of the GAA', Conor Cruise O'Brien (ed.), *The shaping of modern Ireland* (1960), 74–84; J. Hurley, 'The founders of the GAA', *Capuchin Annual, 1960*, (1960), 195–7; Mark Tierney, *Croke of Cashel: the life of Archbishop Thomas William Croke 1823–1902* (1976), 192–9; W. F. Mandle, 'The IRB and the beginnings of the Gaelic Athletic Association', *Irish Historical Studies*, vol. 20, no. 80 (September 1977), 418–38; Marcus de Burca, *The GAA: a history* (1980); L. P. Ó Caithnia, *Micheál Ciosóg* (1982); W. F. Mandle, *The Gaelic Athletic Association and Irish nationalist politics, 1884–1924* (1987); Marcus de Burca, *Michael Cusack and the GAA* (1989); Séamus Ó Riain, *Maurice Davin (1842–1927): first president of the GAA* ([1994])

Beauchamp Day

1881–1972

PROFESSIONAL RUNNER

Beauchamp (Bert) Rochfort Day was born 25 December 1881 at 14 Clarinda Park North, Kingstown (Dún Laoghaire), Co. Dublin, son of Beauchamp John Day, gentleman, and Geraldine Isabella Day (née Rochfort). He was educated locally at Corrig School, where at seventeen he won the 100-yards race at the school sports in the tremendous time of 10.2 seconds. Running with the Haddington Harriers, he came to prominence at the Irish Amateur

Athletics Association championships in 1900 when, at just eighteen, he won the 220- and 440-yard titles. Later that year he won the 440-yards at the Dublin Metropolitan Police Sports in 49.4 seconds, a time so quick that it was not believed. Although it was clearly a new Irish record, the timing officials amended his winning time to 50.8 seconds, making it the minimum measurable increment (0.2 seconds) inside the then Irish record of 51.0 seconds. He also raced in the north of England that year, winning several handicap races and defeating the English champion Alfred Tysoe over 440 yards, benefitting from an eight-yard start.

Despite his respectable upbringing, he was drawn into what was perceived as the 'ungentlemanly' sport of professional racing and shocked Irish athletics by turning professional in April 1901 even though it was said that he had been settled with a comfortable income. (Immediately prior to turning professional, he was working in Dublin as a bicycle agent.) He based himself in the north of England, which was a hotbed of professional running, and burst onto the professional racing scene in January 1902 by winning the premier event of the time in Britain, the Powderhall New Year Sprint in Edinburgh. Initially quoted at 20/1 in the betting markets, eventually going off in the final at 4/6, he won the 130-yards race in 12.6 seconds off a 10-yard handicap. Day's backers were said to have won several thousand pounds from skilfully targeting a race that had been seen as too short for him.

Piecing together his professional career is difficult, not least because such runners often raced under assumed names. He was contracted for much of this time to gambling syndicates and participated in many exhibition and handicap events running under the instructions of his employers, which often meant strategically losing races. Professional runners made most of their money from betting on themselves (or others) to win. Noted for his geniality and for his clean-living lifestyle, he was at his best over 440 yards and considered a championship standard runner anywhere from 100 yards to 880 yards.

From 1902, he established himself as Britain's best professional runner, winning numerous handicaps and also 'matches' against other leading runners. He won high-profile matches against Britain's leading professional sprinter Bill Growcott over 120 yards in August 1903 and against the British amateur champion R. W. Wadsley over 220 yards in September 1903; in July 1904, however, he lost to the US champion Tom Keane over 130 yards at Oldham, in what was billed as a world title match. Increasingly, he found himself having to concede insurmountable starts in handicaps while other big names learned to preserve their reputations by not taking up his challenges. During 1905–06 he staged a series of crowd-pulling exhibition matches against trotting horses, generally winning over distances of 100 yards to 110 yards.

With professional running losing popularity in Britain, he arrived in Western Australia in autumn 1906 to take on the celebrated Australian sprinter Arthur Postle for the title of world professional sprint champion. The Australian newspapers were struck by Day's gentlemanly manner, with one terming him a 'Johnny English' (*Sunday Times* (Perth), 28 October 1906). For all that, a moderate brogue was detectible, and Day played up his Irish roots, often sporting a shamrock insignia on his race gear. His match with Postle was staged in Kalgoorlie, Western Australia, a gold-mining area, and involved races over three distances: 75, 130 and 300 yards. On 5 December 1906, before a crowd of 20,000 people, Postle won the 75 by two yards and the 300 by three yards, and as a result the

130 was not run. Day's defeat in the 300 came as a rude shock to the many local Irish who had backed him heavily. Disgruntled gamblers noted how he had come under the wing of the controversial Australian promoter Rufe Naylor, and some even claimed that Day was an imposter.

Day maintained that while he was fairly beaten in the 75, the partisan crowd had interfered with his progress in the 300 (*Sport*, 12 January 1907). A rematch was arranged over 200, 440 and 300 yards, distances more likely to favour Day. On 10 April 1907 some 8,000 spectators gathered at Boulder, Western Australia, to see Postle win all three races convincingly, with Day giving up before reaching the line in the 440-yards event. If he did not run to form in his contests with Postle, he performed impressively in numerous handicap races during his time in Australia. Prior to a 440-yards handicap held on 1 April in the Perth suburb of Claremont, he bet all his money on himself before learning to his horror that five other runners were also being heavily backed. A highly motivated Day proceeded to win in a time of 47.8 seconds, breaking the thirty-four-year-old world professional record by half a second.

Soon after his second defeat to Postle, he departed for New Zealand where he emerged victorious from his matches held in Dunedin (4 June) and Auckland (29 June) against the local champion Lachlan Campbell McLachlan; he won four out of the six races in distances varying between 175 yards and 440 yards. The New Zealand Athletic Union refused to sanction the second match. Progressing onwards to the USA, he participated in exhibitions and won his 100-yard match against W. D. Walker in Goldfield, Nevada, on 12 October, but what would have been a lucrative coup came unstuck when one of the principal stakeholders absconded owing nearly $2,000. He reached Britain in November 1907, bringing his fifteen-month-tour to an end.

There, he resumed his rivalry with Postle by defeating him on 17 August 1908 in a 440-yard race for the world title in front of a record crowd of over 15,000 people in Salford, winning easily in 49.2 seconds. The first man to beat Postle on level terms, Day's victory was hugely popular in the north of England, allowing him to embark on a series of well-paid exhibitions. That November he defeated Growcott in another well-attended match for the 220-yard world title. A month earlier Day had won the Welsh Powderhall Handicap over 130 yards at Pontypridd, running off a handicap of three-and-a-half yards. Postle, who was running from scratch, had to withdraw from the final due to an injury but admitted he would not have beaten Day. Day's matches against Postle and Growcott, as well as his participation in handicap races featuring Postle, Growcott and other internationally renowned athletes, revived interest in professional running in the north of England during 1908.

The next year he travelled to South Africa where he lost his 220-yards world title to Postle in a race in Johannesburg, held on 20 March 1909; shortly afterwards he also surrendered his 440-yards world title to Postle in the same city. Back in England that May, his defeat to Postle over 220 yards at Higginshaw, Oldham, aroused suspicion, as he had just run a much faster time in a trial.

Although he spent his best years 'running to order', which meant that his full potential was never fulfilled, the times Day ran suggest that he deserves to be considered as one of the greatest Irish athletes of his time, and as possibly the greatest Irish sprinter ever. Yet his achievements have not been properly acknowledged. The widely held view among the middle and upper classes that professional athletics was not respectable, coupled with the cult of amateurism and the rise of the Olympic games, has obscured the fact that the best athletes of this time were often professional. (It is hard to make direct comparisons as amateur and professional races were timed differently, with Day being of the view that amateur races were timed more generously.) Many Olympic champions subsequently turned professional, and professional running attracted tremendous interest and large crowds, particularly in the north of England, Scotland, the US and the southern hemisphere.

One consequence of this neglect is that little is known about his life once he faded from the professional athletics scene after 1910. He enlisted in the Sportsman's Battalion upon the start of the first world war in 1914 and served on the front lines in France before being transferred to the motor transport division in September 1916, suffering from shellshock. By then he had married (September 1915) Hilda E. Baker from Fylde, Lancashire. They had a daughter, Enid, in 1916 and lived in the village of Bispham, near Blackpool. After divorcing his first wife, he married Margaret Barnes, a widow, in 1934, by which date he was living in Blackpool. Both his daughter Enid's birth certificate (1916) and his second marriage certificate (1934) refer to him as being of independent means. He was resident in Argyle Road, Blackpool, when he died in Rossall hospital, Fleetwood, on 17 November 1972. His death certificate describes him as a retired executive officer.

Jim Shanahan and Terry Clavin

Sources

General Register Office England and Wales (second marriage certificate, death certificate, daughter's birth certificate); National Archives of Ireland, Census of Ireland, 1901; *Evening Herald*, 7 May 1900; 20 April 1901; *Sporting Chronicle*, 11 January 1902; 8, 15, 17 August, 16 November 1908; *Manchester Courier and Lancashire General Advertiser*, 17 September 1903; *Scottish Referee*, 18 July 1904; *Athletic News*, 31 July 1905; *Sunday Times* (Perth), 28 October 1906; 7 April 1907; 4 October 1908; *Referee* (Sydney), 21 November 1906; 5 June, 3 July, 11 December 1907; *Kalgoorlie Miner*, 10 December 1906; *Sporting Life*, 22 December 1906; *Sport*, 12 January, 25 May, 19 October 1907; 6 January, 19 February 1910; *The West Australian*, 11 April 1907; *The Times* (London), 17 August, 6, 19, 30 October 1908; 22, 27 March, 19 April 1909; *The Northern Miner*, 17 May 1909; *The Sportsman*, 27 October 1914; *The People*, 24 September 1916; *Sporting Globe* (Melbourne), 25 January, 1, 8 February, 1, 22 March, 12, 19, 26 April 1933; P. D. Mehigan ('Carbery'), *Fifty years of Irish athletics* (1943); William Dooley, *Champions of the athletic arena* (1946); Arnold E. H. Bousefield, *Corrig School, Kingstown* (1958)

Jack Dempsey

1862–95

BOXER

Jack ('The Nonpareil') Dempsey, world middleweight boxing champion, was born John Edward Kelly on 15 December 1862, near Clane, Co. Kildare, son of Martin Kelly and Alicia Kelly (née Lennon). In 1867, aged four, he emigrated with his family to America, where he attended public school in Brooklyn, New York. His father died while he was still a child, and his mother married Patrick Dempsey, whose surname he assumed. On leaving school he worked as a cooper and earned money on the side as a professional wrestler, enjoying considerable success. He fought his first professional boxing match against the Irish-born Ed McDonald, whom he knocked out in twenty-one rounds, in a dilapidated hall on Staten Island, New York (7 April 1883). For most of his career he boxed under the rules of the London prize ring, based on fighting bare-knuckled (or, latterly, in skin-tight gloves), in rounds that lasted until one of the men was knocked to the ground. Such fights were illegal in many jurisdictions, yet often widely reported in the newspapers. The contestants fought for stake money supplied by backers, by the small crowds in attendance and by gamblers.

Dempsey defeated Jack Boylan, the Irish lightweight champion, in twenty-three rounds in Flushing, New York (14 August 1883). Several of his early fights were interrupted by the arrival of police (and scored as 'no contests'), including his match against the highly experienced Harry Force, whom he was beating well after eleven rounds, in Coney Island, New York (3 September 1883); Force failed to appear for a rematch set by the referee. Amid a run of impressive results—he scored knockouts in eight of his first fourteen bouts—Dempsey decisively defeated Billy Dacey for the lightweight championship of New York (6 March 1884), and briefly claimed the world title. He soon abandoned the lightweight class, however, to his friend and protégé, the Cork-born Jack McAuliffe, and competed in the middleweight division. Accepting the challenge of George Fulljames, the Canadian champion, who offered to fight any claimant for the vacant world title, Dempsey scored a knockout victory in the twenty-second round in Great Kills, New York (30 July 1884). Though boxing historians date his world middleweight championship from this victory (1884–91), his claim was disputed until 1886, when he successively vanquished two highly regarded rival claimants, Jack Fogarty and George LaBlanche, thereby securing universal recognition.

Throughout the 1880s Dempsey was the second most famous athlete in America, behind only heavyweight champion John L. Sullivan. Handsome, personable and well mannered, despite being a heavy drinker, Dempsey enjoyed a respectability denied to the rough-hewn Sullivan. This lent force to efforts to legalise the sport and attracted many women to his legion of admirers. Standing 5ft 8in. (1.73m) in height, he weighed several pounds over 10st. (63.5kg), placing him within the welterweight limit. By fighting in the middleweight division (the limit of which was raised in 1889 from 11st. (69.8kg) to 11st. 4lb (71.7kg)), he routinely fought heavier opponents. Skilful, quick, clever and agile, he had a sharp left jab and a potent stiff-armed right. He was expert at feinting an opponent to create openings and land his accurate, perfectly timed punches. Cool under pressure, normally he relied on outboxing his foe but could stand his ground and out-slug a man when necessary. His nickname, 'The Nonpareil', meaning 'unique' or 'unequalled', signified his absolute dominance and was derived from the agnomen of Jack Randall, a London-based middleweight of the 1820s.

Through his four prime years (1884–7), Dempsey was unbeaten in fifty-two fights, none of his non-title contests lasting longer than ten rounds. The period culminated in his most famous fight, a titanic struggle against Johnny Reagan at two separate outdoor seaside locations on Long Island, New York (13 December 1887). When, after eight rounds, the ring was engulfed by the rising ocean tide, the contestants and their attendants travelled twenty-five miles by tugboat to a second site on higher ground. Early in the fight, Reagan's sharply spiked shoes opened a four-inch gash in Dempsey's shin (Reagan had been observed paring the spikes before the fight). After the resumption Dempsey took command, Reagan repeatedly saving himself by going to ground intentionally. With another interruption looming amid a blinding snowstorm, Dempsey concluded proceedings with a knockout blow to the jaw in the forty-fifth round. His rematch against George LaBlanche (27 August 1889) was declared a non-title fight when the challenger weighed in over the limit. In the thirty-second round, LaBlanche, struggling desperately and nearing defeat, suddenly knocked Dempsey unconscious by pivoting on his heel, and sweeping his stiffened right arm in an arc to land a backhand blow with the knuckles on the champion's jaw. Though the 'pivot blow' (also called the 'LaBlanche swing') was widely decried as unethical and soon was officially outlawed, the referee refused to call a foul, and Dempsey, while retaining his title, lost his unbeaten record.

Dempsey defeated Australian Billy McCarthy over twenty-eight rounds in San Francisco in the first world middleweight title fight contested under marquis of Queensberry rules, with padded gloves and three-minute rounds (18 February 1890). Competing for a record purse of $12,000, he lost his title to the Cornish-born, New Zealand-reared Bob Fitzsimmons in New Orleans (14 January 1891). Though a two-to-one favourite, Dempsey was comprehensively outmastered, unable to fathom Fitzsimmons's unorthodox style. Knocked out in the thirteenth round, he lamented that he would be less troubled to have lost the title to an Irishman or an American, 'but to an Englishman, that's what kills me' *(The fighting Irish,* 54). His fitness rapidly declining, suffering the early stages of tuberculosis, he fought only three more times. In his last fight he was beaten in three rounds by Tommy Ryan for the world welterweight title (18 January 1895).

Over a twelve-year professional career, Dempsey was defeated only three times in sixty-eight contests; his forty-eight victories included twenty-five knockouts. Bridging the transition between the London prize ring and the Queensberry rules, he is listed as the first modern world middleweight champion. Probably the greatest Irish-born boxer in any class, he is widely regarded as one of the best ever 'pound-for-pound' fighters. Boxing historian Tracy G. Callis (of the International Boxing Research Organisation) ranked him third in this regard, behind only Fitzsimmons and Sugar Ray Robinson. He was elected to the *Ring* Hall of Fame in 1954 and to the International Boxing Hall of Fame in 1992. The even more famous eponymous heavyweight champion of the 1920s—born William Harrison Dempsey in Manassa, Colorado—boxed as Jack Dempsey in tribute to the Nonpareil.

Dempsey married (27 July 1886) Margaret Brady, of Portland, Oregon, whom he met while touring the west coast in 1885; they had two daughters. He made his home in Portland, where he died 2 November 1895.

Lawrence William White

Sources

J. B. McCormick, *The Square: stories of the prize ring* (1897); *Dictionary of American biography* (1928–58); Gilbert Odd, *The fighting blacksmith: a biography of Bob Fitzsimmons* (1976); Benny Green, *Shaw's champions* (1978); Bert Randolph Sugar (ed.), *The Ring record book and boxing encyclopaedia* (1981 edition); Patrick Myler, *The fighting Irish: Ireland's role in world boxing history* (1987), 51–5, 172, 177; Gilbert Odd, *Hamlyn encyclopaedia of boxing* (1990 edition); Nat Fleischer, Sam Andre *et al.*, *A pictorial history of boxing* (1998 edition); Patrick Myler, *Gentleman Jim Corbett* (1998); Tracy Callis, 'Pound for pound', *Wail! The CBZ Journal* (August 1998), www.cyberzoneboxing.com; Tracy Callis, '"Nonpareil" Jack Dempsey: slick and quick', *Wail! The CBZ Journal* (January 1999), www.cyberzoneboxing.com; Harry Mullan, *The world encyclopedia of boxing: the definitive illustrated guide* (1999 edition); *American national biography* (1999); '"Nonpareil" Jack Dempsey' (boxing record), www.cyberboxingzone.com/boxing/non-jack.htm (all internet material accessed April 2012)

Dan Donnelly

1788–1820

PUGILIST

Dan Donnelly was born in Townsend Street, Dublin,
eldest surviving son among seventeen children of Joseph
Donnelly, carpenter, of Dublin; his mother's name was
Gore. His life is one in which reality and mythology are
not easily separated. The main source of information is

a 120-page biography, entitled *The life of Dan Donnelly* (1820), written by T. G. Hazard with help from Donnelly's sister and widow. This account aimed, quite successfully, at burnishing the growing Donnelly legend. Thus, the doctor who attended his birth allegedly predicted that he would perform great deeds for Ireland.

He had a rudimentary education, played hurling on the streets of Dublin and worked as a carpenter for his father. Standing 6ft (1.83m) tall and weighing 14st. (*c.*90 kg), his life was a pursuit of merriment, facilitated by an astonishing capacity for alcohol. Hazard acknowledged his wildness while also depicting him as honourable and patriotic: he fought only with bullies and even then, with regret. His first recorded fight came in a public house when he beat up two men following an insult to his father. On foot of this his fame spread throughout the city. Reluctant to inconvenience his socialising, he eschewed all offers of combat before eventually fighting and defeating a man previously regarded as the best in Dublin.

His reputation drew the notice of Captain William Kelly of Maddenstown House, the Curragh, Co. Kildare. A sports-obsessed racehorse trainer, Kelly was looking for an Irish boxer capable of matching the English bare-knuckle prize fighters who were touring Ireland. Kelly put Donnelly up in a house in Calverstown, Co. Kildare, where he was trained for several months by a Scotsman, Robert Barclay Allardice (known as 'Captain Barclay'). In summer 1814 Donnelly challenged a touring English boxer, Tom Hall, who accepted. Donnelly went into intensive training during which Kelly was said to have posted sentries to prevent any escape to local hostelries.

On 14 September 1814 a large crowd, purportedly 40,000-strong, arrived mainly from Dublin to see the fight in a natural amphitheatre, then called Belcher's Hollow, in the Curragh, Co. Kildare. During the fight the much lighter Hall quickly realised he was outmatched and took to dropping intentionally to the ground, which under the prevailing rules ended the round, permitting him half a minute to recover. (The rules also permitted butting, eye-gouging, hair-pulling and wrestling.) The fight ended with both sides claiming victory when an exasperated Donnelly hit Hall while he was down. The Turf Club, which adjudicated on the bets waged for this match, declared it a tie; neither contestant received the £200 stakes. Donnelly's supporters wildly celebrated his 'victory', and he was hailed as a national hero on his return to Dublin.

In late 1815 a more formidable English boxer, George Cooper, arrived in Ireland to challenge Donnelly. Once more housebound under Barclay's supervision, Donnelly demonstrated uncharacteristic restraint in training diligently for the fight, which was held at the same Curragh venue as before on 13 November 1815. In what was the best performance of his career, Donnelly overwhelmed Cooper in the eleventh round and claimed the £60 purse before a large and vociferous attendance. He made his way back towards Dublin in a carriage pulled by his admirers. The site was subsequently renamed Donnelly's Hollow. Pugilism had been for long a disreputable and illegal activity in Ireland, but Donnelly made it popular and semi-respectable.

After a wealthy merchant set him up as a publican in Capel Street, Dublin, marriage and children tempered Donnelly's lifestyle as the pub traded well off his name. He soon reverted to form, however, by drinking through his profits. Periodic sobriety and attempted industry saw him open further public houses in Poolbeg Street and the Coombe. Aside from engaging in several well-attended sparring exhibitions held in the Olympia Theatre, Dublin, he showed little interest in returning to the ring. Moreover, his reputation, along with the certainty of having to cope with a partisan home crowd, deterred English boxers from fighting him in Ireland.

Needing to clear his debts, he began a tour of England in February 1819 by sparring against the Lancashire boxer Jack Carter in exhibitions held at Liverpool and Manchester, both cities with large Irish immigrant communities. The contrast between Donnelly's power and Carter's skill made these exhibitions a great success. Arriving in an expectant London in March, he sparred before packed houses in various venues against Carter, Harry Harmer, Ben Burns and Tom Spring, showing clear signs of inebriation in his entertaining engagement with Burns. Spring was probably England's best boxer, and Donnelly acquitted himself well against him.

He came under pressure from spectators to commit to a prize fight, particularly after an injury forced his withdrawal from an exhibition against the English champion, Tom Cribb. Like most pugilists, Donnelly preferred the steady money to be earned from sparring exhibitions fought with gloves to the hazards of outdoor bare-knuckle brawling. Rather than lose his popularity, he agreed to take on the veteran Englishman, Tom Oliver, at Crawley Downs on 21 July 1819. The fight was eagerly anticipated, not least because of the nationality of the combatants, with heavy betting occurring in England and Ireland. Some 10,000 people saw Donnelly claim the £210 purse after thirty-two rounds (lasting seventy-two minutes). It was an unimpressive display, however, as his preparations had been far from ideal.

His boundless charm and humour, combined with his unquenchable thirst, had brought him to the fore of London society. He later restyled himself 'Sir Dan', claiming to have been knighted by the Prince Regent for bravery. Women proved as great an attraction as alcohol, and his boxing performances undoubtedly suffered from the venereal disease he contracted. English boxers were less wary of him after the Oliver fight, and he received various challenges, but he was not to be diverted. Eventually running out of money, he returned to Dublin where he received the customary hero's welcome and was led through the city astride a white horse.

In August 1819 he staged sparring exhibitions at Donnybrook Fair before his adoring Irish public, who curtailed his performances by plying him with drink. He then contracted to fight Carter only for this to fall through when they disagreed over the financial terms. Reverting to managing a public house at Pill Lane, he died there on 18 February 1820, after a sudden illness provoked by his lifestyle. His funeral drew a huge crowd as it passed through the streets of Dublin, before his remains were buried at Bully's Acre, Kilmainham. Bully's Acre was regularly targeted by grave robbers, and riots ensued on foot of reports that Donnelly's body had been snatched.

His death was widely reported in Britain, albeit less reverently than was the case in Ireland. Donnelly fought in only three official contests, none of which was against the champion of England, though Cooper and Oliver were strong opponents. Experts were impressed by the strength of his right hook and his skill at throwing opponents to the ground but considered him a little raw; it was said he leant back too much. Regardless, he achieved lasting fame and was commemorated in numerous ballads and dirges, all lauding him for vindicating his country's honour by conquering English opponents. He can be seen as Ireland's first sports celebrity. Pugilism in Ireland declined markedly in popularity after his demise.

In 1888 a memorial obelisk was erected at Donnelly's Hollow in the Curragh, where footprints can still be seen, allegedly those of Donnelly dug out by a rapturous crowd following his passage from the ring after defeating Cooper. A mummified arm, said to have been severed from Donnelly's body by the surgeon who received his corpse from the graverobbers, was displayed in the Hideout public house in Kilcullen, Co. Kildare, for four decades from 1953. During 2006–10 the arm was exhibited in New York and Boston, and in Omagh, Co. Tyrone and Croke Park, Dublin.

Paul Rouse

Sources

Freeman's Journal, 14 November 1815; 17 May 1819; *Carlisle Journal*, 31 July 1819; anon., *A monody on the death of Daniel Donnelly, late champion of Ireland* (1820); T. G. Hazard, *The life of Daniel Donnelly* (1820); *Blackwood's Magazine*, May 1820; 'An operator', *The Fancy*, vol. 1, no. 16 (1826); Pierce Egan, *Boxiana; sketches of modern pugilism during the championship of Cribb …* (1829), vol. 3, 71–126; *Journal of the County Kildare Archaeological Society*, vol. 3 (1899), 26–9; H. D. Miles, *Pugilistica: 144 years of British boxing*, vols 1–3 (1906); Bohun Lynch, *The prize ring* (1925); Henry Funiss, *The by ways and queer ways of boxing* (n.d.); A. J. Liebling, *The sweet science* (1958); Patrick Myler, *Regency rogue: Dan Donnelly: his life and legends* (1976); John Gleeson (ed.), *Fyffes dictionary of Irish sporting greats* (1993); Neal Garnham, '"To die with honour or gain the day": Dan Donnelly as a sporting hero', *Irish Historical Studies*, vol. 37, no. 148 (November 2011), 535–49; James Kelly, *Sport in Ireland, 1600–1840* (2014); Adam Chill, *Bare-knuckle Britons and fighting Irish* (2017); *Kildare Nationalist*, 4 October 2020; Ray Esten, 'Using the gloves to turn a shilling or a crown', www.theirishstory.com/; Ray Esten, 'Scrapping: the early years', www.theirishstory.com/ (all internet material accessed April 2021)

Jack Doyle

1913–78

BOXER

Jack Doyle was born Joseph Alphonsus Doyle on 31 August 1913 at 12 Queen Street, Queenstown (Cobh), Co. Cork, eldest son among four sons and two daughters of Michael Doyle, sailor, of Queenstown, and Anastasia Doyle. His schooling at St Joseph's Presentation Brothers school, Cobh, ended prematurely when his father was invalided out of the navy, forcing Jack to work as a farm labourer, on local coal boats and as a quay labourer. Inspired by a boxing manual, *How to box*, by former world heavyweight champion Jack Dempsey, he worked on his boxing technique in the evenings and was reputed to have knocked out a donkey with one right-hand blow. On being refused entry to the Irish army on account of his youth, he joined (September 1930) the British army and pursued his boxing career in the Irish Guards. His amateur record of twenty-eight straight wins (twenty-seven by knockout) attracted the attention of promoter Dan Sullivan, who contracted him to fight professionally and bought him out of the army for £28 (February 1932).

An imposing 6ft 4in. (1.93m) frame, along with handsome features and relentless charm, earned him such soubriquets as 'The gorgeous Gael', 'The body beautiful', and 'The king of clout'. In 1932 he began his professional career with a flourish, as ten straight knockouts (by courtesy of a powerful right hand) brought him massive publicity. Soon after Sullivan sold Doyle's management contract to a greyhound syndicate for 5,000 guineas (£5,250). Doyle's spectacular victories, backed by his looks and a whirl of hype, allowed him to embark on a lifestyle that neutered his talent even as it developed. An insatiable desire for women was unleashed as he courted the socialites of the West End in London and accommodated the many who sought his company. His training suffered, and by the time he was granted a fight for the British heavyweight championship against Jack Petersen (July 1933), he was suffering from venereal disease. In front of a 70,000 crowd in White City, London, he was disqualified for a series of low blows in the second round, inducing a mini-riot as the crowd stormed the ring, throwing chairs, before carrying him shoulder-high to Marble Arch. He was later fined almost £3,000 (his purse) and banned for six months by the British Boxing Board of Control—a decision he never forgave. He won his next fight in eighty-three seconds, but then turned his back on British boxing amid a breakdown in his relations with his management and continued wrangling with the British boxing authorities over his purse for the Petersen fight.

The break did enable him to pursue a career in singing, and with a fine tenor voice he recorded such songs as 'Mother Machree', which sold heavily. Returning to an adoring Irish public, who viewed his disqualification as part of a British conspiracy to deny him greatness, he packed out the 3,500-seater Theatre Royal in Dublin and the Opera House in Cork. In 1935 he turned to the movies, appearing as a fearsome fighter and robust lover in the buccaneering *McGlusky the sea rover* and later starring in the equally inauspicious *Navy spy* (1937). In Hollywood he married the actress Judith Allen (28 April 1935). Their passionate romance did not stop him embarking on a series of affairs with other women, but attempts at reform saw the couple travel to London, where their concert tour was well received. In Dublin, however, distaste at his marriage to a divorcee forced cancellation of shows at the Theatre Royal, and he returned to America, forming a carousing friendship with Errol Flynn and Clark Gable. He resumed boxing and won his first three fights but lost his fourth when he was unluckily beaten on a technical knockout in the first round by Buddy Baer in Madison Square Garden, New York.

Chastened, he went to Britain as his wife issued divorce proceedings. He re-entered the ring there in January 1937 and, when in an unassailable position, was disqualified against Alf Robinson for hitting him as he sat on the bottom rope of the ring. He won his next two fights, the second, against King Levinsky, being his only contest to go the full distance, before losing what interest he still had in boxing. When fighting former British heavyweight champion Eddie Phillips (27 September 1938), he sought to finish the contest with a haymaker, but missed and fell through the ropes and into the back row of press seats, where he was counted out. Many believe that having failed to defeat Phillips in the first round, he knew his lack of fitness would be exposed and so took a dive by throwing himself through the ropes. He remained a huge draw, and it was estimated that some 250,000 people attempted to get into White City arena for his return fight with Phillips on 10 July 1939. After putting Phillips on the canvas twice, he rushed in to end the fight, ran into a jab and was knocked out. From 1938 he fought on only a handful of occasions, and in 1943 his career was effectively ended by his first-round defeat at the hands of Chris Cole, a Mullingar blacksmith, before a huge crowd at Dalymount Park, Dublin. His seventeen professional wins were achieved through the ferocity of his punch, but his six defeats were the product of non-existent fitness and of a glass jaw, protected by a minimalist defence. Few of his fights lasted more than two rounds.

Even by the standards of his sport, he was an outrageous self-publicist whose flamboyance was not tempered in defeat. He earned a vast amount of money and at the height of his fame kept a large mansion at Ascot, attended by an entourage that included bodyguards, servants, chauffeurs and a singing maestro. There were numerous affairs, including one with the automobile heiress Delphine Dodge, as well as with her fifteen-year-old daughter and her sister-in-law. The Dodge family later paid him £10,000 and threatened him at gunpoint to stay away from the women of the family. Another actress, Betty Strathmore, took poison in front of him in a hotel. He then met Movita, a Mexican actress who had appeared with Clark Gable in *Mutiny on the Bounty*, and they married in Mexico (January 1939) and then in St Andrew's church, Westland Row, Dublin (February 1943). The couple toured and performed on stage in London and Dublin, including a successful run at the Theatre Royal, but their marriage collapsed due to his womanising, alcoholism and physical abuse. His violence towards Movita became so extreme that acquaintances began to fear for her life. She left him in 1945, later marrying the actor, Marlon Brando.

A period of homelessness in Dublin followed, during which he slept in the back of a broken-down taxi on Henrietta Street, was incarcerated in Mountjoy Prison for fourteen days for hitting a garda and pursued a brief and tempestuous relationship that led to him being charged with assault. He then made something of a recovery and became a wrestler for a time. For many years, he also performed intermittently on the cabaret circuit. He lived in London with Nancy Kehoe but continued to woo many women while mistreating Kehoe. Having squandered and been cheated of a fortune, he was plagued by alcoholism and lived in poverty. In 1972 he returned to Cork, where he played to a cabaret in the Commodore Hotel, drawing large crowds. His circumstances deteriorated rapidly once Kehoe finally left him in 1976, and he died 13 December 1978 in London after a long illness; following services in London, Dublin and Cobh, he was buried in the Old Cemetery, Cobh. A large crowd attended his funeral.

Paul Rouse

Sources

Cork Examiner, 4 December 1972; 14, 21 December 1978; *Irish Press*, 14, 21 December 1978; *Daily Telegraph*, 14 December 1978; John Gleeson (ed.), *Fyffes dictionary of Irish sporting greats* (1993); Michael Taub, *Jack Doyle: the gorgeous Gael* (2007)

John Doyle

1930–2010

HURLER

John Doyle (pictured centre) was born on 12 February 1930 in Glenbane, Holycross, Co. Tipperary, the only child of Timothy Doyle, farmer, and his wife Margaret (née Spillane). His mother died forty-six days later, and

John was sent to live with his maternal aunt in Dungarvan, Co. Waterford. In 1934 he returned to Glenbane and spent a year in the Sacred Heart College for Little Boys in nearby Thurles, which catered for orphans and motherless children.

He was then enrolled in the local national school at Moycarkey and later attended Thurles Christian Brothers School (CBS). Stubborn, bad tempered and hyperactive, he was obsessed with hurling and at age twelve lined out for the Thurles CBS under-15 team. When his father fell ill, he left school aged fourteen to work the farm and hurl for the Holycross-Ballycahill ('Holycross') juveniles. By then he was 6ft (1.8m) tall and built like a man, and the farm labour made him stronger still. During 1946–8 he played for the Tipperary minors in various defensive positions, latterly in midfield, winning two Munster titles (1946–7) and an all-Ireland (1947). He was captain in 1948.

Shuttling between the left-corner- and left-half-back slots, he broke into the Holycross senior team in 1947. He inspired Holycross to their first county title in 1948 and made his senior inter-county championship debut the next year in the Munster first-round replay against Tipperary's arch-rivals, Cork. Displaying maturity beyond his years, he earned a reputation as a tenacious, teak-tough defender in a succession of ferociously contested championship encounters with Cork during 1949–54. He contained elusive forwards through close marking and clever positioning, being deceptively nimble for such a sturdy and ungainly looking figure. Under the high ball, he concentrated on stopping his man from either catching or pulling overhead, before using his strength and assured ground hurling to prevail. At club level, he was an accurate long-range free-taker and appeared in midfield and among the forwards.

He was an undervalued member of a fearsome defence as Tipperary won three consecutive all-Irelands (1949–51). Then, during a frustrating period in the championship for Tipperary from 1952, he was acknowledged as hurling's foremost corner-back and captained his county to a National Hurling League title in 1955. He was pugnacious and easily provoked, flinging his hurley into the jeering crowd after being sent off in the 1953 Munster semi-final.

Isolated by the deaths in 1953 of his father and his aunt—a surrogate mother—he intensified his courtship of Anne Reidy, marrying her in 1955. The distractions caused by marriage and by his mixed dairy and tillage farm undermined his form during 1956–7, and he was criticised after Cork's Paddy Barry scored three goals off him in the 1957 Munster semi-final. He announced his retirement from hurling later that year but was talked out of it by his mentor, the chairman of the Tipperary selection committee, Paddy Leahy. Anne's willingness to help with the farm rejuvenated his hurling.

In 1958 the Tipperary selectors experimented with placing him at left-half-back. There he could risk bursting forward, barging opponents aside while tipping the ball along the ground, ultimately gaining the space to lift and drive. He found the perfect foil in Tipperary's centre-half-back, Tony Wall, who covered his forays and for his relative lack of pace. Doyle attained talismanic status in Tipperary during 1958, as his ability to turn defence into attack powered a relatively average team to all-Ireland victory, the first of five within eight years. He preferred to go through rather than around opponents, performing with an aggressive swagger that roused the Tipperary players and supporters and infuriated everyone else. His provocations and open hurling exposed him to constant punishment, which he bore contemptuously. He rarely went to ground and never missed a championship match despite countless blows that chipped and scarred his shins. Subjecting markers to bone-crushing challenges and verbal menaces, he eschewed malicious strokes and was not a notably dirty player. He did not have to be—given the leeway then permitted.

He was bested by speedy wing-forwards in both the 1960 and 1961 all-Ireland finals, albeit in mitigating circumstances: Tipperary had overtrained for the 1960 final (lost to Wexford), while in 1961 their final opponents, Dublin, were rampant through the middle until Tipperary's switching of a fit player to the centre-half-back position allowed Doyle to assert himself late on and turn the match with two epic sallies. By 1962 his legs were unable to cope with the demands of the half-back line and he retreated to the right corner where he continued his relieving charges out of defence. During 1962–6, he formed a Tipperary full-back line along with Kieran Carey and Mick Maher that compensated for its seniority and slowness with unscrupulous physicality. With the half-backs cutting off low passes into open space, the powerfully built trio devoured their markers under the high ball, as the area around the Tipperary goal became known as 'Hell's Kitchen'. He capped his career by becoming the Caltex Hurler of the Year for 1964 and by claiming a joint-record eighth all-Ireland medal in 1965, drawing level with his celebrated contemporary, Christy Ring of Cork.

Retiring voluntarily following Tipperary's loss to Kilkenny in the 1967 all-Ireland final, Doyle ended his senior inter-county hurling career with fifty-four championship appearances, a Tipperary record at the time; a joint-record ten Munster medals (1949–51, 1958, 1960–62, 1964–5, 1967); a then joint-record eight all-Ireland medals (1949–51, 1958, 1961–2, 1964–5); and a record eleven National Hurling League medals, including one as a non-playing substitute (1949–50, 1952, 1954–5, 1957, 1959–61, 1964–5). He also won eight Railway Cup medals with Munster, including two as a substitute (1951–3, 1955, 1960–61, 1963, 1966). Playing with Holycross for another year, he finished his club career with two Tipperary minor medals (1947–8), five Mid-Tipperary senior medals (1947–8, 1951, 1954, 1966) and three Tipperary senior medals (1948, 1951, 1954).

A Fianna Fáil representative on North Tipperary County Council (1967–74), he ran unsuccessfully in the 1969 and 1973 general elections for Tipperary North and served one term in Seanad Éireann (1969–73). He was a Tipperary hurling selector (1976–8), also managing Tipperary in 1976. As Tipperary's representative on the Gaelic Athletic Association (GAA) central council (1975/6, 1978/9, 1983–90), he was broadly progressive and non-doctrinaire. Nonetheless, he bemoaned the imposition of stricter rules for taking the manliness out of hurling and opposed opening up Croke Park to rugby and soccer, though he enjoyed watching both. His bluntness antagonised elements within Tipperary GAA, and he had to campaign hard for his annual election to central council, losing on several occasions.

After being hospitalised in a hit-and-run car accident in 1985, he retired from farming to work as an auctioneer. He died 29 December 2010 in the Community hospital of the Assumption, Thurles, Co. Tipperary, and was buried in Holy Cross Abbey. He and his wife had five daughters and two sons. His sons, John and Michael, both played for the Tipperary senior hurling team; Michael also managed Tipperary. Named the left-corner-back on the hurling teams of the century (1984) and the millennium (1999), Doyle was simultaneously immortalised and diminished by his assiduous self-mythologising, as somewhat-embellished accounts of 'Hell's Kitchen' and the 'Holycross Hercules' obscured a fine hurler.

Terry Clavin

Sources

General Register Office Dublin (birth certificate, marriage certificate); *Irish Press*, *passim*, esp.: 5 September 1962; *Sunday Independent*, *passim*, esp.: 5, 12, 19, 26 May 1963; *Irish Independent*, *passim*, esp.: 13 January 1966; 17 March 1993; 6, 13 April 2004; *The Irish Times*, *passim*; *Tipperary Star*, *passim*; *Nenagh Guardian*, *passim*; *Cork Examiner*, *passim*; Tommy Doyle, *A lifetime of hurling* (1955); *Gaelic Sport*, September–November 1962; June 1964; February 1965; September 1967; Tony Wall, *Hurling* (1965), 47, 51, 70–71; *Irish Farmers' Journal*, 30 October 1965; 19 May 1984; Seamus Ó Braonáin, 'That ninth medal', *Our Games* (1967), 107–08; Raymond Smith, *The clash of the ash* (1972), 146–51, 281, 293–4, 298, 321; Seamus J. King, *Tipperary's hurling story, 1935–84* (1988); Raymond Smith, *The greatest hurlers of our time* (1990), 54; Brendan Fullam, *Giants of the ash* (1991); Bob Stakelum, *Gaelic games in Holycross and Ballycahill 1884–1990* (1992), 219–21; Norman Freeman, *Classic hurling matches 1956–75* (1993); Michael Keating, *Babs: a legend in Irish sport* (1996), 46–51, 61; Colm Keane, *Hurling's top twenty* (2002); *Sunday Tribune*, 18 August 2002; 30 January 2005; Séamus McRory, *The all-Ireland dream* (2005); Diarmuid O'Flynn, *Hurling: the warrior game* (2008); Ralph Riegel, *Three kings: Cork, Kilkenny, Tipperary: the battle for hurling supremacy* (2008); Conor McMorrow, *Dáil stars: from Croke Park to Leinster House* (2010); John Harrington, *Doyle: the greatest hurling story ever told* (2011)

This entry and the related sources have been abridged for publication. The full version is available at www.dib.ie

Henry Dunlop

1844–1930

Henry Wallace Doveton Dunlop was born in February 1844 in Bombay (Mumbai), India, the only son of (William) Henry Glasgow Dunlop (d. 1869), deputy superintendent of the Bombay Water Police, and his wife Mary Anne (née Pilkington). His mother was originally from Dublin, his father from Prestwick in Ayrshire. In 1848 Henry and his older sister moved into the care of relatives in Plymouth, England.

While his mother worked as a governess in Europe, Henry spent time in Germany and attended a secondary school in Montauban, France, before entering Trinity College Dublin (TCD) on 11 October 1861, aged seventeen, to study engineering; he graduated as a licentiate in civil engineering (1864) and BA (1866). On 24 July 1863, he joined the Irish civil service as a junior clerk in the record of title office of the landed estates court, housed in the Four Courts, Dublin. He spent over five decades there, rising to 'second clerk in the land court'; from 1879 he was also keeper of deeds.

A champion sprinter, he won the 100- and 400-yard races at the inaugural Irish civil service athletics championships (31 August 1867). Becoming a speed walker ('pedestrianism' then being a mainstay athletics event), Dunlop won the 3-mile and 7-mile races at the second civil service championships (4 July 1868), and the 2-mile race at the Dublin University (TCD) athletics sports (14 June 1869). The 'college races', held at TCD's College Park, were the focal point of athletics in Ireland, drawing over 20,000 spectators each summer. After victory in the 2-mile race at the third civil service championships (26 June 1869), he retired unbeaten in competition.

During 1871–2 Dunlop was honorary secretary of the Dublin University Athletic Club, which managed the TCD college races. Other TCD sporting clubs, however, repeatedly thwarted his attempts to lay a running path around College Park. As a result, he was the key founder of the Royal Irish Athletic Club, which was established on 28 June 1872 to stage an annual national athletics championship. Renamed the Irish Champion Athletic Club (ICAC) in November 1872, its executive committee comprised prominent representatives of athletic and sporting clubs in Dublin, Ulster, Cork, Galway and Limerick. The club adopted amateur rules from English rowing that explicitly excluded professional athletes, mechanics, artisans and labourers. It held its first 'championships of all Ireland' meeting at College Park on 7 July 1873.

After the TCD board revoked permission for future ICAC events to be held in the college, Dunlop drew on his contacts in the land trade to lease an 8.5-acre plot to the east of Lansdowne Road train station in December 1873. He deployed his engineering skills in laying out the new sportsgrounds, which boasted a 586-yard cinder track (Ireland's first) enclosing cricket and archery grounds, and croquet and rugby football pitches. The Lansdowne Road complex was officially opened by the viceroy, John Poyntz Spencer, fifth Earl Spencer, on 23 May 1874. By December the cinder track was overlooked by a covered 400-seat grandstand with open seating for another 600; the grounds also included a separate gate lodge and a dressing room. The development of the complex was assisted by the fact that many civil servants, professionals and military officers resided locally while the adjacent Lansdowne Road train station permitted easy access from both the city centre and the affluent coastal suburbs. In 1880 the *Irish football annual* noted that the ICAC 'possessed the best ground, and the most complete dressing arrangements of any club in the vicinity of Dublin'.

Envisioning an athletics and cricket club active over spring and summer, with members playing rugby football to maintain fitness in winter, Dunlop helped establish a range of affiliated clubs at the Lansdowne Road grounds, also making ICAC facilities available for hire by other sports clubs. He readily agreed to the request in November 1873 by Wanderers Football Club for use of the football pitch (a rugby club, Wanderers officially shared the ground from 1880). Lansdowne Football Club emerged in the 1873/4 season, initially known as the 'Irish Champion Football Club, or Lansdowne Road FC'. Codified football was in its infancy, and the nebulous terminology makes it hard to distinguish between rugby football and association football, though both Lansdowne and Wanderers clearly played an early form of rugby. In November 1874 Lansdowne became a founding club of the Irish Football Union (predecessor of the Irish Rugby Football Union (IRFU)). Dunlop served as the Lansdowne football club's first honorary secretary (1872–9) and president (1872–1904), and coached the Lansdowne second XV in the late 1870s; under his watch the Lansdowne 'seconds' formed a nucleus of players around which a strong club spirit developed.

By 1877 the ICAC was parent to seven affiliated clubs—cricket, football, archery, croquet, tennis, lacrosse and cycling—which involved Dunlop in various Irish sporting firsts, including the ICAC's arranging of a 'grand croquet champion meeting' at Marino, Dublin, in August 1874 and a 'champion archery meeting' at Lansdowne Road in September 1874. The Irish Champion Bicycle Club (established November 1875 by the ICAC) held its first Irish cycling championship in June 1876. The ICAC ground also hosted the first inter-provincial rugby game played in Dublin, when Leinster took on Ulster (16 December 1876). In 1875 the All-Irish Lawn Tennis Club (from 1880 the Lansdowne Lawn Tennis Club) was established by Dunlop under ICAC auspices.

Annual summer athletics championships were held at the grounds from 1874 to 1880, attracting first-class competitors from across the country and on occasion from Britain and America. On 5 June 1876 the ICAC hosted the first ever international athletics meeting, when an Ireland team competed against an England selection. The last ICAC-hosted Irish athletics championships were held 17 May 1880 at Lansdowne Road, but even after the club's demise in 1880, the 'Irish championship meeting' continued to be held there each summer until 1884. Dunlop regularly acted as a judge, starter and handicapper at athletics events held by other clubs in Dublin (often in the Lansdowne Road grounds) and Belfast. He was honorary secretary of the Civil Service Athletic Club (1874–5), which, added to his earlier involvement with Dublin University Athletics Club, meant he was a crucial figure in the three main athletic sporting clubs in Dublin (and Ireland) in the mid-1870s, and thus integral to nascent Irish sporting and associational culture.

In summer 1877 Dunlop launched a chancery suit to indemnify himself against debts personally assumed as ICAC honorary secretary, for which creditors were then pursuing him. Hampered in his attempts to fund improved facilities by ICAC members committed to a purely amateur ethos, he resigned as honorary secretary in December 1877, while continuing to manage the club's activities. ICAC's deteriorating finances eventually forced Dunlop and other executive committee members (including Gaelic Athletic Association founder Michael Cusack) to agree unanimously on dissolving the club in November–December 1880, selling property and cups to discharge its liabilities. The tenancy of the ground transferred to Lansdowne Football Club (and later personally to Henry Sheppard, honorary secretary of the IRFU, passing on his death in 1906 to the IRFU).

Dunlop's lasting contribution to Irish sport was his founding of Lansdowne Football Club and the creation of the Lansdowne Road ground, the home of Irish rugby. The first rugby international was held there on 11 March 1878 when Ireland played England. Prior to its redevelopment during 2006–10, Lansdowne Road was regarded as the oldest international rugby ground in continuous use in the world. The redeveloped stadium opened in May 2010, with a suite named in Dunlop's honour.

Dunlop exhibited a range of interests embodying late-Victorian associational culture in Ireland. A keen sculptor, good enough to exhibit at the Royal Hibernian Academy (1871, 1872 and 1887), he was honorary secretary (1879) of the Irish Kennel Club, performed in amateur dramatics and was a member of the Dublin Naturalists' Field Club. He also promoted sanitation schemes to prevent the spread of typhoid via the River Liffey and to abate noxious sewerage fumes in Clontarf. Arising from his experience revising the catalogue as assistant librarian to the Royal Dublin Society (November 1869–April 1876), he patented a system of slotted index cards (1871). His other patented inventions included a suspension railway truck (1891), a T-shaped pneumatic cushioned bicycle saddle (1901) and a carrier for bicycles on railways (1902).

On 6 August 1873 he married Georgina Rebecca (d. 1906), daughter of George Lambert Cathcart, solicitor, at Molyneux Chapel, Leeson Park, Dublin; they had a daughter and five sons. Dunlop married secondly (13 May 1911) Ethel, youngest daughter of William Hinch, at St Peter's church, Aungier Street, Dublin, and with her had a daughter and two sons. Henry Dunlop died at his home, 40 Sydney Avenue, Blackrock, on 16 April 1930.

Turlough O'Riordan

Sources

General Register Office Dublin (marriage certificate, death certificate); National Archives of Ireland, Census of Ireland, 1901, 1911; Trinity College Dublin [TCD] Manuscripts and Archives Research Library, 'TCD entrance book 1847–76'; Royal

Dublin Society [RDS] Library, 'Minute book of the foot-race committee 1865–73', 'RDS library committee minutes 1869–1880'; Irish Rugby Football Union archives, 'ICAC minute book 1872[–1874]'; *Freeman's Journal, passim*; *Irish Sportsman and Farmer, passim*; *The Irish Times, passim*; *Thom's Irish almanac and official directory*, (1865–1925), *passim*; J. T. H. [James T. Hurford] (ed.), *John Lawrence's handbook of cricket in Ireland* (1865/6–1880/81); *Dublin University Calendar 1868*, 107; *The Times*, 14, 28 June 1869; *Times of India*, 27 August 1869; *London Gazette*, 8 August 1871; *Return of the names and employments of the officers and clerks of the landed estates court*, House of Commons (1873); *Daily News*, 22 May 1877; R. M. Peter, *Irish football annual* (1880); *Catalogue of graduates of the University of Dublin*, vol. 2 (1896), 71; Michael J. O'Connor (ed.), *The history of Lansdowne Football Club* (1951); Ann Stewart (ed.), *Royal Hibernian Academy of arts: index of exhibitors 1826–1979*, vol. 1 (1987), 236; Padraig Griffin, *The politics of Irish athletics 1850–1990* (1990); R. C. Cox, *Graduates in engineering* [TCD] *1843–1993* (1993); Tony O'Donoghue, *Irish championship athletics 1873–1914* (2005); Brian Griffin, *Cycling in Victorian Ireland* (2006), 34; Tom Higgins, *The history of Irish tennis* (2006), vol. 1, 231; Abstracts of Church of Ireland parish records (marriage and baptismal) for the diocese(s) of Dublin, Church Records at www.irishgenealogy.ie (internet material accessed December 2021)

This entry and the related sources have been abridged for publication. The full version is available at www.dib.ie

Joey Dunlop

1952–2000

MOTORCYCLIST

Joey (William Joseph) Dunlop was born 25 February 1952 at Unshinagh, near Dunloy, Co. Antrim, second among seven children of William Dunlop, motor mechanic, and his wife May (née Barkley). Joey received his early education at Ballymoney High School, Co. Antrim. His motorcycle racing career commenced, at age seventeen, in 1969, when he rode a Triumph Tiger Cub in a 200cc event at a meeting organised by the Motor Cycle Road Racing Club of Ireland on the Maghaberry airfield circuit near Moira, Co. Armagh. His first race on a closed public roads course was in the 200cc handicap at the 1970 Temple 100, which was held on the Saintfield circuit in Co. Down. A motorcycle racing career which started out as a 'bit of fun' had, within a few years, become much more serious, though lack of finance and sponsorship hampered Dunlop's progress. Within a relatively short period of time, however, he had established himself as a fast, safe and successful competitor on both short circuit and road courses, riding Italian Aermacchi and Japanese Yamaha machines.

After stints in the family steel erection business and working as a diesel fitter, truck driver and roofer, Dunlop bought and ran the Railway Tavern pub in Ballymoney, renaming it 'Joey's Bar'. Each job allowed him to focus on building and racing motorbikes. He excelled at engine management, being a self-taught mechanic who brought his encyclopaedic knowledge to bear on his bikes. In 1977 Dunlop adopted a yellow helmet dissected by a central black stripe, which became a lucky talisman; similarly, he always put on his left glove first at the start of a race. He was indifferent towards fame or wealth and travelled to races in his works van, where he often happily slept during competitions. A shy yet determined character, his approachability in the race paddock contributed to his immense popularity among racing fans.

Dunlop's first major victory came in July 1975, when he won the 500cc class at the Temple 100. In 1976 he made his debut at the Isle of Man TT, finishing sixteenth in the Junior (350cc) and eighteenth in the Senior (500cc) races. The following year (1977) he had his first victory on the daunting 37.73-mile (60.7-km) TT Mountain Circuit, winning the four-lap (150.92-mile; 243-km)

Jubilee Classic TT at an average speed of 108.86mph (175.2kph) on his 750cc Yamaha. He also had the fastest lap in the race at 110.93mph (178.5kph). Success followed success, and towards the end of the 1980 season he was signed by the Suzuki (Great Britain) team as a back-up for their rider, New Zealander Graeme Crosby, in the remaining rounds of that year's World and British Formula One Road Racing Championships. His stay with Suzuki was a short one. In 1981 he signed a contract to ride for the Honda Britain Racing Team.

In his first year as a Honda team rider (1981), Dunlop finished third in the Formula One World Championship behind winner Graeme Crosby (Suzuki) and his Honda teammate Ron Haslam. The Dunlop–Honda union proved very successful, as Dunlop went on to win the Formula One World Championship for five consecutive years (1982–6). In the 1987 championship Dunlop finished second to Italian Virginio Ferrari (Bimota–Yamaha), and in 1988 he was second to English rider Carl Fogarty (Honda). Due to injuries sustained in a race accident at Brands Hatch at Easter 1989, he did not contest that year's championship. The Formula One World Championship was dropped from the international calendar after 1989; a replacement Formula One World Cup, run for just one year (1990), was won by Carl Fogarty (Honda), with Dunlop taking second place.

It was on the Isle of Man, where he was particularly adept at plotting the fastest line, that he really tore up the record books. From his Isle of Man debut (1976) to his final appearance there (2000), he won a total of twenty-six TTs—an all-time record as of 2022. Dunlop was also one of just a handful of riders who have won three TT races in one week. This he achieved three times, in 1985, 1988 and 2000. His TT wins are as follows: 1977, Jubilee TT; 1980, Classic TT; 1983, Formula One; 1984, Formula One; 1985, Formula One, Junior, Senior; 1986, Formula One; 1987, Formula One, Senior; 1988, Formula One, Junior, Senior; 1992, 125cc; 1993, 125cc; 1994, 125cc, Junior; 1995, Lightweight, Senior; 1996, 125cc, 250cc; 1997, 250cc; 1998, 250cc; 2000, Formula One, 250cc, 125cc. Dunlop's sensational victory in the 2000 Formula One TT race was built on his unrivalled knowledge of the Manx course. Coming twelve years after his last win there in that class, Dunlop, aged forty-eight, took pole position with almost a minute to spare, in his twenty-fifth year of racing at the TT.

Dunlop's success brought many accolades. In 1984 readers of the top-selling British weekly *Motor Cycle News* voted him their Man of the Year—the first time an Irish rider was so honoured. That same year, the sports editors of the Irish national newspapers (north and south) nominated him Texaco Motorsport Star of the Year, a title he again received in 1985. In 1986 he was awarded the MBE for services to motorcycle sport. A decade later he received another royal award—the OBE—for his outstanding work in bringing aid to the destitute children in Romanian orphanages. During the off-season period, when he was not busy with racing commitments, Dunlop raised money for the children, purchasing supplies of food, clothing and medicines. He would then load his race transporter and drive single-handed across Europe to deliver the goods to their destination. On one of these trips Dunlop detoured to the Imola racetrack in Italy to pay his respects to Ayrton Senna, who had died there in a tragic crash. Dunlop also assisted in fund-raising for Our Lady's Hospital for Sick Children in Crumlin, Dublin. At the annual autumn congress of the Fédération Internationale Motocycliste (FIM; the world governing body of motorcycle sport), which was held in Dublin in October 1993, Dunlop was awarded the prestigious FIM silver medal for his career achievements.

Renouncing cigarettes in his early forties, Dunlop worked hard to improve his physical fitness later in his career, essential in wrestling larger bikes around circuits. Indeed, his fastest-ever lap of the TT Mountain Circuit—123.87mph (199.3kph)—was set on Saturday 10 June 2000, in what was his final race in the Isle of Man. Other records set by Dunlop include twenty-four wins in the Ulster Grand Prix, thirty-one wins in the Southern 100 (Castletown circuit, Isle of Man) and 117 wins in Irish national road races. He won the prestigious Hutchinson Trophy—premier award at the Leinster 200 (Mondello Park)—five times (1975, 1976, 1977, 1980, 1984). While he was most closely associated with Honda, Dunlop also rode other makes of machine—Triumph, Suzuki, Aermacchi, Yamaha and Benelli.

A cautious racer who knew his limits, he survived two serious accidents during his thirty-one-year career. At the Brands Hatch circuit in Kent, England, during the Eurolantic Motor Cycle Challenge meeting on Good Friday, 24 March 1989, he was involved in a crash with Belgian rider Stephane Mertens at Paddock Bend, suffering multiple injuries, breaking a leg, a wrist and his ribs. He never raced again on short, enclosed circuits, regarding them as leaving him vulnerable to the mistakes of others, unlike road racing. After four months of recuperation, he returned to racing in mid-July, though still far from fully fit. A second serious crash happened during the 125cc race at the 1998 Tandragee 100 meeting in Co. Armagh. In the tumble, which happened at high speed, Dunlop lost the tip of his left-hand ring finger, as well as suffering a cracked pelvis, broken collarbone and a broken bone in his right hand.

Joey Dunlop lost his life in a crash during a 125cc race at an international meeting at Tallinn, Estonia, on Sunday 2 July 2000. In wet conditions, his Honda machine ran off the road and crashed into trees, killing him instantly. His death resulted in a great outpouring of grief in Ireland and overseas. Over 50,000 people attended his funeral at Garryduff Presbyterian church, near Ballymoney, Co. Antrim.

His younger brother Robert was killed in a crash at the North West 200 in 2008. One of Robert's sons, William, died in 2018 in a crash at the Skerries 100; in June 2022 another son, Michael, won his twenty-first Isle of Man TT title, placing him third behind his uncle Joey in the all-time list.

Statues of Joey Dunlop were erected in Ballymoney, Co. Antrim, and at the 'Bungalow' bend, Snaefell, on the Isle of Man. The Joey Dunlop Cup is awarded annually to the most successful rider at the Isle of Man TT. He married (22 September 1972) Linda Patterson from Ballymoney. They had five children: Donna, Gary, Joanne, Julie, and Richard.

Harry Havelin

Sources
Motor Cycling Ireland archives; Mac McDiarmaid, *Joey Dunlop: his authorised biography* (2010); personal knowledge

Shay Elliott

1934–71

<small>CYCLIST</small>

Shay (Seamus) Elliott (pictured left) was born 4 June 1934 at Old County Road, Crumlin, Dublin, the second of three sons of Jim Elliott, garage owner of Rathfarnham, Co. Dublin, and his wife Nell (née Farrell). His parents were part of the republican contingent that seized the Four Courts in Dublin in 1922 at the outset of the Irish civil war. The family moved to Crumlin during Shay's childhood. He attended the Christian Brothers School in Crumlin, where he played hurling and football, and he did not take up cycling until he was fourteen.

Riding successively for St Brendan's, the Southern Road Club and (from 1952) the Dublin Wheelers, he achieved various successes, winning the Grand Prix of Ireland (1952) and the Irish Road Race Championships (1953–4). In 1954 he came second in the An Tóstal race, winning the 'king of the mountains' title, and placed fourth overall in the 1954 Route de France, a prestigious under-25s amateur race. In early 1955, having just completed his apprenticeship as a panel beater, he joined a training camp for aspiring professional cyclists in Monte Carlo. Soon after he joined the Athletic Club Boulogne-Billancourt team, based in Paris. He won six races and was awarded the title of best amateur rider in France for 1955. Cycling on indoor tracks late in the season, he broke the world records for the 1,000m flying start, the 5km and the 10km.

He turned professional in 1956, joining the Heylett team, and impressed in his early seasons by regularly winning minor races and showing well in the important one-day classics. In 1958 he missed out on becoming the first native English speaker to win a stage of the Tour de France when he was blocked and had his jersey pulled in the final sprint. Within the space of eight days that year, he seemed poised for victory in the Paris–Roubaix and Paris–Brussels classics only to be thwarted both times by mechanical faults. Winning either race would have catapulted him into cycling's elite. His victory the next year in the Het Volk in Belgium, considered a semi-classic, failed to prevent him from having to settle for the role of *domestique*, albeit a highly regarded and well-paid one. He rode for his team leaders, the five-time Tour de France winner, Jacques Anquetil, and Jean Stablinksi, who was Elliott's close friend and later his best man and godfather to his child. Quickly integrating into French society, he married Marguerite 'Gigi' Steiger of Mulhouse, France, in early 1961; they had a son and lived in Paris.

An aggressive rider and a powerful sprinter, he was not a general classification contender for a Grand Tour event, as he struggled in the mountains and in individual time trials but was capable of landing either the World Championship or a big classic: his failure to do so can be put down to selflessness, *peloton* politics and naivety. Being one of the first anglophones to make an impression in professional cycling, he suffered from the clannishness that characterised the sport.

He won a stage of the Giro d'Italia in 1960 and of the Vuelta a España in 1962, leading that year's Vuelta for nine days before coming third. In the 1962 World Championship race he looked the strongest member of the leading group of four and went clear near the finish. Stablinksi, however, struck a deal with the other two pursuing riders who worked hard at successfully catching up and then did nothing when Stablinski attacked decisively, leaving Elliott to trail in second. Elliott continued this great form into 1963 when he won another stage in the Vuelta a España and became the first English-speaking rider to hold the *maillot jaune* of overall leader of the Tour de France, heading the race for three days after winning the third stage with help from Stablinski. This also made him the first anglophone rider to win stages on all three Grand Tours.

His best years were behind him when his career hit a crucial turning-point in August 1965. A rider of immense loyalty to his team, he was devastated when, with his victory all but assured in the four-stage Paris–Luxembourg race, some of his teammates (including Anquetil and Stablinski) conspired to deny him victory. His friendship with Stablinksi broken, he left the team at the end of the year, joining the arch-rival Mercier team. In late 1965 he borrowed heavily to open his 'Hôtel d'Irlande: chez Seamus Elliott' in Loctudy, Brittany. The hotel was immediately in difficulties, and the attendant strain undermined both his marriage and his cycling. In desperation he took Benzedrine, a banned substance, in an unsuccessful attempt to cover his debts with prize money. At the end of a disappointing 1966 season, he left the sport and abandoned his hotel venture. He returned to Ireland penniless while his wife stayed in France with their son.

Thoroughly disillusioned, he sold a three-part exposé to the *People* newspaper in Britain on the widespread drug taking and race fixing within professional cycling. He admitted to helping other riders win in return for money but only in open races, such as the World Championship, where cyclists competed as individuals rather than as part of a team. Suspicions had been aroused when he came last in the seventeen-man sprint for the 1960 World Championship, and there is a photograph of him braking before the finishing line of the London–Holyhead race in 1965; conversely, the British cyclist Tom Simpson recalled how Elliott once refused his £1,100 blandishment. Elliott stated that he had not knowingly taken performance enhancing drugs prior to 1966 but was sure drugs had been put in his drinks by team doctors. On one occasion, a team car he was driving into Belgium was searched by police, who found drugs concealed inside a seat and arrested him; the case against him was eventually dropped.

He used the £500 he received for these articles to set up a garage on South Princes Street, Dublin, where he lived in a flat at the premises and built up a moderate trade. He cycled in the 1970 London–Holyhead race, was reinstated as an amateur and was to help prepare the Irish team for the Munich Olympics. He was on anti-depressants when, on 4 May 1971, he seemingly killed himself in his flat with a shotgun that had been his prize for winning a stage of the Vuelta a España in 1963. His family and friends always disputed the generally held view that it was a suicide. He was buried at Kilmacanogue, Co. Wicklow, beside his father, who had died two weeks previously. In 1998 the Tour de France passed his grave as a mark of respect; Bray Wheelers stage an annual event in his memory.

Paul Rouse

Sources

People, 20, 27 November, 4 December 1966; *Irish Independent*, 5, 7 May 1971; *The Irish Times*, 5 May 1971; 8 July 1998; Paul Kimmage, *A rough ride* (1990); John Gleeson (ed.), *Fyffes dictionary of Irish sporting greats* (1993); Peter Matthews and Ian Buchanan, *The all-time greats of British and Irish sport* (1995); *Irish Press*, 5 May 1998; *Sunday Independent*, 5 July 1998; Graham Healy, *Shay Elliott: the life and death of Ireland's first yellow jersey* (2011)

Dick Fitzgerald

1882–1930

GAELIC FOOTBALLER

Dick (Richard) Fitzgerald was born 2 October 1882 in College Street, Killarney, Co. Kerry, one of at least three sons and three daughters of Michael Fitzgerald, a merchant of College Street, and his wife Bridget (née Healy). His primary education was with the Presentation Brothers in Killarney, his secondary successively with St. Brendan's, Killarney; Mungret College, Limerick; and the Presentation Brothers in Cork city. He would eventually take on the family business, earning his livelihood from trading butter, poultry and eggs.

His Gaelic football career began with the Nils club in Cork city before he returned to Killarney to play for Dr Crokes. Mainly a centre-half-forward, though also appearing in other forward positions, he was one of the earliest stars of Gaelic football. Considered the best player of his generation, he was an exceptionally talented and accurate scorer, a good distributor of the ball, and possessed of a wide range of skills, including difficult overhead kicking. He did not figure on any teams of the century or millennium, because he played so long ago.

He won the first of his five all-Ireland senior football championship medals with Kerry in the 1903 championship (played in 1905), Kerry's first ever all-Ireland football title, after an epic three-match encounter with Kildare that raised the profile of Gaelic football nationally. The first game was abandoned after a pitch invasion when the referee deemed that the Kildare goalkeeper had carried the ball over the goal-line while attempting to clear a free taken by Fitzgerald. The replay resulted in a draw (Kerry 0–7, Kildare 1–4), and Kerry finally triumphed in the third game by 0–8 to 0–2 with Fitzgerald the star of the game.

He won four more all-Ireland championships with Kerry (1904, 1909, 1913, 1914), captaining the side and peaking as a footballer on the last two occasions. Furthermore, he was on the losing side in the all-Ireland finals of 1905, 1908 and 1915 (as captain); and was due to have played in the 1910 final but, because of a dispute between Kerry and the Great Southern Railway, Kerry refused to travel, and Louth was awarded a walkover. Between 1903 and 1916 he played fifty-eight senior inter-county championship matches, placing him fourth on the list of all-time Kerry championship appearances as late as 2008.

With Dr Crokes, he won four Kerry senior champion-ship medals (1901, 1912–14) at a time of intense rivalry between Dr Crokes and the Tralee Mitchels club. During an encounter between the two sides in March 1911, he led his team off the pitch over a disputed decision. The authorities banned Dr Crokes for six months, render-ing its players ineligible for the Kerry team for the du-ration. Fitzgerald would have returned for the 1911 all-Ireland final, but a weakened Kerry surprisingly lost in the Munster final.

In 1914 he published a book entitled *How to play Gaelic football*, in which he portrayed Gaelic football as a scientif-ic game, superior to soccer and rugby. It included detailed descriptions of every position and the duties attached to them, photographs illustrating the principal skills, discus-sions on the roles of team captain and referee, and a fasci-nating account of how to play with thirteen-a-side teams, which he thought might happen in the future. The book also espouses his preference for attacking rather than de-fensive football and his fear of professionalism creeping into the game, which led him to condemn training camps for teams. It was still being read by aspiring young Gaelic footballers into the mid-twentieth century.

From the 1910s he was active in the GAA as a match official, coach, selector and administrator. He coached the Clare team that reached the 1917 all-Ireland football final. In the 1920s he coached Dr Crokes and served as a member of the Kerry county board, the vice-chairman of the county selection committee, and a Kerry represen-tative on the Munster and central councils; he was team manager for Kerry's 1927 American tour. In 1924 he sup-ported unsuccessful attempts to remove the ban that pro-hibited GAA members from playing soccer, rugby, hockey and cricket. He was involved in a controversial incident in the 1925 all-Ireland football semi-final between Cavan and Kerry; Kerry won by one point after Fitzgerald, acting as umpire, signalled a point for Kerry that the Cavan players believed to be wide. Both teams were subsequently ejected from the competition.

He joined the Killarney company of the Irish Volunteers in 1913 and influenced its decision to declare for the McNeillite Volunteers in 1915. He was second lieutenant of the company. In 1916 he was arrested after the Easter rising and interned in Frongoch, where he organised Gaelic football matches until his release on 2 August 1916. Rearrested on 22 September and returned to Frongoch, he was released for good towards the year's end. An active organiser for Sinn Féin in the Kerry East constituency from 1918, he was elected to Killarney urban district council for Sinn Féin in 1920. Local lore maintains that he drew upon his national network of Gaelic Athletic Association (GAA) connections to play an important role in organising safe houses for Michael Collins. In the last months of the war of independence (1919–21), he went on the run as a member of the local flying column. A supporter of the Anglo–Irish treaty (1922), he served as a Cumann na nGaedheal member of Killarney urban district council (east ward) from June 1925 until his death. Latterly he was described as being disillusioned with politics.

In 1925 he married Catherine Dillon, of Kenmare Place, Killarney; she was the sister of his former teammate Paddy Dillon. They had no children, and her death in 1927 hit him hard. Dick Fitzgerald died 26 September 1930 after a fall from a roof in Killarney. An inquest jury found that he died 'from shock and haemorrhage due to internal injuries to abdomen and chest by a fall from some height' (*Kerryman*, 4 October 1930). Witnesses stated that he was coming down from the roof when he slipped and fell. He was buried in the New Cemetery, just outside Killarney. Two days after his death, Kerry reluctantly contested the all-Ireland football final, which they won; the match at Croke Park was preceded by the playing of Chopin's 'Funeral march' by the Artane Boys' Band. In 1935 the new GAA stadium in Killarney was named Fitzgerald Stadium in his honour.

Marie Coleman

Sources

National Library of Ireland, Piaras Béaslaí papers; Dick Fitzgerald, *How to play Gaelic football* (1914); *Kerryman*, 4 October 1930; P. D. Mehigan ('Carbery'), *Gaelic football* (1941); Patrick Foley, *Kerry's football story* (1945); Raymond Smith, *The football immortals* (1968); Seán O'Mahony, *Frongoch* (1987); *Killarney urban district council, local election results, 1899–1994* (1999); Jack Mahon, *A history of Gaelic football* (2000); T. Ryle Dwyer, *Tans, terror and troubles: Kerry's real fighting story, 1913–23* (2001); Joe Ó Muircheartaigh and T. J. Flynn, *Princes of pigskin: a century of Kerry footballers* (2007); Tom Looney, *Dick Fitzgerald: king in a kingdom of kings* (2008); Richard McElligott, *Forging a kingdom: the GAA in Kerry 1884–1934* (2013); information from Sean Moran of *The Irish Times*

Dave Gallaher

1873–1917

RUGBY PLAYER

Dave Gallaher was born on 30 October 1873 in Castle
Street, Ramelton, Co. Donegal, son of James Henry
Gallagher, a shopkeeper trading at Market Cross there,
and (Anna) Maria Hardy Gallagher (née McCloskey),
a schoolteacher originally from Belfast. James had two

sons from his first marriage; Dave was James's and Maria's fourth child of seven surviving children born in Ireland. The family emigrated to New Zealand in May 1878, henceforth spelling their surname 'Gallaher'. Eventually settling in Katikati, near Tauranga, Bay of Plenty, James struggled to farm, defaulting on his mortgage. Before dying from cancer in September 1887, Maria taught in Katakati, providing a £2 weekly wage and a 'teacher's house', where the family resided and where she gave birth to four more children. Dave Gallaher left school around 1887 to work for the local stock agent.

The family moved to Auckland in 1889 where Dave Gallaher worked as a labourer with the Northern Roller Mills Company, playing on the company's cricket team. After James died (30 November 1894), Dave lived with his eldest brother Joseph and his family. The hooker on the Parnell Rugby Club second fifteen, Dave joined the Ponsonby District Rugby Club in the winter of 1895 and played for the Auckland provincial side from 1896. Undertaking hard manual work as a labourer, later foreman, with the Auckland Farmers' Freezing Company no doubt benefitted his fitness. Gallaher was known for wearing his distinctive black shin pads over his socks. Volunteering for service in the Boer War, he was a scout in the 16th (Auckland) Company of the Sixth New Zealand Contingent of Mounted Rifles. He participated in clearing the Northern Transvaal of Boers as part of the British 'scorched earth' policy and endured harsh conditions skirmishing across the veldt. Promoted to sergeant major, he returned to Auckland in August 1902. His war service, and the attendant weight loss, cost him two seasons of provincial rugby.

Gallaher, almost 6ft (1.8m) tall, weighing 13st. (82.5kg) and known for his fitness and physicality, was selected as hooker for New Zealand's 1903 tour of Australia. He first played as wing-forward for New Zealand in their 28–0 victory over Queensland (8 August), harrying the half-backs around the scrum and thriving in the space created by his skilful dribbling rushes. Making the position his own, he played wing-forward in New Zealand's first international test (15 August), a 22–3 away win over Australia. In New Zealand's 9–3 victory (13 August 1904) over a touring 'Great Britain' side in Wellington—their first home international test—Gallaher, again wing-forward, smothered the opposition's half-backs. A week earlier, he had played for Auckland in the inaugural defence of the Ranfurly Shield, a 3–6 loss to Wellington

His appointment as captain for the seven-month tour 'home' to Great Britain and Ireland caused some disquiet amongst the twenty-four-man squad, as past All Black captains had been elected by players. He called a meeting at sea to address perceptions of partiality in favour of 'North islanders'; stressing the importance of team unity, his offer to resign was rejected by a player vote. With his vice-captain Billy Stead, he drilled the squad daily at sea. After New Zealand's 55–4 victory in their first match of the tour (16 September 1905), against Devon, a leading English side, newspapers in Britain and New Zealand initially assumed the score had been mistakenly inverted by telegraph operators. New Zealand held fourteen of their first eighteen opponents scoreless.

Their dominance emanated from their 'wedge formation' (2–3–2) scrum, intricate back line passing and agile movement, all based on exemplary fitness and handling skills. Scrum formation then varied greatly. In Britain the eight forwards, with no fixed position, formed the scrum in the order they arrived. As slower, larger forwards invariably arrived last, they joined the side and rear. In New

Zealand forwards were assigned to seven (and not eight) specific scrum positions, leaving Gallaher as a roving 'wing-forward'. Integral to rugby in New Zealand, the position was unknown in Britain and Ireland. The wing-forward position, as then conceived, was essentially an extra half-back. After feeding the ball into the scrum, the wing-forward stood in line with the scrum front rows, either shielding his own half-back (scrum-half) or pressurising the opposition, depending on who secured possession. Critics held that when New Zealand secured possession in the scrum Gallaher, in front of the ball, was in an offside position; adept positional play was required to stay onside. The position was effectively abolished in 1931.

New Zealand's well-drilled forwards and dexterous backs dominated, engendering much soul searching in the British sporting press. The unmarked Gallaher, conspicuous in his distinct shin pads, became the focal point for the ire of home spectators and of press commentary which emphasised the 'illegality' of his positional play. The *London Chronicle* noted Gallaher 'may be described as a scrum-half who claims the privilege of a forward in the scrum. His part is that of a passive and active obstructionist' (*Dave Gallaher*, 156). Such claims ignored his fitness, keen tactical awareness and footballing skills.

New Zealand were undefeated in nineteen games and had scored over 600 points as they prepared to face the four 'home' nations. Troubled by a leg injury sustained during the 12–7 victory over Scotland in icy conditions in Edinburgh (18 November), Gallaher missed New Zealand's 15–0 victory over Ireland in Dublin (25 November) and had not recovered fully when he returned for the 15–0 defeat of England in London (2 December). The fatigued squad was subject to mounting injuries, forcing the New Zealand selection committee to ruminate for five hours on their team to face Wales, the 1905 Triple Crown and Home Championship winners.

In front of forty thousand spectators at Cardiff Arms Park (16 December), Wales were awarded repeated penalties, the referee adjudging Gallaher's feeding of the ball into the scrum illegal. To prevent further penalties, Gallaher ordered his forwards to concede their own scrums, allowing New Zealand to defend aggressively. Wales won 3–0 with New Zealand having a try disallowed in highly contentious circumstances. Gallaher graciously congratulated the Welsh captain, publicly praising the Welsh performance. Suffering a bite to his finger in a 9–0 victory over Glamorgan, he missed one match before returning to cover as hooker in the 4–3 victory over Cardiff. After a 38–8 win over France in Paris (1 January 1906)—France's inaugural test match—the New Zealand government funded an extension of the tour to the USA, where exhibition games were played in New York and San Francisco. On this tour, New Zealand played 35 games, scoring 976 points (243 tries) while conceding only 59 points.

Gallaher had played in twenty-six games and led the tour's triumphant return to Auckland on 6 March 1906. Met by the New Zealand premier (prime minister) Richard Seddon, who praised their exhibition of sporting prowess in the 'mother country', the squad was widely fêted across the country. His captaincy of 'the Originals', as the squad rapidly became known, brought Gallaher universal acclaim. He played thirty-six games for the All Blacks, captaining them thirteen times. Of these appearances, six were in test matches, in four of which he was captain.

Emphasising how teamwork underpinned New Zealand's success, he justified the legality of the wing-forward position in his contribution to *Why the All Blacks triumphed* (1906), compiled by J. A. Buttery of the *Daily*

Mail. Gallagher also contributed to *The complete rugby footballer on the New Zealand system* (1906), which outlined the origins of rugby there and narrated the 1905–06 tour. Discussing tactics, preparation, training and set-piece play, it even extolled the calming virtues of pipe smoking.

Gallaher married Nellie (Ellen Ivy May) Francis (the sister of his Ponsonby and New Zealand teammate, Arthur Francis), on 10 October 1906 at All Saints Anglican church, Auckland. A daughter, Nora, was born in September 1908. He played his last ever game of rugby 4 September 1909, for Auckland versus Maniapoto, in Te Kuiti, a 16–0 victory; he represented Auckland twenty-six times in inter-provincial competition. He was sole selector and coach of Auckland (1906–15), successfully implementing agile backline play, as Auckland defended the Ranfurly Shield twenty-three times in a row between 1905 and 1913. His last game of coaching inter-provincial rugby was for Auckland against Wellington in August 1915. Gallaher's record as Auckland sole selector was 48 wins, 11 losses and 6 draws. A New Zealand selector (1907–14), he also coached Auckland Grammar School for a time.

He again volunteered for military service, underwent an army medical (23 May 1916) and commenced training in July 1916. Commanding a platoon in 2nd Battalion, Auckland Regiment, he was promoted to sergeant. During an onslaught on Passchendaele Ridge, Flanders, at the third battle of Ypres, Gallaher was mortally wounded by a German artillery barrage on 4 October 1917. Of the five Gallaher brothers who served in the first world war, three were killed on active service in Europe.

Gallaher was buried in Nine Elms cemetery, Poperinge, Belgium. The New Zealand team who toured Britain in 1924 visited Gallaher's grave, as have many subsequent touring New Zealand sides. The Gallaher Shield, inaugurated in 1922, is awarded annually to the leading club in Auckland. In 2000 the French and New Zealand rugby unions agreed to contest a cup named after Gallaher. When Letterkenny Rugby Football Club opened its Dave Gallaher Memorial Park in 2005, the ceremony was attended by that year's touring All Black squad, who also visited Gallaher's birthplace in Ramelton. A bronze statue of Gallaher was unveiled outside Eden Park, Auckland, in 2011. In 2015 the jersey he wore on the 'Originals' tour sold for £180,000 at auction.

Gallaher's leadership by example, dominant on the pitch and gracious in infrequent defeat, was crucial to establishing rugby as New Zealand's national sport. His successful leadership of the All Blacks 'Originals' 1905–6 tour, seen as embodying the spirit of fair-play and muscular competition, alongside his subsequent military sacrifice, rapidly conferred a sanctified aura that contributed to New Zealand national identity.

Turlough O'Riordan

Sources

General Register Office Dublin (birth certificate); *Auckland Star, passim; Observer* (New Zealand), 20 August 1904; Jock Philips, *A man's country? The image of the Pakeha male—a history* (1996), 117–124; Matt Elliott, *Dave Gallaher: the original All Black captain* (2012); 'Casualties of Passchendaele: Serjeant David Gallaher', Commonwealth War Graves Commission, 4 October 2017, www.cwgc.org/our-work/news/casualties-of-passchendaele-serjeant-david-gallaher/; Denis McLean, 'Gallaher, David', *Dictionary of New Zealand Biography* (1996), Te Ara—the Encyclopedia of New Zealand, teara.govt.nz/en/biographies/3g1/gallaher-david; 'Dave Gallaher #97', stats.allblacks.com/asp/profile.asp?ABID=300; 'Dave Gallaher 1905 All Blacks jersey sells for £180,000' BBC News, 9 October 2015, www.bbc.com/news/uk-wales-south-east-wales-34486830 (all internet material accessed December 2020)

Philomena Garvey

1926–2009

AMATEUR GOLFER

Philomena Kathleen Garvey was born 26 April 1926 in the village of Baltray, Co. Louth, the youngest of six children (two daughters and four sons) of James Garvey, a seaman, and his wife Kathleen (née Owens), whose father had been a ship's captain. Philomena went to the girls' national school in Termonfeckin, Co. Louth. From an early age, like her siblings, she played golf at every opportunity at their local links course at Baltray, the County Louth Golf Club. Her brother Kevin Garvey won the East of Ireland championship in 1942.

That same year, Philomena, aged sixteen, won the captain's prize at Baltray; from then on, golf was the most important thing in her life. She worked first as a clerk in the Irish Hospitals Sweepstakes office in Ballsbridge, Dublin, and later as a sales assistant in Clery's department store but returned to Baltray as often as she could to play her home course. She was fortunate that the shop's owners, Denis Guiney and his wife Mary Guiney, were interested in golf and allowed her to take unpaid leave during the summer to practise and compete. In 1947 she considered accepting an offer of marriage, but since it was conditional on her giving up golf, she turned it down and never married. (A contemporary English male golfer publicly expressed the view that a married woman playing golf well enough to win championships provided sufficient grounds for divorce.)

In 1944 Garvey was defeated in the Leinster Cup by Clarrie Reddan, ten years her senior and also a member of the County Louth club, but in subsequent encounters Garvey triumphed. The two women were never friendly. The final of the 1946 Irish ladies' championship, in Lahinch, was particularly thrilling, with Garvey winning a play-off decided by a stymie on the thirty-ninth green. Commentators marvelled at her focus and concentration, as much as at her technique. For most of her playing career, she was the pre-eminent woman golfer in Ireland; she won fifteen Irish ladies' amateur championships from 1946 to 1970 without ever losing a final in that competition.

In 1950 Garvey reached the quarter-finals of the US Open championship. Normally, she could not afford to travel to the United States to compete there, but that year her way was paid as a member of the British and Irish Curtis Cup team. Garvey was selected by the Ladies' Golf Union (LGU) for the prestigious Curtis Cup team in 1948, 1950, 1952, 1954, 1956, 1958 and 1960, and in 1952 contributed to the first ever victory of the Great Britain and Ireland team over the United States. In 1958, however, the LGU produced a new emblem for the Curtis Cup team, representing only the Union Jack, and Garvey refused to play if there was no recognition of Ireland. She offered to wear the earlier version of the badge, representing emblems of all four home countries, but the LGU was immovable. Her stand was supported by the non-playing captain of the Curtis Cup team, Daisy Ferguson from Royal County Down, and by many other individuals and organisations in Ireland, including the Irish Ladies' Golf Union (ILGU). Garvey, a reserved and private person, tried to avoid publicity in the matter, and, when a more acceptable badge was issued for the 1960 event, she felt able to play when selected for the team. She was not chosen again, though at the peak of her prowess in competition, and some commentators believed she had become *persona non grata* with the LGU.

Earlier in her career, the sport's governing body, the Royal and Ancient Golf Club of St Andrews, investigated her amateur status, in doubt because her job in Clery's required her to sell golf clubs. In February 1949 the authorities ruled that she was an amateur player, allowing her to continue her participation in the women's blue riband event, the British ladies' amateur open championship. She lost in finals four times (1946, 1953, 1960, 1963), but won the 1957 event at Gleneagles. In the last stages of that match against Scotland's Jessie Valentine, Garvey twisted her ankle. Her friend Kitty MacCann (a previous British open champion) was a spectator along with her husband Pat MacCann, a veterinary surgeon. He used a handkerchief to bind the ankle, allowing Philomena to continue to victory by 4 and 3. She was accorded a civic reception in Drogheda in June 1957 and a hero's welcome back to Baltray.

During 1964–7 Garvey allowed her amateur status to lapse as she attempted to make a career as the first woman professional golfer in Ireland. She gave lessons, endorsed the 'Philomena Garvey golf club' and contributed fifteen weekly articles to the *Evening Herald*, but she found that the opportunities were insufficient for her to be able to maintain her income and develop her game. In 1968 she regained her amateur status. Admitting that she was tired of reading about the apparently unbeatable twenty-one-year-old Mary McKenna, the 1969 Irish close champion, Garvey went all out in 1970 to win the Irish ladies' championship, doing so for the fifteenth time at Royal Portrush on 23 May 1970. Shortly afterwards, she announced her retirement from international golf competition.

Garvey received numerous sporting awards throughout her career: she was nominated as the 1963 Texaco Sportsperson of the Year, had honorary life membership of the Baltray club and was made a life vice-president of the ILGU. In 1980 the Irish Golf Writers' Association gave her its distinguished services to golf award. In old age she was robbed of her mobility by osteoporosis and was sometimes forced to use a wheelchair. Philomena Garvey died of a heart attack as she entered the Baltray clubhouse on 5 May 2009.

Linde Lunney

Sources

Irish Independent, passim, esp.: 29 June 1957; 10 May 2009; *The Irish Times, passim*, esp.: 19 December 1980; 16 May 2009; Dermot Gilleece and John Redmond, *Irish Ladies' Golf Union: an illustrated centenary history 1893–1993* (1993); John Gleeson (ed.), *Fyffes dictionary of Irish sporting greats* (1993); Paul Garvey, *Philomena Garvey: queen of the Irish fairways* (2009); *Irish Examiner*, 29 December 2009

Mollie Gill

1891–1977

CAMOGIE PLAYER AND ADMINISTRATOR

Mollie Gill (Máire Ní Giolla) was born Mary Anne Gill on 24 March 1891 at Murphystown, near Leopardstown, in south Co. Dublin, the daughter of James Gill, a shoemaker, and his wife Jane (neé Daly). Census records suggest that she was the middle child of four daughters and three sons.

In 1908 she became an 'assistant printer', possibly at first with Dun Emer Industries, before joining Cuala Press, which was founded that year when Elizabeth (Lollie) Yeats and Susan (Lily) Yeats, sisters to W. B. Yeats, broke away from Dun Emer Industries to create their own venture. The Yeatses sent Mollie to art school and arranged Irish classes for her; there were also regular visits to the Abbey Theatre and the opera. She recalled 'We met all the top people. There was Michael Collins coming in, and George Bernard Shaw' (*The Irish Times*, 21 November 1975). She worked at Cuala Press for six decades, as it moved from its first base at Churchtown (1908–23) to W. B. Yeats's residence at 83 Merrion Square (1923–5), on to Lower Baggot Street (1925–42) and on again to Palmerston Road (1942–69). For most of her adult life, she lived in Rialto, Dublin.

From her first days at the press, Gill worked closely with Esther (Essie) Ryan (1887–1961), from Churchtown. Gill and Ryan were inseparable, and together they were active members of Cumann na mBan. During the civil war they supported, or at least sympathised strongly with, the republican side, which presumably led to their arrest in a raid on the Cuala Press premises on 19 May 1923. Gill spent two months in Kilmainham Gaol before being released on 20 July. Though the extent of her activity in Cumann na mBan is uncertain, in 1948 both she and Ryan were awarded service medals for the period 1917 to 1921. Gill also served on the executive of the Irish Republican Prisoners' Dependents' Fund.

She began playing camogie with the Crokes club, which had a team from *c*.1906; its members were to the fore in the second phase of the game's development, including the re-invigoration of An Cumann Camoguidheacht (the Camogie Association) in 1911. During the 1910s, Gill played for Crokes in the Dublin League. She said of this period that 'Respectable citizens regarded them [camogie players] as unsexed young women,' while 'the girl carrying a camogie through the streets of Dublin, took the precaution to wrap it in brown paper in order to avoid unpleasant notice' (Loretta Murray Clarke collection, 'Transcript of interview', folder 18, box 3, subseries C, MS.2016.016). In January 1915 she was invited to train University College Dublin's new camogie club in preparation for the first iteration of the Ashbourne Cup, which they won, defeating University College Cork (UCC) that April.

She established her reputation as a player at representative level during the 1920s. Her performance on 18 March 1923 for a Dublin League selection that defeated UCC was praised in the *Evening Herald*, which described her as the 'pivot' of the side, reporting that she 'shone out above all the others … leading, attacking, defending'. She scored both of her side's points and set up their only goal. Dublin played three inter-county contests in 1923 but such matches were irregular and would remain so throughout the decade. She captained Leinster to victory in inter-provincial camogie competitions held as part of the 1928 and 1932 Tailteann Games.

The first inter-county all-Ireland camogie championship was held in 1932. Having overcome Wexford in the semi-final, Dublin, captained by Gill, played Galway in the 1932 final, which did not take place until 30 July 1933. While the correspondent for *An Camán* was generally unimpressed, the report acknowledged that 'Miss Gill was best in the second half' as Dublin won 3–2 to 0–2. Less than five months later, the final of the 1933 championship was played on 17 December at Killester, Dublin. *An Camán* was more enthusiastic on that occasion, recording that Gill, who played in midfield, 'was outstanding and time and again fed the forwards'. Dublin scored 9–2 as they defeated Galway again. In November 1935 Dublin returned to the final, losing to Cork (3–4 to 4–0) in an exciting match at the Athletic Grounds, Cork. The *Irish Press* lauded 'Dublin's grand defence', characterising Gill as one of its 'stars'. This was her last appearance in the all-Ireland decider: she was forty-four-years-old. That Gill was admired for her play in attack, midfield and defence suggests a versatility that almost certainly prolonged her career.

In parallel with, and after, her playing career, she was an important camogie official. In June 1917 the Dublin League was re-organised and she became chair (remaining so till 1935), while she refereed matches from as early as September 1917. The Gaelic Athletic Association's (GAA) Dublin county board offered to manage the Dublin League's finances and administration, but she turned this offer down in order to preserve the Camogie Association's independence. In leading the league during the 1920s, she worked with Ryan, who was an assertive secretary, to achieve the allocation to camogie of first one, then a second pitch at the Phoenix Park. In a 1936 radio interview Gill explained that by 1928 camogie in Dublin had expanded sufficiently to sustain senior, intermediate, junior, schools and college leagues, while acknowledging that progress was far more modest in rural areas.

From 1922 Gill and Ryan represented camogie on the executive committee charged with organising the proposed Tailteann Festival. Then, in January 1923, Gill was elected president of the Camogie Association. Her election coincided with the establishment of a three-person *ard coiste*, or executive committee: in 1923 the other members of that triumvirate were Kathleen Ryan, as vice-president, and Áine Ní Riain (Essie Ryan) as secretary. In

July 1924, the Camogie Association withdrew camogie from the upcoming Tailteann Games, claiming it had not received sufficient financial support to facilitate participation. When a team from Wicklow turned out as 'Ireland' and played 'England' in an exhibition match, the *ard coiste* expelled sixteen women from the association, including Lucy Byrne, wife of the Cumann na nGaedheal TD for Wicklow, Christopher Michael Byrne. Civil war politics may have been a factor—establishing the Camogie Association's authority certainly was. The assertive approach of the determined group fronted by Gill generated resentment and, over time, enduring rancour within the association, not least because they were sometimes viewed as a Dublin clique.

From the mid-1920s their continued efforts can be tracked in incremental development: the appointment of Seán O'Duffy as national organiser, the holding of an inaugural annual congress (April 1925), the adoption of less constrictive on-field attire for players, the proliferation of clubs and the consequent emergence of a series of county boards. The introduction in 1929 of a second horizontal bar above the goalmouth, thereby creating a rectangular 'points space', unlike in hurling, may represent a further assertion of the Camogie Association's independence from the GAA. In 1932 congress sought to broaden the geographic base of the central council (though Gill and Ryan remained president and secretary) while pursuing an extension of the association's effective jurisdiction. The first all-Ireland championship followed that year. By 1935 the association boasted 423 clubs, totalling some 10,000 players, but it was vulnerable to the hostility of the Catholic church and beset by internal disputes. Conscious of provincial resentment at the urban dominance of the association, in 1936 Gill stressed the desirability of extending the game's reach in rural areas, pointing to the establishment of provincial councils (in 1934) as a measure of achievement in this regard.

During the mid-1930s this urban–rural division exacerbated a deep rift inside camogie over the merits of a GAA-style ban on foreign games; in reality a ban on hockey. When, at the annual congress held in February 1934, delegates from Galway and Antrim proposed a motion to introduce 'the ban', Cork and Dublin delegates led the opposition. Ryan was, perhaps, the most determined opponent. During a long and heated debate, Gill intervened, as chair, to ask pro-ban speakers 'not to introduce politics' and 'requested the delegates present to act in the interests of camoguidheacht [camogie]', reminding them that 'this was not a GAA convention' (Croke Park Archive, Minutes of the Camogie Association 1932–1947, Minutes of congress, 24 February 1934). So clear was her anti-ban view, that an Antrim delegate accused her of delaying the vote in the hope that provincial delegates would have to leave for their trains. When Gill called it, the vote was carried by twenty-six votes to seventeen.

Banning hockey players had little effect in much of rural Ireland whereas in Dublin and Cork it ensured that existing and potential players were deterred from playing camogie. If Gill's opposition had a pragmatic reasoning, it also reflected her general attitude to sport. She lauded camogie as the 'best game for women' and stressed that it was 'a national game' but railed against gendered and class attitudes that restricted women's access to sport. 'There is', she said in 1936, 'a broader attitude towards the game [camogie] now. Towards every game. Time was when tennis, golf, hockey were only for the favoured few, now the humblest fireside may have its representative on the playing fields' (Loretta Murray Clarke collection 'Transcript of interview').

The 1934 vote led to a series of aftershocks that further hobbled the Camogie Association. Senior voices believed that the ban had been pushed through by men who were not primarily concerned with the well-being of a woman's sport. Consequently, the congress of February 1935 passed a motion that only women delegates could be sent by county boards to congress or central council or provincial councils. Then, in 1939, the anti-ban faction achieved a repeal of the ban by using the mechanism of a special delegate meeting, which gave Dublin more clout given its strong player and club base. This prompted the establishment of a rival pro-ban organisation, the National Camógaíocht Association, which drew strong support from a wide range of counties, notably in Ulster. While influential loyalists such as Seán O'Duffy and Agnes O'Farrelly urged compromise, Gill and Ryan held out for two years until it became evident that theirs was the rump organisation. Despite their objections, in October 1941 their colleagues accepted mediation from Pádraig Ó Caoimh, the general secretary of the GAA, prompting the re-emergence of a single camogie organisation, led by pro-ban officials, in December. Thereafter, Gill lost all influence over the Camogie Association.

In 1937 she had become the principal compositor at the Cuala Press, and from 1939, following a reorganisation, she had a small shareholding. From 1961 she worked alone: indeed, the business had contracted in 1946, when it ceased producing books. She was still working for Cuala Press in 1971, two years after it had been revived upon passing into the ownership of a new generation of the Yeats family. Retiring in the early 1970s, she was described in 1975 as 'amazingly energetic and cheerful' (*The Irish Times*, 21 November 1975). Mollie Gill died at her residence in South Circular Road, Dublin, on 15 March 1977. Her remains were buried at Glencullen cemetery.

William Murphy

Sources

General Register Office Dublin (birth certificate, death certificate); National Archives of Ireland, CSPS 1/5721, Petty Sessions Order Books; National Archives of Ireland, Census of Ireland, 1901; Boston College, Burns Library, Loretta Clarke Murray Collection of Women in Revolutionary Ireland, 'Máire Gill papers'; Croke Park Archive, 'Minutes of the Camogie Association, 1932–1947'; Trinity College Dublin MS 11535, 'The Cuala Press Business Collection'; *An Claidheamh Soluis*, 22 September 1917; *The Irish Times*, 15 April 1922; 19 March 1923; 9 February 1971; 21 November 1975; *Evening Herald*, 24 March 1923; *Wicklow People*, 26 May 1923; *An Camán*, 12 August, 23 December 1933; *Irish Press*, 25 November 1935; Liam Miller, *The Dun Emer Press, later the Cuala Press* (1973); *Scéal na Camogaíochta* (1984); Joan Hardwick, *The Yeats sisters: a biography of Susan and Elizabeth Yeats* (1996); Mary Moran, *Camogie champions* (1998); Ann Saddlemyer, *Becoming George: the life of Mrs W. B. Yeats* (2002); Sineád McCoole, 'Mollie Gill, 1891–1977: a woman of Ireland', *History Ireland* vol. 13, no. 2 (2005), 10–11; Mary Moran, *A game of our own: camogie's story* (2011); Ríona Nic Congáil, '"Looking on for centuries from the sideline": Gaelic feminism and the rise of camogie', *Éire-Ireland* vol 48, nos 1–2 (2013), 168–90; Ciara Daly, 'Women of the Cuala—Maire 'Molly' Gill', www.tcd.ie/library/manuscripts/blog/2021/03/women-of-the-cuala-maire-molly-gill/ (internet material accessed October 2021)

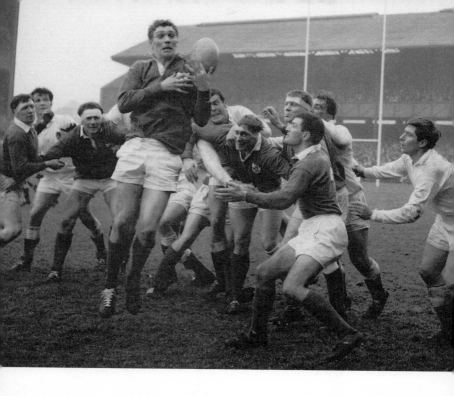

Ken Goodall

1947–2006

RUGBY PLAYER

Ken (Kenneth George) Goodall was born 23 February 1947 at St Mary's hospital, Leeds, England, to George Goodall, a roofer, and his wife Kathleen (née Daly). George, a Yorkshireman, had married Kathleen, from Derry, during the second world war; the family moved to Northern Ireland when Goodall was an infant. He was educated at Foyle College, Derry city, and played in the second row there and for Ulster schools. Playing junior rugby with City of Derry from the 1965/6 season, he commenced a chemical engineering degree at Newcastle University in September 1965. Featuring in the second row, as wing-forward or as number 8, Goodall played for club and university concurrently over the next few years. He declined an England trial and offers to play for Gosforth, a leading English club.

Goodall made his Ulster debut in their 6–6 draw with Australia in December 1966. He was a surprise selection for Ireland, given his youth and inexperience, as number 8 against Australia (21 January 1967). His grandmother, a staunch unionist, draped a cloth over her television as the Irish national anthem was played before his international debut. Aged nineteen (the second-youngest Irish forward, after Karl Mullen (1926–2009)), Goodall was commanding in a 15–8 victory, dominating the lineout. After playing as number 8 in that season's five nations championship, Goodall was selected for the Barbarians' Easter tour of Wales.

Touring Australia with Ireland, Goodall demonstrated his versatility by playing at wing-forward in the only test of the tour. Ireland's 11–5 victory at Sydney Cricket Ground (13 May 1967) was Australia's first loss to a touring 'home nation'. Playing again as wing-forward in Ireland's 6–16 loss to France (27 January 1968) he featured as number 8 in Ireland's remaining Five Nations games that season. Although the form Irish back-row-forward, he was not selected for the 1968 British Lions tour to South Africa due to his university exams clashing with the first test. He had missed his exams the previous spring when he toured Australia and could not delay them again. Called up by the Lions as a replacement, Goodall played in the 37–9 victory against Eastern Transvaal on 29 June. He injured his hand five minutes into the game but played on. The multiple fractures he sustained required surgery, which ended his tour.

Goodall was selected as wing-forward for Ireland against Australia, scoring the second try in Ireland's 10–3 victory (26 October 1968) in Dublin, his third win with Ireland over Australia in twenty-one months. He distinguished himself as Ireland's most effective forward in victories over France and England, becoming untouchable at number 8, retaining that position for all his subsequent international caps. Commanding in the lineout, impactful off the scrum and domineering in the loose, in many respects a precursor to the all-round ability of the professional-era rugby union player, Goodall was regarded as perhaps the best back-row-forward in world rugby in 1969, certainly the best in the northern hemisphere. He was critical to Ireland's then-record achievement of six successive international victories (February 1968–February 1969). After he injured his ankle in the away victory over Scotland— the last in the sequence—Ireland greatly missed him in their 21–11 loss to Wales in the Triple Crown decider.

It was the only international game Goodall missed in four seasons during which he maintained a gruelling playing schedule for City of Derry, Newcastle University, Ulster, Ireland and occasionally for English Universities. Goodall was one of a number of especially talented Ulster players, including Mike Gibson, Syd Millar and Willie John McBride, playing together for the province and Ireland. Goodall shone in inter-provincial games, the apex of Irish domestic rugby, as Ulster shared the title in 1967 and won it outright in 1968 and 1970.

Following Ireland's losses to France and England in the 1970 Five Nations Championship, he scored a try in the

16–11 victory against Scotland (28 February 1970). The final championship game (14 March 1970) in Lansdowne Road, against a Wales team chasing its second successive Triple Crown, saw Goodall score a memorable try in a 14–0 victory. Catching a loose clearance, Goodall ran fifty metres, chipped the Welsh full-back J. P. R. Williams, collected the ball, and then won a footrace against scrum-half Gareth Edwards to the line. The try, one of the finest seen at Lansdowne Road, sealed Ireland's biggest win against Wales since 1925.

Goodall's dominance of the lineout was hugely valuable—he was probably the best lineout jumper in the world—during a period when the use of the outside arm, and lifting, in lineouts was prohibited and games could feature between fifty and eighty lineouts. (Direct kicks to touch were allowed until 1970, with the ensuing lineout taking place where the ball left the field of play; after that date, a direct kick to touch was only allowed from behind the kicking team's '22'.) Despite being 6ft 3in. (1.9m) tall, and weighing over 14 stone (89kg), Goodall was also highly mobile, the standout back-row member of an imposing Irish pack. He was *Rugby World* magazine's International Player of the Year for 1970, the first Irish player to receive this prestigious award.

After Goodall graduated B.Sc. (June 1969), he struggled to find work in the chemical industry and took up a teaching position with Limavady Grammar School, Co. Derry. He married (23 December 1969) Wilma Lyttle, a teacher and international track and field athlete, in Waterside Presbyterian church, Derry. Still aged twenty-two, he had won nineteen Irish caps. Although selected for the autumn 1970 Irish tour to Argentina, he put an end to mounting speculation by signing professional papers with English rugby league club Workington Town on 6 July

1970. He was drawn by a salary significantly higher than that earned by a teacher; he had been living with his wife in his mother's home and struggling financially.

Goodall started in rugby league by scoring thirteen tries in his first eleven matches for Workington Town. Going on to score 20 tries in 35 games that season, he became the first forward to top the club's annual scoring table. His lineout skills and capacity to dominate broken play, however, were almost useless in rugby league. Moreover, his prolific scoring made him a marked man. Taller than his fellow forwards and more vulnerable to the incessant tackling innate to rugby league, he succumbed to injury. A knee injury limited him to ten appearances during his second season, before a compressed nerve in his lower back required surgery in January 1974; after a lengthy convalescence he retired on medical advice at the end of his fourth season with the club. Playing eighty-two games over four seasons (1970–74), he added only five more tries over his final three injury-plagued seasons. Goodall worked as a physics teacher at Moorclose School while living in Workington.

He returned to Derry with his wife and young son and took up a teaching post with Faughan Valley High School where he introduced rugby union. But Goodall had committed the greatest sin possible in the eyes of the rugby union establishment; the Irish Rugby Football Union (IRFU) and International Board rules that opposed professionalism were sacrosanct and essentially directed at one sport, rugby league. The tenets and officious culture of rugby union demanded that he be refused admittance to any rugby union ground in the decade or so after his move to rugby league. He kept up friendships in the union game, and gradually the warmth in which he was held denuded the formal ostracism demanded by rugby union officialdom. Covering club rugby in Ulster with BBC Radio from the mid-1970s, he was part of the coaching staff of Irish Schools and Ulster under-21 teams (c.2000).

In April 1989 Goodall, along with other converts to rugby league, was formally reinstated to rugby union by the International Rugby Board. He took up his allotment of international match tickets from the IRFU, bearing no ill will towards the code. Having taken early retirement as vice-principal of Faughan Valley High School, Goodall died in Derry on 17 August 2006 after a short illness, and was buried in Ballyoan cemetery. He was aged fifty-nine. He was survived by his wife Wilma, son Gareth and daughter Gail. The Ulster branch of the IRFU instituted the Ken Goodall Award for the provincial club player of the year, presented annually by the City of Derry club. Goodall was selected at number 8 on the 'greatest Ulster team' in 2005.

Turlough O'Riordan

Sources

General Register Office England and Wales (birth certificate); *The Irish Times*, *passim*, esp.: 16 March, 9 April, 29 October, 30 December 1968; 23 December 1969; 19 August 2006; *Irish Independent*, 1 December 1966; 19 August 1967; *Irish Press*, 17 November 1967; 11 March 1968; John Reason, *The 1968 Lions: the British Isles tour of South Africa* (1968); *Sunday Independent*, 11 January 1970; David Orr (ed.), *City of Derry Rugby Football Club: centenary 1881–1981: a club history* (1981); *Belfast Telegraph*, 19 September 2000; *Sunday Times*, 13 November 2005; Tony Collins, *Rugby league in twentieth-century Britain: a social and cultural history* (2006); BBC Sport online, 17 August 2006, news.bbc.co.uk/sport2/hi/rugby_union/irish/5260460.stm (internet material accessed May 2013); *Times & Star*, 22 August 2006; Tom English, *No borders: playing rugby for Ireland* (2016), 42; 'Barbarians fixtures and results, 1966–67', www.barbarianfc.co.uk/results-fixtures/1966-1967/ (internet material accessed January 2021)

This entry has been abridged for publication. The full version is available at www.dib.ie.

Vere Goold

1853–1909

Tennis player

Vere Thomas St Leger Goold was born 2 October 1853
in Waterford, sixth son among seven children of George
Ignatius Goold, justice of the peace and resident magistrate of Waterford, and his wife Clara, daughter of Major-
General James Webber-Smith. He was born into a wealthy,
long-eminent catholic family.

Waterford was one of the earliest regions to hold competitive lawn tennis events. Goold took to the game and was often known as 'Vere St Leger' when playing incognito. In 1878 he travelled to Limerick to play in the open lawn tennis championships. He duly won the singles title. St Leger also won the first Irish Open. In those inaugural Irish championships, held in 1879 at his home club, Fitzwilliam Lawn Tennis Club in Dublin, he beat C. D. Barry (also Irish) 8–6, 8–6 in the final of the men's singles. The first prize was valued at £20, a considerable amount at the time. A total of fifteen players had entered in the singles. He was known to have a splendid backhand and was expected to win the Wimbledon championships a few weeks later. In his first and last appearance at 'The Championship', he reached the final, beating F. Durant (6–1, 6–2, 6–3), J. D. Vans Agnew (6–2, 6–3, 6–1), A. J. Mulholland (6–4, 2–6, 6–1, 6–4), and G. E. Tabor (6–2, 6–5, 5–6, 6–3). But he seems to have been nursing a bad hangover in the final and was beaten by the Reverend John Thorneycroft Hartley, 6–4, 6–2, 6–2. Hartley wrote about his opponent: 'He was then a cheery wild Irishman, Irish champion, and a very pretty player. I think he volleyed more than most of us that year; but there were some weaknesses I suppose in his play, as being fit and well after a night's rest I won three sets straight off' (*50 years of Wimbledon*, 15). Hartley had returned to Yorkshire after his semi-final to give his church sermon. On Monday 15 July, after a train journey and a rushed horse-and-carriage ride, he arrived just in time for the final. About 1,100 spectators watched this match. St Leger did win the play-off for second prize, beating C. F. Parr 4–6, 6–2, 5–6, 6–4, 6–4.

Back in Dublin, Goold was a prominent member of the Fitzwilliam club and was involved in handicapping as well as in the purchasing of equipment. The club colours had been chocolate and blue, but in deference to Goold's play and that of Ernest de Sylly Hami Browne, the new colours of chocolate and maize became affectionately known as 'Browne and Goold'. The wearing of cap, tie and waist scarf in the club was at first compulsory. Goold acted on the committee that ran the championships in 1879 and 1880. According to O'Connor, 'He was the bright spark of Fitzwilliam in this period. In the minutes his name constantly comes up. "Mr Goold was selected to handicap." "Mr Goold reported that he had ordered four nets from Messrs Caylers at £1 each and they had promised to present one net to the club"' (*Fitzwilliam story*, 5).

In his early days Goold was in the public service in Dublin as secretary of the municipal boundaries commission. This gave him plenty of time to play tennis. In October 1879 he returned to England to play in an open tournament at the Imperial Winter Gardens, Cheltenham. Play took place on outdoor asphalt and on a covered court. William Renshaw came back from 4–1 down in the fifth set to beat Goold in the final, 6–4, 6–3, 5–6, 5–6, 6–4. Goold played at Fitzwilliam Lawn Tennis Club the following year, but illness prevented practice and he lost his Irish title to the same William Renshaw in three easy sets (6–1, 6–4, 6–3) in the challenge round. Renshaw later won three Irish singles titles and seven Wimbledon singles titles between 1880 and 1889.

Goold continued to play till about 1883. His only noteworthy tennis win was in 1881 when he and W. H. Darby defeated the highly rated English pair, H. F. Lawford and A. J. Mulholland, in an unofficial Irish–English international, the first match between two countries in the sport of lawn tennis. Ireland beat England two matches to one, all doubles. Lawford was in six Wimbledon finals, beating Ernest Renshaw in 1887, and won the Irish Open three times (1884, 1885, 1886).

Goold later moved to London, where he met a Frenchwoman, Marie Violet (née Girodin). By the time she met him in 1886 she had already been widowed twice, had sold her jewellery and was a court dressmaker. Both aged thirty-eight, they married (22 August 1891) at St Mary of the Angels, Paddington; they had no children. They emigrated to Canada for a few years and then returned to London in 1903. After losing money in a laundry business, they moved to Monte Carlo to try their luck on the gaming tables. On Tuesday 6 August 1907 the 5.38 a.m. train from Monte Carlo arrived at Marseilles. A porter noticed an unusual smell coming from a trunk and large handbag, deposited by the Goolds with instructions to be forwarded to London. When a dismembered body of a lady was found, both were arrested.

The trial commenced on 2 December and lasted for three days. Among the thirty witnesses was Isobella Girodin, a niece of Mrs Goold, who indicated that Goold often drank and quarrelled with his wife. The murdered woman, Emma Liven, a Dane, had been visiting the Goold's flat to reclaim a loan, when she was struck during a furious argument. Goold was sent to Devil's Island, French Guiana, on 19 July 1908 and died there on 8 September 1909. His wife was imprisoned in Montpellier and died in 1914. Vere Thomas St Leger Goold might be remembered as the first winner of the Irish Open at the age of twenty-five, but thirty years later he was to die ignominiously. He is remembered as the only Wimbledon finalist convicted of murder—so far.

Tom Higgins

Sources

John Burke, *A general and heraldic history of the peerage and baronetage* (1912), 840; A. Wallis Myers, *Fifty years of Wimbledon* (1926), 15; J. J. Treacy, *Fitzwilliam's first fifty: half a century of Irish lawn tennis* ([1927]); Ulick O'Connor, *The Fitzwilliam story* (1979), 4–6 (with group photo); Alan Little, *St Leger Goold: a tale of two courts* (1984); 'The Irish murderer of Monte Carlo', www.independent.ie/lifestyle/the-irish-murderer-of-monte-carlo-26806963.html (internet material accessed November 2021)

Lady Mary Heath

1896–1939

(Sophie) Mary Heath (née Peirce-Evans; Eliott-Lynn) was born Sophie Catherine Theresa Mary Peirce-Evans on 17 November 1896 in Knockaderry, Co. Limerick, the only child of Jackie Peirce-Evans and his wife and former housekeeper, Kate Doolin (or Dowling) of Kerry. She was baptised into the Church of Ireland. Jackie Peirce-Evans lived in Knockaderry House on 350 acres of land he had inherited. He subjected his wife to physical and sexual abuse. In December 1897 Kate Peirce-Evans was found dead in Knockaderry House, with Sophie wrapped up beside her, sleeping. Jackie admitted beating his wife to death and was charged with murder, found insane and placed in a mental institution for the rest of his life.

Sophie was reared by her grandfather, Dr George Peirce-Evans, and by her aunts in Newcastle West, Co. Limerick, and educated in St Margaret's Hall School, Dublin. Enrolling as an associate student in the Royal College of Science (RCS) on Merrion Street in 1914, she was an excellent and popular student. In November 1916 she married William Elliott-Lynn, a forty-one-year-old army officer. Soon, she abandoned her studies to volunteer in England for the Women's Auxiliary Army Corps as a motorcyclist dispatch rider. In 1917 she went to France, operating close to the front. She was the subject of a portrait, in uniform, by the official war artist Sir John Lavery in 1918. Demobilised in July 1919, she resumed her studies in the RCS, graduating first in her class in July 1921 with an associateship in agriculture. She based herself in London while her husband farmed at Pangani in east Africa's Tanganyika territory. Although she visited him in 1922, and again in 1923, the Elliott-Lynns, who had never spent much time together, then drifted towards divorce.

Having become obsessed with athletics during 1921, she competed in athletics meets held in and around London and further afield in the early to mid-1920s. Of Amazonian proportions, she stood 6ft (1.83m) tall, weighed 11st. (70kg) and excelled in several events, notably the high jump and the Greek two-handed javelin throw (which involved adding together throws out of each hand). Soon after representing Britain in the shot at the first Women's Modern Olympic Games held in Paris (August 1922), she helped set up the Women's Amateur

Athletic Association (WAAA), becoming its secretary and treasurer. At the inaugural English Women's Athletics Championships, held in August 1923 at the Oxo Sports Ground, Bromley, she became England's two-handed javelin champion. She claimed to have jumped 4ft 10in. (1.47m) in the high jump at Brentwood that October and this was listed, probably incorrectly, as a world record. Her finest hour came at the 1924 English Women's Championships, held in the Woolwich Stadium, London, where she won the high jump and javelin, smashing the two-handed javelin world record by throwing an aggregate of 173ft 2in. (52.78m). This achievement, however, was not officially recognised due to a slight breeze.

She became vice-president of the WAAA in autumn 1923, which boasted 25,000 members in 500 clubs by 1925, and was active in the National Playing Fields Association, which sought better sports facilities for deprived children in urban areas. Cultivating a high profile, she spoke at sports and health conferences, and published a coaching manual, *Athletics for women and girls* (1925); she read out the book's preface on BBC Radio. She spoke in favour of women's participation in sport as a member of the Fédération Sportive Féminine Internationale (FSFI) delegation at the International Olympic Congress held in Prague (29 May–4 June 1925). Immediately after coming fourth in the two-handed javelin in the 1926 Women's World Games at Gothenburg 1926, she participated in the ensuing FSFI conference held there and argued against women joining the Olympic movement, probably because she preferred for the WAAA to remain independent.

From 1925 aviation replaced athletics as her main interest. She was the first woman member of the London

Light Aeroplane Club when it opened in August 1925 before qualifying that November for her private ('A') licence. Incensed by the International Commission for Air Navigation's ban on commercial licences for women, she bombarded the commission with statistics on women's fitness and offered herself for medical tests. The commission took up her offer but obliged her to undergo the required fitness tests while she was menstruating. She began studying for her commercial ('B') licence in January 1926 and went on to become Britain's first officially recognised woman commercial pilot on 26 June. Her success obliged the authorities in Britain and in several other countries to rescind their ban on women commercial pilots.

Flying successively in a De Havilland Moth, a SE.5a Viper (from July 1926) and an Avro Avian MK II (from July 1927), she earned a living giving joyrides and flying lessons, and by performing stunts and participating in races in air shows in Britain and on the continent. In numerous air races she showed herself to be the best woman pilot in the country and well capable of beating most men also, mainly through her skill at cornering. Under a blaze of publicity, she became the first woman pilot to make a parachute jump in public in April 1926, set altitude records of 15,748ft (4,800m) in May 1927 and of 19,200ft (5,852m) in October 1927, and defeated her fellow Irishwomen and main rivals, Sicely O'Brien and Lady Bailey, in a ladies' race at Bournemouth in June 1927. On a one-day publicity tour of British aerodromes in July 1927 she covered 1,250 miles (2,011km) and touched down seventy-nine times in eighteen hours. Later that month she made a triumphal visit to Ireland as an honoured guest of the Irish Air Corps, before re-crossing the Irish Sea to claim the Grosvenor Cup, the main short race at the Nottingham aviation meeting. Her Grosvenor Cup victory in a field of fourteen with only one other woman was publicised as the first by a woman pilot over men. To pay for her expensive recreation, she married a seventy-five-year-old industrialist Sir James Heath in October 1927, but only after delaying the wedding until he agreed to settle her with an income of £925 a year. Thereafter, she styled herself Lady Mary Heath, Mary being one of her middle names.

In February 1928 came the escapade that made her world-famous: the first solo flight by a woman from South Africa to England. Setting off from Pretoria on 17 February in her new Avro Avian Mk III, she suffered sunstroke near Bulawayo, Southern Rhodesia (Zimbabwe), and made an emergency landing but recovered to arrive in Khartoum on 1 April. This made her the first woman to fly across the equator. She attributed her safe progress to her assid-uousness in maintaining her aircraft. On reaching Cairo she headed west along the north African coast because she disliked crossing long stretches of water. The locals liked to shoot at airplanes passing overhead, and she later found a bullet hole in one of her wings. Making the short hop to Europe from Tunis, she landed in Croydon, London, on 17 May and stepped out of the aircraft wearing a silk dress, fur coat and black straw hat, proclaiming that 'it is so safe that a woman can fly across Africa wearing a Parisian frock and keeping her nose powdered all the way' (*Daily Express*, 17 May 1928). She had covered about 10,000 miles (16,093km) in flying from Pretoria to London. Honoured with a dinner from the African Society and lunch from the Overseas League, she made clear her imperialist leanings, expressing the hope that her flight would strengthen the ties between the dominions and Britain.

In summer 1928 she was second pilot on the large Fokker planes operated by KLM, the Dutch airline, accumulating thirty hours experience carrying passengers on the London–Amsterdam route; on some of these flights the first pilot hardly touched the controls. She was thus the first woman to fly a commercial aircraft, but to her disappointment KLM did not hire her, fearing that having a woman pilot would deter passengers. On 4 October 1928 she claimed to have set a new altitude record of 23,000ft (7,010m) for a light aircraft, but the barographs on her plane conflicted, with the other reading 19,000ft (5,791m). Her claim was discredited, and she was criticised for engaging in another of her publicity stunts. The British press had always disliked her forceful personality and self-promotion, dubbing her 'Lady Hell-of-a-din'—this was a play on Elliott-Lynn, the surname by which she first became famous, though she has gone down in history as Lady Heath.

In November 1928 she escaped the jealousy towards her in Britain by moving to America, where she was received rapturously and toured the country, flying in air shows and races. Her title and accent led Americans to treat her as an aristocrat of long pedigree, and she thrived off lecturing and by acting as sales agent and test pilot for the Cirrus company, which made aviation engines. As well as writing regularly for US journals and newspapers, she published another book, co-written with Stella Wolfe Murray, *Women and flying* (1929), in which she encouraged more women to become aviators. On 29 August 1929, however, she crashed into a factory beside Cleveland Airport while practicing a dead stick landing. She was not expected to survive, suffering two factures of the skull and a fractured jaw amongst other injuries: steel plates were inserted in her skull. Though she recovered and flew again, it was never to the same standard. She became far more eccentric and drank heavily. Her second marriage ended in divorce in 1930: it had been in difficulties even before the accident due to her financial profligacy, an issue which had also undermined her first marriage. In November 1931 she married a black aviator, Reggie Williams, yet another man of means, originally from Trinidad.

Unable to earn a living in America, she returned to Ireland in 1932, settling in Dublin to work as a pilot and flight instructor for Iona National Airways, based in Kildonan, Co. Dublin. She helped set up flying clubs, most significantly the National Irish Junior Aviation Club, inaugurated in May 1933. After Iona closed in 1933, she and her husband bought out its successor company at Kildonan, Dublin Air Ferries, in 1935. The venture went bankrupt in 1936, whereupon she separated from her husband and moved to London. Her last years were scarred by instability, poverty and alcoholism; she was prosecuted several times for drunkenness and placed on probation. She died in St Leonard's hospital in Shoreditch, London, on 7 May 1939 after falling from the top floor of a bus. There was no alcohol in her system, and the accident probably arose from a blood clot in her brain. Her third husband scattered her ashes over Surrey. None of her marriages produced any children.

Although she was forgotten for a time, her achievements in women's athletics and aviation, and her role in their promotion, stimulated renewed interest in her from the late twentieth century. She was commemorated on an Irish postage stamp in 1998.

Bridget Hourican

Sources

Harald Penrose, *British aviation: the adventuring years, 1920–29* (1973); Wendy Boase, *The sky's the limit* (1979); Michael Barry, *Great aviation stories* (1993), vol. 1; Newcastle West Historical Society, *Annual Observer* (June 1983), 62–7; Rosanne Welch, *Encyclopaedia of women in aviation and space* (1998); Noel Henry, *From Sophie to Sonia* (1998); Stephanie Daniels and Anita Tedder, *A proper spectacle: women Olympians, 1900–36* (2000); John Haughton, *The silver lining* (2003); Lindie Naughton, *Lady Icarus* (2004); Mark Pottle, 'Heath [née Peirce-Evans; other married name Eliott-Lynn], Sophie Catherine Theresa Mary, Lady Heath', *Oxford dictionary of national biography* (2012), doi.org/10.1093/ref:odnb/67141 (accessed December 2021); Michael Traynor, *Petticoat pilots: biographies and achievements of Irish female aviators, 1909–1939* (2019)

Kevin Heffernan

1929–2013

GAELIC FOOTBALLER AND COACH

Kevin Heffernan was born 20 August 1929 at 51 Pembroke Cottages, Donnybrook, Dublin, the second eldest of seven children of John Heffernan, a garda originally from Co. Offaly, and Mary (née Burke) from Co. Kilkenny. The family moved to Turlough Parade, Marino, Dublin, where Kevin grew up. He attended Scoil Mhuire

Boys national school, Marino, and St Joseph's Christian Brothers School in Fairview, Dublin, before joining the Electricity Supply Board (ESB) accounts department in 1949. He later entered Trinity College Dublin (TCD) where he graduated B.Comm. in 1957.

His family had no tradition of involvement in the Gaelic Athletic Association (GAA), and he began playing football and hurling, mainly at left-corner-forward, through his schools and the local St Vincents GAA club. In 1948 St Vincents adopted a policy that restricted membership to those born into, or residing in, the local parish, thereby precluding the selection of country-bred footballers living elsewhere in Dublin. The newly 'nativised' St Vincents team developed a revolutionary short-passing game, also based on running with the ball and a great deal of movement off it. This was ideal for Heffernan who made up in bravery, skill and intelligence for what he lacked in strength and physique. By breaking with a tradition predicated on a simple 'catch and kick' philosophy and on confining players to their selected positions on the field, St Vincents dominated Dublin football from 1949, outmanoeuvring rival club sides composed mainly of players born outside Dublin.

At inter-county level Heffernan won Leinster minor medals for Dublin in football (1946) and hurling (1947), following this with Leinster and all-Ireland football medals playing for the Dublin junior footballers in 1948. He was on the Dublin senior football team from the late 1940s and was a good enough hurler to be either a starter or a substitute for the Dublin senior team during the mid-1950s. When he first began playing football for Dublin, the team included many country-born, Dublin-resident players. In the early 1950s, however, Dublin adopted the

St Vincents' policy of selecting 'natives' and by April 1953 all fourteen outfield players on the Dublin team that defeated Cavan in the National Football League final were St Vincents men, Heffernan amongst them.

In 1955 Heffernan began playing as a roving full-forward for Dublin. By dropping deep, he found the space he needed to link up with teammates, gather possession and swerve past lumbering full-backs. He ran amok against Paddy 'Hands' O'Brien of Meath, long considered the best full-back in Ireland, in both the 1955 National Football League final and the 1955 Leinster football final. Heffernan's scintillating attacking play drove Dublin to the 1955 all-Ireland final where they faced Kerry in an eagerly anticipated match, billed as a clash between the slick-passing Dublin 'machine' and the 'catch and kick' purists of Kerry. Carrying an injury into the final, he failed to shine and was guilty in the second half of prematurely going for goals, as Dublin tried in vain to overturn Kerry's lead.

Two barren years followed for Dublin whereupon Heffernan, who was effectively the player-manager, decided that the defence was over elaborating with the ball and put in place a full back line that was tough, strong and cleared its lines without delay. A more determined and pragmatic Dublin captured the National Football League and all-Ireland titles in 1958, with Heffernan playing a starring role as captain in the all-Ireland final against Derry. He was disappointed not to win another all-Ireland or to avenge the 1955 all-Ireland final defeat, as Dublin lost all-Ireland semi-finals to Kerry in 1959 and 1962.

He retired from inter-county football in 1962 with one all-Ireland medal (1958), four Leinster medals (1955, 1958–9, 1962) and three National League medals (1953, 1955, 1958); playing for Leinster, he won seven Railway

Cup medals (1952–5, 1959, 1961–2). His achievements were recognised by his inclusion at left-corner-forward on both the GAA's team of the century and team of the millennium. He stopped hurling in 1962 but continued playing club football until 1967, scoring 1–4 in his last match as St Vincents won the county final. At club level he won fifteen Dublin county medals (1949–55, 1957–62, 1966–7) in football and six county medals (1953–5, 1957, 1959, 1962) in hurling.

He remained heavily involved with St Vincents, acting as the club's football manager for most of the 1960s and 1970s. Amid an evenly and ferociously contested rivalry with University College Dublin (UCD) for the Dublin championship during the early to mid-1970s, he guided St Vincents to two Leinster senior championships (1973 and 1976) and an all-Ireland club championship (1976). From 1963 he was also generally a Dublin selector but was unhappy in this role, as the yearly shuffling of selectors led to a lack of continuity in management and on the team. The Dublin inter-county teams lost competitiveness and spectator appeal.

In 1973 the chairman of the Dublin county board Jimmy Gray convinced Heffernan to take over a stream-lined, three-man selection committee, given three years' tenure. In practice he rapidly assumed complete control at a time when other county teams were being run by un-wieldy committees. He brought an unprecedented level of sophistication to the team's physical conditioning and tactics, combining this with old-fashioned belligerence. The impact was transformative: in 1974 an initially unheralded Dublin team set a new standard of strength and fitness for Gaelic football, and on 21 September Heffernan's players defeated Galway in the all-Ireland final to secure the county's first all-Ireland title since 1963. Their success spawned a social and cultural phenomenon. 'The Dubs' achieved significant popular support in the capital, appealing to a cohort of urban youth, known as 'Heffo's army', that had no previous relationship with the GAA.

In just over a decade—from 1974 to 1985—Dublin footballers contested nine senior all-Ireland football finals and won four. Heffernan was not at the helm for all of them, having stepped down following Dublin's victory in the 1976 all-Ireland final. In his absence, Dublin retained their all-Ireland title in 1977, after which he returned. Before the decade was out, he had led Dublin to two more all-Ireland finals both of which were lost to a similarly outstanding Kerry team. During 1975–9 Dublin and Kerry played each other in four all-Ireland finals and one all-Ireland semi-final, with Kerry winning three times and Dublin twice. This rivalry represented a particular high point for Gaelic football, not only for the outstanding matches it produced, but also because it provided a sporting clash of rural and urban Ireland. In the distinctive personalities of Kevin Heffernan and Mick O'Dwyer, his Kerry counterpart, the Dublin–Kerry rivalry fuelled the emergence of the cult of the manager in Gaelic sports.

After 1979, Dublin retreated to the sporting shadows. But when they re-emerged in 1983, Heffernan was still in charge and with a new team, full of youth and a few veterans of the 1970s. He delivered an unlikely all-Ireland title to the capital, his new-look team's campaign ending in a remarkable, if ill-tempered, all-Ireland final against Galway in which four players were sent off, three of them from Dublin. Two more all-Ireland final appearances followed in 1984 and 1985 but Kerry again proved Dublin's nemesis. He stepped down again as Dublin manager after the second of those defeats, but in 1986 the GAA appointed him to manage an Irish team of Gaelic footballers travelling to Australia to contest an 'international rules' series against a team of professional Australian rules footballers. The choice of Heffernan over Mick O'Dwyer—then the manager of seven all-Ireland winning teams—created a mini-controversy and led some Kerry footballers to decline the offer to travel to Australia. The tour was a success, with Ireland winning the series by two games to one, and it cemented Heffernan's reputation as a brilliant sporting tactician and motivator.

A deep intelligence was critical to Heffernan's success in sports management. Thus, after Dublin lost the 1975 all-Ireland final to Kerry he successfully reconstructed and redeployed his half-back line to cope with Kerry's flying forwards. In 1983 he astonished the rest of the Dublin panel by converting Joe McNally from being the substitute goalkeeper into an all-star corner-forward. There could be ruthlessness to his managerial style, though the range of perspectives from those who played under him suggest a manager who knew when to gently coax and when to sharply prod his players to best effect.

Heffernan left a deep impression on all of those he managed, yet, with exceptions, the relationship between mentor and mentored was not personally close. He was too exacting of his players for that. When one player approached him to make representations on behalf of another who had not been selected, he replied: 'Look, I would drop my own mother if I thought she was not worth her place' (*Giants of Gaelic football*, 58). He was also, perhaps, too reserved a personality to forge strong personal relationships with those he managed, his reticence extending to his dealings with the press, whom he did not ignore but seldom indulged.

Outside of sport as inside it, he excelled as a leader. Appointed an industrial relations manager at the ESB in 1970, he revamped its approach to staff relations, eschewing confrontation in favour of a more open and collaborative approach. After taking early retirement in 1985, he was nominated to the Labour Court as a representative of the Federated Union of Employers, later serving as the Labour Court's chairman (1989–94). A regular at greyhound tracks—his other sporting pastime was golf—he was also chairman of Bord na gCon (1994–5), the semi-state body responsible for greyhound racing in Ireland, and of an independent body established to oversee the policing of greyhound racing for doping offences (2007–9).

Yet he remained forever associated in the popular consciousness with Dublin GAA. It was for his contribution to Gaelic games that he received honorary degrees from TCD (1988) and UCD (2004), the latter coming months after he was also honoured with the freedom of the city of Dublin (2004). He continued to contribute in administrative and advisory capacities to St Vincents and Dublin GAA. In the early 1990s he chaired a county board development committee that oversaw the implementation of new coaching programmes, including the appointment of full-time coaches to support clubs in forging links with their local schools. This would feed into subsequent success for the county at underage and adult levels.

Kevin Heffernan died, after a lengthy illness, on 25 January 2013 in Dublin. He was survived by his wife Mary, daughter Orla and two grandchildren. His funeral mass at St Vincent de Paul church in Marino drew a large attendance. He was buried at St Fintan's cemetery, Sutton, Co. Dublin.

Marc Duncan

Sources

Gaelic Weekly, 21 October 1967; Raymond Smith, *The football immortals* (1968 edition), 213–26; *Dublin GAA county board yearbooks 1975–87;* Paddy Donnelly, *Cumann Iomáine and Peile Naomh Uinsion 1931–1981* (1981); David Walsh, 'Return to the hill: the remarkable story of Heffo's heroes', *Magill*, January 1989; *Labour Court forty-second annual report* (1990); Brian Carthy, *Football captains: the all-Ireland winners* (1993); *IPA administration yearbook and diary* (1995); Dáil Eireann debates, 16 October 1996, www.oireachtas.ie/en/debates/debate/dail/1996-10-16/36/ (accessed April 2019); *The Irish Times*, 21 February 2004; 11 January 2007; 25, 29 January 2013; William Nolan (ed.), *The Gaelic Athletic Association in Dublin, 1884–2000* (2005); Tom Humphries, *Dublin v Kerry: the story of an epic rivalry that changed Irish sport* (2006); Seán Óg Ó Ceallacháin, *Giants of Gaelic football* (2007); Liam Hayes, *Heffo: a brilliant mind* (2013); *Sunday Independent*, 21 December 2014; conversation with John Costello, CEO Dublin GAA, 3 April 2019; information from Orla Heffernan, daughter, April 2019

This entry and the related sources have been abridged for publication. The full version is available at www.dib.ie.

May Hezlet

1882–1978

May (Mary) Hezlet was born 29 April 1882 in Gibraltar
to a landed Co. Londonderry family, one of six surviving children of Richard Jackson Hezlet, an officer in the
Royal Artillery and his English-born wife Emily Mary
Linzee Hezlet (née Owen). May grew up in Ireland
where her family lived at Bovagh House in Aghadowey,
Co. Londonderry, while also spending time at their other

residence in Portrush, Co. Antrim. The Hezlets were a famous golfing family, linked to the Royal Portrush Golf Club. Her father and her brother, Charles, and her mother and three sisters, Florence (Jackie), Violet and Emmie, all captained the men's and ladies' clubs, respectively, and all were accomplished golfers. Her mother was also associated with the founding of the Irish Ladies' Golf Union (ILGU).

May started playing golf when she was nine, won her first competition in 1893, aged eleven, and by the age of twelve she was playing off a handicap of sixteen. In 1898, aged fifteen, she was runner-up in the Irish amateur championship, which she won in 1899 at Newcastle, Co. Down, when she defeated her clubmate Rhona Adair. A week later, she recorded a surprising victory in the British amateur championship, again at Newcastle, and became the youngest ever winner of the tournament, having celebrated her seventeenth birthday during the intervening week. These sensational victories had involved playing two rounds of golf a day for ten days out of eleven. Her routine of cycling the eighteen miles from Bovagh House to Portrush to play thirty-six holes helped her to outlast competitors on the golf course.

She lost form for the next couple of years, mainly because she was sent to a school in London and could not practice enough. In 1902, by which date she was living back home, she regained the British championship at Deal in Kent by overcoming E. C. Neville in an exciting final, which she won on the second extra hole. After losing the 1904 final on the final green to the tennis star and archer, Lottie Dod, she claimed her third British championship, then a joint record, in 1907 amid appalling weather at Newcastle, Co. Down, where she defeated her sister Florence in the final. Meanwhile, a three-in-a-row of Irish championship victories was recorded from 1904 to 1906, and then a fifth and final Irish championship was added in 1908. She defeated her sister Florence in three Irish finals. A five-time beaten finalist in the Irish championship, Florence also lost a second British championship final in 1909. Of her other sisters, Violet reached the final of one British championship and two Irish championships; Emmie the final of one Irish championship. Their younger brother Charles (1891–1965) won the Irish amateur close championship in 1920 and the Irish amateur open championship in 1926 and 1929, also becoming Ireland's first Walker Cup golfer.

Outside her family, May's main rival was her fellow Portrush clubmate Rhona Adair. Between them they won four British amateur championships during 1899–1903. Although she could not drive the ball as far as Adair, Hezlet was more accurate. Her stylish swing led many to account her the most complete golfer, man or woman, they had seen. Also admired for her consistency, outstanding iron play and capacity for rallying from a losing position, she was widely acknowledged as the finest women golfer of her day. In 1907 T. H. Miller, the vice-president of the Ladies' Golfing Union, brought over a team of four men from England to challenge May Hezlet, Violet Hezlet and Rhona Adair at Royal Portrush; May played two matches. The men were beaten soundly with May thrashing Miller 10 and 8. Miller insisted they continue until he won a hole only to find himself sixteen down on the seventeenth tee; she let him halve the final two holes.

That same year she captained the Irish ladies' team, which included her sisters Violet and Florence, to victory in the Women's Home Internationals held at Newcastle. This 'triple crown' over the Welsh, Scottish and English teams was not repeated for seventy-three years. She also played on the Irish teams that won the Home International competition in 1901 and 1903. In 1904 May, Violet, Florence and their mother were all chosen for the Irish team. In 1905 she participated along with Florence in the British team that defeated a visiting US team 6–1 at the Royal Cromer Golf Club. May won her match against Margaret Curtis. The Hezlets became friends with the Curtis sisters, Margaret and Harriet, who were America's best women golfers. (This 1905 event would lead eventually to the inauguration in 1932 of the biennial Curtis Cup, contested between teams representing the USA, and Great Britain and Ireland.)

She retired from championship golf upon her marriage in April 1909 to the rector of Ballymena, Arthur Edwin Ross, although she represented Ireland one last time in the 1912 Home Internationals. In 1921 she was elected an honorary member of the ladies' committee at Royal Portrush, and in 1922 she was instituted as the first president of the ladies' club, having already served the club as captain in 1905. She was also a life vice-president of the ILGU.

She published one book, as well as numerous articles, on golf and was praised for being a clear, precise and witty writer. Her book, *Ladies' golf* (1904, revised edition 1907), was replete with good practical advice and sold well. In it she wrote that golf was the ideal game for women: 'the exercise is splendid without being unduly violent, as is sometimes the case in hockey or tennis … The girl of the present day must have some outlet for her superfluous energy, and she is not content with the life which women were expected to lead in former years' (*Ladies' golf* (1907 edition), 3). Lauding golf as a means for achieving serenity and self-reliance, she encouraged women club members to manage their club finances instead of leaving it to the men. At a time when women golfers had to wear impractically long and heavy skirts, she advocated shorter skirts—by which she meant about a foot off the ground. (In the picture above she is wearing an elastic belt around her waist, designed to slip down below the knees as she swung, to preserve her modesty in windy weather.)

Her husband served in the 1914–18 war and was awarded the military cross; he was appointed bishop of Tuam in 1920. He died suddenly in May 1923, and she moved subsequently to England. She worked for the Society for the Propagation of the Gospel and became president of the Mothers' Union, although she had no children herself. For many years she lived with her sister Violet, by then Mrs Violet Hulton, in Trowbridge, Wiltshire, before entering a nursing home in Sandwich, Kent, in the mid-1970s. She died there on 27 December 1978. A portrait by Harry Douglas of her aged seventeen hangs in the Portrush Ladies clubhouse.

John Rouse and Terry Clavin

Sources

Belfast News Letter, 31 May 1902; 18 January, 6 May 1907; *Scotsman*, 17 May 1904; *The Times* (London), 20 May 1905; 11 May 1907; *Illustrated sporting and dramatic news*, 19 December 1908; *Irish Independent*, 4 January 1958; Ian Bamford, *Royal Portrush Golf Club* (1988); Rosalynde Cossey, *Golfing ladies* (1984); William A. Menton, *The Golfing Union of Ireland 1891–1991* (1991); Kath Stewart-Moore, *Royal Portrush Ladies* (1991); *Belfast Telegraph*, 4 June 1992; Lewine Mair, *One hundred years of women's golf* (1992); Dermot Gilleece and John Redmond, *Irish Ladies' Golf Union: an illustrated centenary history 1893–1993* (1993); John Gleeson (ed.), *Fyffes dictionary of Irish sporting greats* (1993); *The Irish Times*, 28 September 1999; Paul Gorry, 'Hezlet [married name Ross], Mary Elizabeth Linzee [May]', *Oxford dictionary of national biography* (2004), doi.org/10.1093/ref:odnb/51537 (accessed December 2021); David L. Hudson, *Women in golf* (2008); Julie Ganz (ed), *The best golf stories ever told* (2013); Ivan Morris, *A history of women's golf in Ireland* (2018); information from Royal and Ancient Golf Club Museum, St Andrews; 'The Reverend Ross's remarkable golfing wife', snake43.webs.com/rev-ross-s-golfing-wife; 'The story of Portrush's original golfing superstar' www.nationalclubgolfer.com/the-open/news/may-hezlet-portrush-open/ (all internet material accessed September 2020)

Alex ('Hurricane') Higgins
1949–2010

Alex ('Hurricane') Higgins was born 18 March 1949 in Belfast, the only son of Alexander Gordon Higgins, a labourer of Abbingdon Drive, Sandy Row, Belfast, and his wife Elizabeth (née Stockman); he had three sisters.

Educated locally at Mabel Street primary school and Kelvin secondary school, he was a restless child with little interest in schoolwork. Aged eleven, he wandered into the Jampot snooker hall off the Donegall Road, where he earned a few pennies keeping score for other players. He soon discovered a talent for snooker, particularly when playing for cash, and honed his skills and competitive instinct in the Jampot against older players. He left school in 1964 and worked briefly as a runner for the Irish Linen Company but spent most of his time playing snooker.

Aged fifteen, he left home to train as a jockey with trainer Eddie Reavey in Berkshire. The hard work required held little appeal, and he spent more time backing horses than riding them. This habit continued for the rest of his life: rarely a day went by without his placing a (usually losing) bet. After almost two years, Reavey let him go. He then lived in the East End of London, working the night shift in a paper mill and spending his days playing snooker. Returning to Belfast in late 1967, he resumed his hustling at the Jampot and other snooker clubs. In 1968 he captained the YMCA team that won the UK team championship, and he also won the individual Northern Ireland and all-Ireland amateur snooker championships. Afterwards he based himself in Lancashire (a snooker hotbed), sleeping in squats and playing all comers. Local promoters dubbed him 'Hurricane Higgins' to advertise his rapid-fire play, and the name stuck. At Accrington, he challenged the world champion John Spencer to play for £100 and won, which encouraged him to turn professional at the age of twenty-two.

In January 1972 Higgins won the Irish professional championship, beating Jack Rea, who had held the title for twenty years. He also beat Spencer to win the World Snooker Championship at his first attempt in February 1972. His prize was £480. Snooker was a marginal working-class sport, but already his game showed the unique combination of edginess, speed and grace that would massively broaden its appeal. He also showed signs of being a troublemaker: he was fined £100 for misconduct at the 1973 world championship and ushered out of the 1974 tournament after abusing the referee. Many senior players in the World Professional Billiards and Snooker Association (WPBSA) worried that he would destroy the sport's veneer of respectability. Some, though, believed that his flamboyant style and bad-boy image were just what was needed. He was the subject of a documentary, *Hurricane Higgins*, broadcast by Thames TV in summer 1972. Snooker began receiving more television coverage, notably on BBC 2's *Pot black*, its appeal transformed by the growing availability of colour television. Higgins appeared on *Pot black* before he won his world title in 1972 but offended the commentator and was not invited back until 1978.

As its profile grew, snooker needed distinctive personalities, and Higgins duly obliged. His style was like no other player's, breaking many conventions. He had a high unorthodox stance, and his cueing action included a trademark body swerve. Waiting his turn to play, he twitched, fidgeted and chain-smoked before he would spring up to the table, radiating nervous energy, potting balls instinctively and racking up mesmerising breaks. Snooker had revolved around long periods of safety play, but Higgins disdained cautious tactics. His daredevil style inspired the kind of adulation and raucous cheering normally heard in football stadiums.

When a system of world rankings was introduced in 1976, Higgins took second place, and the mid-1970s to early 1980s were his heyday. He won five major titles: the world championship (1972, 1982), Benson & Hedges UK Masters (1978, 1981) and Coral UK Championship (1983), completing snooker's triple crown of world, UK and UK masters titles. Other titles included the Irish professional championship (1972, 1978, 1979, 1983, 1989), Canadian Open (1975, 1977), Watney Open (1975), Benson and Hedges Ireland tournament (1977), British Gold Cup (1980), Tolly Cobbold Classic (1979, 1980) and the Irish Masters (1989). In 1984 he and Jimmy White (one of his few close friends on the snooker circuit) won the world doubles championship, and Higgins won the World Cup three times with an all-Ireland team (1985–7). At his best he was almost unbeatable, but his game lacked consistency, and in terms of major titles won he did not fully deliver on his early promise. Although an astute tactician capable of playing a cagey game, he rarely had the discipline to maintain it over a full match. In 1976 he was runner-up in the world championship final to Ray Reardon, and in 1980 to Cliff Thorburn. In the latter, his showmanship was his undoing: 10–6 ahead, he started playing to the gallery, allowing the relentless Thorburn to win 18–16.

The seventeen days of continuous play required to win a world championship was ill-suited to Higgins's restless personality and helter-skelter style, but in the 1982 tournament he combined tenacity with brilliance to play some of the best snooker of his career. His 16–15 win over Jimmy White in the semi-final was regarded as one of the classic all-time matches, and its penultimate frame among the best seen on television, with Higgins rarely in position but sinking a succession of daunting pots that few other players would have contemplated. He beat Ray Reardon in the final to win his second world championship. This time the prize money was £25,000 (with £1,000 surrendered in disciplinary fines for offences such as urinating in a plant pot). By 1982 the world final at the Crucible theatre in Sheffield was a major televised event, and Higgins's tearful post-match celebration with his wife Lynn and baby daughter Lauren became one of the classic scenes of 1980s sport. He proclaimed himself to be 'the people's champion' and enjoyed large followings in Ireland, Britain, Australia and the Far East. For many of his fans, his flaws were part of his appeal, and they lauded him for spicing up snooker by challenging its outmoded conventions.

In 1983 Higgins achieved the most dramatic of all his victories, coming from 0–7 down to beat Steve Davis 16–15 in the final of the UK championship. This was a rare victory over Davis, who dominated snooker in the 1980s and beat Higgins in twenty-five of their thirty-one tournament matches. Higgins was contemptuous of Davis's methodical playing style and colourless personality, likening him to a robot. Their contests had an extra edge, often portrayed as a clash between the mercurial Celt and the stolid Englishman.

TROUBLES AND DECLINE, 1983–97

Primarily because of his gambling, Higgins was never financially comfortable enough to limit the number of tournaments and exhibitions he played and reserve his energies for the important games. His lifestyle often left him physically and mentally exhausted, and in 1983 he attempted suicide after a domestic row. He was a bad loser and, as he lost with greater frequency and his personal troubles mounted, he became more aggressive, particularly towards referees and officials. In 1986, after being asked to take a drugs test at the UK Open at Preston, he headbutted the tournament director. He was convicted and fined £200 for assault in a magistrate's court, and the WPBSA fined him an unprecedented £12,000 and suspended him for five tournaments. His treatment added to his contempt for the WPBSA, which he believed had unfairly hounded him and given him no recognition for his role in popularising snooker.

From this time his decline accelerated. His marriage collapsed, and he indulged in self-destructive excess, gambling recklessly, drinking heavily, taking marijuana and cocaine, and enjoying the company of hell-raisers such as the actor Oliver Reed. He was involved in several brawls and violent domestic incidents, reported in lurid terms in the tabloid press, and was regularly barred from pubs, betting shops and hotels. Higgins craved popular adulation, but he bitterly resented press intrusion into his life and often regarded meeting the public as a chore. He could be amusing and charming, and friends recalled acts of kindness and unpublicised visits to children in hospital, but being in his presence was rarely easy. He relied on a relay of friends and hangers-on to get him out of trouble, chauffeur him around (he never learned to drive), run his errands and lend him money. Although he had a sharp mind (he was adept at crosswords and Sudoku puzzles), he was incapable of dealing with mundane tasks and unwilling to take advice. All his failings were blamed on others. Higgins bitterly resented the fact that players he thought inferior were financially secure while he was not and became obsessed by the idea that others had made money at his expense. Consumed by his grievances, he inflicted them on anyone available and alienated almost all his friends.

In March 1989 Higgins played the Irish Masters with several broken bones in his foot, having fallen from a first-floor window after a domestic row. Hobbling around the table, he beat Stephen Hendry in the final. This was his last significant victory and, as frustration at his declining prowess grew, controversies followed in quick succession. In March 1990, during a row over prize money while playing for Northern Ireland against Canada, he threatened to have his Catholic teammate Dennis Taylor (whom he had known since they were teenagers) shot by loyalist paramilitaries. Then, after losing in the first round of the 1990 world championship at the Crucible, Higgins punched the WPBSA's press officer. In a rambling, drunken tirade at the ensuing press conference, he announced his retirement from snooker, dismissing it as a corrupt sport. He was banned from snooker for the 1990/91 season, and his world ranking fell to 120th. He was also penniless. What he had not gambled away, he had lost in poor business decisions.

After losing in the first round of the world championship in 1994, Higgins was fined £5,000 for smashing a bottle containing a urine sample. Two years later he assaulted a fourteen-year-old boy; admitting the charge, Higgins was conditionally discharged. His last match on the professional circuit was in August 1997 in a qualifying event in Plymouth, by which time he was ranked 156th in the world. After he lost, he became abusive and was escorted from the venue by police. He was later found sprawled outside a nightclub, the victim, he claimed, of an unprovoked assault.

In 1996 Higgins underwent an operation for cancer of the palate, which spread to his throat two years later. He joined 200 other smokers to sue Embassy and Benson & Hedges, two prominent snooker sponsors, but both actions lapsed. In 1998 he returned to Belfast and lived in sheltered housing on the Donegall Road, cared for by two of his sisters and surviving mostly on state benefits. Friends such as Jimmy White and Ken Doherty organised benefit matches for him. Higgins played occasional exhibition matches and, when his health allowed, he hustled for small stakes, sold signed photographs of himself and frequented the Royal Bar on Donegall Road (where he was later commemorated by a mural).

By early 2010 fifty radiotherapy sessions had virtually cinderised his teeth, leaving him unable to eat solid food. He looked wizened and emaciated, and his voice had degenerated to a faint, croaking whisper. Higgins was found dead in bed in his flat on 24 July 2010, aged sixty-one. The cause of death was a combination of malnutrition, pneumonia, a bronchial condition and throat cancer. After a funeral service in St Anne's Church of Ireland cathedral, thousands lined the streets of Belfast to pay their respects, and his cremated remains were interred in Carnmoney cemetery, Co. Antrim. Prominent snooker figures paid tribute to his importance in popularising the sport; even his great rival Steve Davis described him as 'the only true genius I have encountered in the game' (*Daily Telegraph*, 25 July 2010). Higgins was inducted into the Snooker Hall of Fame in 2011.

In 1991 Higgins released a documentary film on his life, *I'm no angel*; another, *Alex Higgins: the people's champion* (2010), was directed by Jason Bernard. The one-man play 'Hurricane', written and acted by Richard Dormer, was first performed in Belfast in October 2002. Notable portraits of Higgins were painted by Rodney Dickson (1992; Ulster Museum) and Alan Quigley (2010).

Higgins had a son, Chris Delahunty, from his relationship with Joyce Fox; a daughter, Christel, from his marriage in 1975 to Australian Cara Hasler; and a daughter, Lauren, and a son, Jordan, from his marriage in 1980 to Lynn Avison.

James Quinn

Sources

Alex Higgins (with Tony Francis), *Alex through the looking glass* (1986); Jim Meadowcroft, *Higgins, Taylor and me* (1986); *I'm no angel* (VHS documentary, 1991); Alex Higgins, *From the eye of the Hurricane: my story* (2007); *Guardian*, 16 June 2007; 26 July 2010; *Observer*, 25 July 2010; *Sunday Telegraph*, 25 July 2010; *Scotsman*, 25 July 2010; *Belfast News Letter*, 26, 27 July 2010; *Belfast Telegraph*, 26 July 2010; *Irish Independent*, 27 July, 28 October 2010; 7 April 2012; *The Irish Times*, 31 July 2010; *New York Times*, 31 July 2010; *Sunday Independent*, 1 August 2010; *Economist*, 5 August 2010; *Alex Higgins: the people's champion* (BBC TV documentary, 2010); Tony Francis, *Who was Hurricane Higgins?* (2011); John Virgo, *Let me tell you about Alex* (2011)

This entry has been abridged for publication. The full version is available at www.dib.ie

Tom Horan

1855–1916

Cricketer and Journalist

Tom (Thomas Patrick; 'Tommy') Horan (pictured back row, second from left) was born 8 March 1855 near Midleton, Co. Cork, the son of James Horan (d. 1895), a building contractor, and his wife Ellen (née Sheehan) (d. 1876). The family emigrated to Australia soon after Thomas's birth, settling at 186 Fitzroy Street, Melbourne, Victoria. Attending Bell Street School, Fitzroy, Melbourne, Horan made his debut for the Carlton Cricket Club (CC) in 1870, playing for the East Melbourne CC and the state of Victoria from 1874.

Widely regarded as the leading batsman in Victoria by the late 1870s, Horan thrived playing cricket for his state in inter-colonial cricket, the fulcrum of the Australian cricket season. In 1881 he led the table of first-class batsmen in Australia. Nicknamed 'Dutchy', with a stocky build and a notably large head, distinguished by a luxuriant moustache crowning hearty mutton chops, he added to his conspicuousness by wearing distinctive black leg pads. He was also a vegetarian and non-smoker. His defensive right-handed batting, usually deployed in the middle order, was founded on his excellent leg play (deflecting balls aimed at his feet). From 15 to 19 March 1877 he played for Australia at the Melbourne Cricket Ground (MCG) in what was retrospectively regarded as the first ever eleven-a-side international 'test' match. After hitting 12 runs in the first innings, he top-scored with 20 runs in the second innings, as Australia unexpectedly beat England by 45 runs.

Horan joined the 1878 tour of an Australian XI to Britain, the USA, Canada and New Zealand (they also toured Australia at the start and end of their travels), which lasted sixteen months and was self-financed by the twelve players. An insomniac, he spent the overnight train journeys between fixtures composing copy for the English press and *The Age* (Melbourne). His coverage propelled interest in the idea of national teams in both countries, also laying the foundations for his subsequent success as a journalist. He featured in the Australians' famous victory (27 May), in only their second game in England, against a heavily favoured Marylebone Cricket Club (MCC) selection at Lord's Cricket Ground, London. Captained by W. G. Grace, the Goliath of English cricket, the MCC selection was regarded by *Wisden* as one of the strongest ever fielded by that august club. Horan, prefacing the fixture in his newspaper column with the words 'Lord's is to cricket what Rome is to the world' (*Horan's diary*, 83), caught the MCC's last man to close England's first innings and scored the winning runs as Australia won by nine wickets in a single afternoon. This resounding victory by the first ever settler-colonial team to tour England elevated the reputation of Australian cricket from also-rans to equals in first-class cricket. At the tour's close he returned briefly to Cork in mid-September to visit relatives, before rejoining his teammates as they sailed home from Queenstown (Cobh).

Contributing to Australia's 2–0 victory in the four-game series (1881–2) against Alfred Shaw's English touring XI, the first and last games being drawn, he achieved his sole test century, scoring 124, at the MCG in the final test match of the series (31 December 1881–4 January 1882). Later in 1882 Horan joined Australia's thirty-eight-match tour of England, during which he batted two centuries, marking his prowess with the bat on the often more challenging creases there. The first, against a United XI at Chichester, saw Horan top score with 112. Then, at Clifton against Grace's Gloucestershire, the leading county side in England, Horan contributed 141 not out, his highest first-class score. He accumulated a total of 1,175 runs for an average of 25 on the tour, behind only his captain W. L. Murdoch. In the only test match of the tour, however, Horan was easily dismissed during the famous Australian victory over England at the Kennington Oval, London, 28–29 August 1882, from which the Anglo–Australian 'Ashes' competition originated. Having toured England twice, Horan declined an invitation to join the 1884 tour for family reasons.

Appointed Australian captain for the second test of the first-ever five test series, at the MCG from 1–5 January

1885, he took charge of nine newcomers (five of whom were earning their sole cap), and scored 63 in the first innings, in a 10-wicket collapse to England. Losing the captaincy, Horan, a capable right-handed, round-arm medium-pace bowler, took six English wickets for 40 runs in the first innings of their third test, which Australia won by six runs. He was captain again for the deciding fifth test (the fourth change in the captaincy in the series, and Horan's last ever test) in Melbourne. Australia was defeated by an innings and 98 runs, losing the series 3–2.

Horan's 27 innings in 15 tests with the bat for Australia, all against England, produced 471 runs for an average of 18. He also bowled 11 wickets in his 15 tests, for a loss of 143 runs. He kept playing inter-colonial cricket until his retirement in 1892, appearing in forty-two matches for Victoria. Completing eight first-class centuries in total, four of those when at his zenith in 1882, his 126 in Victoria's defeat of New South Wales in December 1883 was regarded as his most commanding. In first-class cricket he bowled 35 wickets for 829 runs. Batting, he made 4,027 runs in 187 innings; his last century, 117 not out for Victoria, came against England in 1886. Joining the Victorian Audit Office in 1873, rising to a senior clerkship there, Horan ensured his annual leave always coincided with inter-colonial and international cricket matches, even after he retired from playing. His regular attendance at practice and his coaching of younger players left an indelible mark on Victoria's cricketing consciousness.

He began his 'Cricket chatter' column for the Melbourne-based *Australasian*, a weekly sister paper of *The Age*, in September 1879, under the pseudonym 'Felix'. His musings appeared regularly during the Australian cricket season and overseas tours (apart from when in England in

1882) until his death in 1916. Indeed 'Felix' was widely quoted in the British and antipodean press. Horan's 'Round the ground' column, which profiled leading cricketers, commenced January 1893. His famous 1902 description, in that column, of the closing overs of the famous August 1882 Australian Ashes victory, became an important and much recounted source for historians. Horan recalled '… that was the match in which for the final half-hour you could have heard a pin drop … when one [English] man's lips were ashen grey and his throat so parched that he could hardly speak as he strode by me to the crease … and when in the wild tumult at the fall of the last wicket, the crowd in one tremendous roar cried "bravo Australia"' (*Australasian*, 11 January 1902). His own playing experience, modestly drawn upon, imbued his highly regarded judgments of players, matches and tours. In 'Round the ground' Horan waxed lyrical about the game of cricket in the broadest sense: the settings, sounds and smells of its grounds, delighting in how the vivid texture of the game emerged anew each spring.

In 1879 he married Catherine Louisa Pennefather, the daughter of a police sergeant, and they had four sons and four daughters together. Two of their four sons, James and Thomas, played cricket for Victoria. Horan died 16 April 1916 of heart disease, aged sixty-two, at his home 'Hillview', 46 Malvern Road, Malvern, Melbourne. He was buried in Melbourne General cemetery. One of only two Irish-born Catholics to represent Australia in his adopted country's national sport, Tom Horan was central to the early evolution of Australian cricket, as sporting prowess reinforced nascent national identity towards the close of the nineteenth-century.

Turlough O'Riordan

Sources

Argus (Melbourne), 17 April 1916; *Referee* (Sydney), 19, 26 April 1916; *Field*, 22 April 1916; *Weekly Times* (Melbourne), 22 April 1916; *Australasian* (Melbourne), 12 January 1918; *Smith's Weekly*, 26 July 1919; *Herald* (Sydney), 8 October 1921; Jack Pollard, *The formative years of Australian cricket 1803–93* (1987); Brian Mathew Crowley and Pat Mullins (eds), *Cradle days of Australian cricket: an anthology of the writings of 'Felix' (T. P. Horan)* (1989); Chris Harte, *A history of Australian cricket* (1993); Frank Tyson (ed.), *Horan's diary: the Australian touring team 1877–1979* (2001); Gideon Haigh, *Silent revolutions: writings on cricket history* (2006), 231–3; John Lazenby, *The strangers who came home: the first Australian cricket tour of England* (2016); 'Thomas Horan', www.blueseum.org/Thomas+Horan; www.espncricinfo.com, *passim* esp.: 'England in Australia, 1884–85', www.espncricinfo.com/wisdenalmanack/content/story/153446.html; 'Tom Horan: first Irish test cricketer, pioneer cricket writer, owner of an imposing moustache', www.cricketcountry.com/articles/tom-horan-first-irish-test-cricketer-pioneer-cricket-writer-owner-of-an-imposing-moustache-699214; findagrave.com; 'Will of Thomas Patrick Horan', Public Record Office Victora, Probate and Administration files, 472/264, VPRS 28, P0004, unit 669, access.prov.vic.gov.au; Probate and Administration files, 143/861, VPRA 28, P0003, unit 615, access.prov.vic.gov.au; death record, Births Deaths and Marriages Victoria, www.bdm.vic.gov.au (all internet material accessed December 2020)

This entry has been abridged for publication. The full version is available at www.dib.ie.

Moss Keane

1948–2010

RUGBY PLAYER

Moss (Maurice Ignatius) Keane was born 27 July 1948 in Currow, near Castleisland, Co. Kerry, the eldest of three sons of Willie Keane and his wife Cassie (née O'Mahony), who were farmers. He was educated in Currow national school before boarding at St Brendan's College, Killarney, renowned for its fine Gaelic football teams. Moss, though, was tall and gangling, and failed to make the school teams. After completing his leaving certificate in 1965 he went to Pallaskenry agricultural college, Co. Limerick, where he played for the college Gaelic football team and was student of the year on graduation in 1966. He also played minor football for Currow and for Castleisland District, winning a Kerry county medal. In 1966 he entered University College Cork (UCC) to study dairy science, graduating with a masters in microbiology (1972) and securing a job in the Department of Agriculture laboratory in Cork. Selected for the UCC Gaelic football team, usually at full-back, he won a Cork county championship (1969) and three Sigerson cups (1969, 1970 (as captain) and 1972), and lost to Bellaghy in the 1972 all-Ireland club final. He played for Kerry at under-21 and junior levels, and was on the Kerry team beaten by Wicklow in an all-Ireland junior home final at Croke Park in 1969 (something of which he never liked to be reminded).

A friend, Johnny Brosnan, advised him that, with his massive build (6ft 5in. (1.96m), and 20st. (127kg) at his heaviest), he would never become a top-class Gaelic foot-baller, and suggested rugby as an alternative. Moreover, Keane's neighbours in Currow, Tom and Mick Doyle, had already played for Ireland. Keane's initial impression of rugby was that 'it was like watching a pornographic movie—very frustrating for those watching and only en-joyable for those participating' (*Independent* (London), 8 October 2010). In December 1970 he turned out for UCC seconds under the pseudonym 'Moss Fenton' to evade the GAA ban on 'foreign games'. When the ban was lifted in April 1971, he began playing rugby more regular-ly. He knew that he had much to learn but reckoned 'you did not need to be a rocket scientist to be a second row' (*Guardian*, 7 October 2010).

Progressing rapidly, he made his debut for Munster against Ulster at Thomond Park on 11 November 1972 and helped the province to a 3–3 draw against New Zealand at Musgrave Park on 16 January 1973. A year later, 19 January 1974, he played his first game for Ireland, alongside Willie John McBride in the second row, as Ireland lost 9–6 to France in Paris. The pace and ferocity of international rugby came as a shock, and he required stitches after a French forward deliberately stamped on his head and severed an artery next to his right ear. Keane played on despite the injury and throughout his rugby career took punishment without flinching, readily dishing it out in return. Ireland drew their next game, against Wales, and beat England and Scotland, to win their first Five Nations title for twenty-five years.

In 1973 Keane moved to the Department of Agriculture in Dublin to become an agricultural inspector, a job he loved. He joined Lansdowne FC (rugby), where he learned much about rugby, especially from the club's kitman, Con Murphy (1914–2002), a former international. At Lansdowne he won three Leinster senior cups (1979, 1980 and 1981) and three Leinster senior leagues (1974, 1977 and 1981), captaining the club to its first ever league and cup double in 1981. To stay in shape, he continued to play Gaelic football with Civil Service, retiring in 1977 to concentrate on rugby.

For about a decade from 1973 Keane was a permanent fixture in the Irish second row, playing 44 consecutive five nations games, earning 51 caps in total and scoring a single try (in a 22–15 victory over Scotland in 1980). While not the most technically gifted second row to play for Ireland, Keane made up for his deficiencies with raw athleticism and whole-hearted commitment. His fierce tackling and ability to disrupt opposition possession were vitally important to Irish teams, especially after McBride's retirement in 1975. Having been a Gaelic footballer, Keane was comfortable with the ball in hand, and his rumbling charges at opposition defences were a memorable sight. He never frequented a gym, maintaining that his upbringing on a farm had given him all the strength he needed. He became a great crowd favourite, and his GAA and farming background did much to popularise rugby in rural areas.

Keane played for the Barbarians in a 22–35 defeat by Moseley on 27 March 1974. Having performed well on Ireland's 1976 tour of New Zealand, he was selected for the British Lions squad to tour New Zealand in 1977. He was injured in the first test, compounding the effects of a concussion received four days earlier. Afterwards, he was restricted to midweek games, playing twelve times against provincial opposition. Keane found the three-month tour wearying; towards the end he lost interest and began drinking heavily. When asked to come on as a substitute in the last game of the tour, he simply refused.

A more rewarding experience was Ireland's 1979 tour of Australia, when Keane was one of only three players selected for all eight matches. In Ireland's most successful tour, the team exceeded expectations to win seven matches, including both tests against a formidable Wallabies team. This was his last international tour. In 1981 he refused to travel on Ireland's tour of South Africa because of his opposition to apartheid.

Some of his most memorable games were for Munster, notably their 12–0 win over the All Blacks in Thomond Park on 31 October 1978. The victory was all the sweeter after his unhappy tour the previous year, but Keane was pushed to his limit by the great New Zealand locks, Andy Haden and Frank Oliver. After a Munster lineout call late in the game, Keane was heard to exclaim: 'Oh Christ, not me again!'

Towards the end of his career, some critics argued that Keane was not mobile enough for international rugby and conceded too many penalties, but his physicality and experience were central to Ireland's Triple Crown in 1982 (the first since 1949) and to sharing the Five Nations Championship with France in 1983. He was then thirty-four and considered retiring but stayed on for another Five Nations campaign, in which an ageing Irish team was whitewashed. His last game for Ireland was a 32–9 defeat to Scotland at Lansdowne Road on 3 March 1984.

He retired from club rugby the following year but took great pleasure in coaching the Lansdowne under-19s to win the McCorry Cup in 1986. Always ready to help charitable causes, he worked for a time in Calcutta (Kolkata) with the charity Goal and was president of the Monasterevin/Portarlington Lions' Club, having moved to Portarlington, Co. Laois, his wife's hometown. He had married Anne Dunne, a teacher, at University Church in Dublin on 11 August 1979, and he always regarded it as the best decision he ever made; they had two daughters, Sarah and Anne Marie. During these years he played golf regularly and maintained an interest in most sports. He had no regrets about missing rugby's professional era, admitting that he would have found its demands excessive.

Although he was something of a hell-raiser, there was more to Keane than that. He prepared carefully for most games and, away from rugby, his interest in herbal medicine, spirituality and meditation belied his reputation. A reflective man with a strong connection with nature, he enjoyed walking his family's land in Currow, thinking about those who had gone before him. He had a deep Catholic faith and before international matches would sometimes drink from a bottle of Lourdes water for protection; on one occasion he sprinkled some over his Ulster Protestant teammates Mike Gibson and Willie John McBride, with the assurance that it would protect them too. His personal warmth, exuberant sense of mischief and razor-sharp Kerry wit made him an immensely popular figure among those who had played with or against him, and he forged strong friendships with opponents such as Bill Beaumont and Jean-Pierre Rives. Those close to him identified kindness and humility as his most characteristic traits; his neighbour Con Houlihan summed him up best as 'a man of few airs and many graces' (*Rucks*, xiv).

In February 2009 he was diagnosed with bowel cancer and faced the trial with courage and humour. He died on 5 October 2010 in Portarlington, Co. Laois, and was buried in the cemetery adjoining St Michael's church, Portarlington.

James Quinn

Sources

Irish Press, 30 October 1972; 2 February 1973; 7, 11, 23 January, 28 March 1974; 15 June 1977; 11 March 1981; 10 September 1993; 14 February 1994; Barry Coughlan, *The Irish Lions 1896–1983* (1983); Edmund Van Esbeck, *The story of Irish rugby* (1986); Terry Godwin, *The complete who's who of international rugby* (1987); *Irish Independent*, 9 September 1993; 6, 8 October 2010; *Hogan Stand*, February 2000; Moss Keane (with Billy Keane), *Rucks, mauls and Gaelic football* (2005); *Sunday Independent*, 20 November 2005; 10 October 2010; *Irish Examiner*, 6 October 2010; *The Irish Times*, 6, 9 October 2010; *Guardian*, 7 October 2010; *Independent* (London), 8 October 2010; *Daily Telegraph*, 18 October 2010

This entry has been abridged for publication. The full version is available at www.dib.ie

Iris Kellett

1926–2011

Iris Kellett was born 8 January 1926 in Lower Baggot Street, Dublin, the only child of Thomas Kellett, of Mespil Road, Ballsbridge, Dublin, and his wife Julia (née

Maron). A veterinary surgeon, her father was also managing director of his family's drapery business in South Great George's Street, Dublin. He had bought the old British army cavalry academy at Mespil Road, opening a riding school there in 1923.

Born into a Church of Ireland family, Iris attended school at St Margaret's Hall, Mespil Road, and delighted in jumping ponies and horses over the natural obstacles built by her father on the family property. From childhood, she rode at agricultural shows and on hunts. The Kellett riding school, which had lapsed, reopened (c.1939) once Iris could help by instructing children and teenagers. She passed the instructor's examination for the certificate of the Institute of the Horse in London in 1945. With her as chief instructor, the Kellett school began training riders and horses for showjumping.

She was Ireland's leading woman showjumper by 1945 and carried the flag for civilian riders in a period when military specialists dominated Irish showjumping. From 1946 she formed a memorable partnership with her half-bred chestnut gelding, Rusty. A hunter and former plough horse, Rusty was a showjumping novice at eleven years of age in 1946 but responded magnificently to her training and riding. In 1947 Kellett was chosen for the Irish civilian team, and in her first competition abroad she and Rusty adjusted readily to the larger and more varied obstacles predominating outside Ireland to claim the British Showjumping Association's national championship at the Blackpool show. Serial winners at the Royal Dublin Society (RDS) Spring Show and at the Dublin Horse Show (also in the RDS), they bested army teams from six countries in winning the Dublin Horse Show's main international competition in 1948.

As countries participating in the International Horse Show at White City, London, had to pick a woman rider, in 1949 she became the first civilian to accompany the Irish army team abroad, though she was restricted to individual events. In ten starts on Rusty at White City during 1949–51, she was unplaced once and won six competitions, including the Selby Cup (for British and Irish riders, men and women) in 1950 and 1951, and Europe's most prestigious women's event, the Princess Elizabeth Cup, in 1949 and 1951. Time being irrelevant in Irish events before 1951, Kellett often struggled for speed, but needing a fast round in the jump-off for the 1951 Princess Elizabeth Cup, she galloped Rusty around the course, vaulting him over fences early and from improbable angles. Following this thrilling victory, Rusty reared during the award ceremony and knocked Kellett into Princess Elizabeth, the future Queen Elizabeth II. A steward commented on Rusty's apparent republicanism.

She also went with the Irish army to the Horse of the Year Show at Harringay, London, in 1949–50, winning the Diana Stakes competition for women riders on Rusty in 1949. On her second-string horse, Starlet, she won four events abroad and shared first prize in the civilian and military competition at the 1950 Dublin Horse Show. In her 1947–51 pomp, she was the leading woman showjumper in Britain and Ireland but was barred from Ireland's Nations Cup team because civilians were ineligible until 1963 and from the Olympics because women were ineligible until 1956.

A freak fall during a jumping exhibition in April 1952 shattered her left ankle, after which she contracted two near-fatal bouts of tetanus: it was doubted whether she would walk again. (This experience made her the prime mover in Ireland for providing riding courses for the disabled.) She was riding again in just over a year and in September 1953 participated in her first event since the accident, being sufficiently undaunted to go on and break her leg, shoulder, wrist and ribs. It took her five years to reach international standard and ten to recover fully, excepting a slight limp, even after which she never recaptured her earlier heights, as the tempting sums offered by foreign buyers led her to sell many promising novices. She was an astute breeder and purchaser, owning the mounts that she rode competitively. By the mid-1960s her riding school and associated livery entailed responsibility for some forty horses, twenty staff, and 200–300 pupils. Furthermore, she ran the Eblana bookshop in Grafton Street with her husband, Benedict Brennan. They had married in London in 1952.

Her patient cultivation from the mid-1960s of an improving string of young horses, particularly the obstreperous Morning Light, allowed her to finish her riding career with a flourish. On Morning Light, she was chosen for Ireland's 1968 Olympic team (but decided against going) and for Ireland's Nations Cup team in 1968–9. Their greatest victory, albeit against a weak field of six, came at the 1969 Dublin Horse Show when they won the ladies' individual European championship.

Kellett retired almost immediately from serious showjumping to focus on her school and on improving the amateurish horse training and rider instruction then available in Ireland. In 1972 she helped establish, and later served as chairman and president of, the Association of Irish Riding Establishments. Contending that rough handling ruined too many Irish horses, she learned from her father how to maintain a horse's health and how to break one in gently. Professionally polite while dealing with riders pursuing a pastime, she was exacting towards those preparing for competition and to become instructors, inculcating a thorough grounding in the classical style: 'balance and heels down and head up and just being in the middle of the saddle' (*Sunday Independent*, 12 August 2001). Eddie Macken blossomed into Ireland's all-time greatest showjumper under her tutelage.

Operating one of the two private yards in Ireland prepared to resist foreign offers for its best prospects, she led Ireland's international showjumping revival. This began with Macken's near-miss in the 1974 World Cup on Pele and continued the next year when his replacement at Kellett's stable, Paul Darragh, won the 1975 Hickstead Derby on the same horse. Darragh, whom she had taught as a boy, was in turn succeeded in 1977 by her second husband, John Hall, an English riding instructor. They married in 1977, two years after her first husband's death.

In 1972 she sold what had become a valuable Mespil Road site and bought a ninety-one-acre farm at Kill, Co. Kildare, where she moved her school in 1974. Developing into one of Europe's finest equestrian centres, Kill eventually comprised stables for eighty horses, accommodation for staff and forty students, a restaurant, two indoor riding schools, a viewing stand, an outdoor arena and a cross-country course. The mainstay of the Irish equestrian industry, especially for breaking horses and producing qualified instructors, Kill drew students from around the world. Kellett efficiently supervised this operation, though its scale prevented her from giving the horses her accustomed attention. Her showjumpers' lack of international success from the late 1970s is also attributable to the roaring trade she enjoyed selling horses to rich Middle Easterners. In 1988 she sold the Kill facility, continuing with a smaller riding school at her farm in Daffodil Lodge, near Naas, Co. Kildare.

A director of the state non-thoroughbred horse board, Bord na gCapall (1976–82), she was active in the Show Jumping Association of Ireland, chairing various committees, and received an honorary doctorate from the University of Limerick in 1999 for her assistance in developing its equestrian science degree course. In 1990 she separated from her second husband; both her marriages were childless. Latterly afflicted by Alzheimer's disease, she died 11 March 2011 in Craddock House Nursing Home, Naas, Co. Kildare, and was buried in Mount Jerome cemetery, Harold's Cross, Dublin. Her will disposed of €1.75 million. Further to gaining international repute as a showjumper, often in competition with men, Kellett contributed more to Irish equestrianism than any other individual in its history.

Terry Clavin

Sources

General Register Office Dublin (birth certificate); *The Irish Times, passim*, esp.: 27 April 1991; 19 March 2011; *Irish Independent, passim*, esp.: 19 March 2011; *Sunday Independent, passim*, esp.: 20 March 2011; *Irish Press, passim*; *The Times* (London), 30 August 1948; 6 August 1969; *Evening Herald*, 30 July 1949; *Irish Field*, 30 July 1949; 4 August 1951; 8, 15 December 1973; 8 February 1975; 7 February 1976; 16 July 1977; 19, 26 March 2011; *This Week*, 3 April 1970; *Pacemaker and The Horseman*, August 1975; A. Norman Jeffares and Antony Kamm (eds), *An Irish childhood* (1987), 312–15; Grania Willis, *The world of the Irish horse* (1992); Michael Slavin, *Showjumping legends: Ireland, 1868–1998* (1998); Noel Mullins, *Horse tales and horse talk: the life and times of 31 equestrians in Ireland, America, France and Australia* (2006); Nicholas O'Hare, *Champions: heroes on horseback* (2007); *Sunday Times*, 6 November 2011

This entry and the related sources have been abridged for publication. The full version is available at www.dib.ie

Jack Kyle

1926–2014

RUGBY PLAYER

Jack (John Wilson) Kyle was born 10 February 1926 on Kinnaird Street, Belfast, the second of five children of John Wilson Kyle and his wife, Elizabeth (née Warren). When Jack was aged seven the family moved to more spacious surroundings at Glenburn Park off Old Westland Road. His father, originally from Co. Londonderry, was the Belfast manager of the North British Rubber Company. The family, though not excessively religious, attended Fort William Presbyterian church. Jack was educated at preparatory and secondary level at Belfast Royal Academy (BRA) from 1930 to 1944. His all-round sporting talent stood out: apart from rugby, he played cricket at schools' inter-provincial level and excelled at athletics. His sister Betty (b. 1928) captained the Ireland women's hockey team to Triple Crown success in 1950, his sister Brenda (b. 1934) played hockey to provincial level and his brother Eric (1924–90) played rugby for Ulster and was an Ireland triallist.

Though the senior rugby team at BRA was unsuccessful while Kyle was a pupil there, he was selected for the Ulster Schools team in 1943 and 1944. In 1944 he also captained the Ulster Schools cricket XI. His senior club career started at Queen's University Belfast (QUB), where he enrolled as a medical student in October 1944. Initially, he was understudy out-half to another future Ireland international, Derek Monteith. An injury to Monteith saw Kyle called up to the Queen's first team, and his career took off rapidly. A running out-half, Kyle was noted for his speed off the mark and ability to spot a gap. His devastating pace over twenty yards and side-stepping ability left defences flat footed and scrambling. He was also an adept left-footed tactical kicker from the hand but tended not to take placed kicks at goal. An instinctive player, he played the field in front of him as he saw it. Kyle was also a skilled defender, noted for his ability to make last-ditch tackles.

In late 1944, within months of leaving school and still only eighteen, Kyle was selected for the Ulster senior XV. Against the Combined Services, he scored a trademark try after a weaving run. Selected again to play for Ulster in a victory over a New Zealand army XV in November 1945, he made his first appearance for an Ireland XV the following month alongside his future Ireland and British Lions teammate, and fellow teenager, Karl Mullen. Ireland comfortably beat the British army XV, though no caps were awarded as it was an unofficial international fixture.

Kyle's performances in 1946, particularly with Ulster, made him a certainty for selection when international rugby officially resumed in 1947 after its wartime hiatus. He earned his first cap against France in January 1947. Although the Irish team lost, new caps were awarded to era-defining players such as Kyle, Mullen and flanker Billy McKay. All three starred in Kyle's second cap for Ireland two weeks later, a record 22–0 victory over England at Lansdowne Road. Though Kyle did not score, he tormented the English defence with penetrating runs, and was acclaimed as not just 'the best out-half in Ireland but better than any in England, Wales, Scotland or France' (*Irish Press*, 10 February 1947).

This was the prelude to a glorious era for Irish rugby. In 1948 Ireland won the Triple Crown for the first time in the twentieth century, finishing the Five Nations Championship campaign with a nail-biting victory over Wales at Ravenhill in Belfast. Kyle was the team's outstanding player, scoring two tries in the campaign, including a crucial score at Twickenham, and providing faultless tactical judgment throughout the championship. By beating France, the team secured what later generations would call the Grand Slam. Hindsight accorded added prestige to the team of 1948 for the latter reason alone, even though until at least the 1960s the Triple Crown and the Grand Slam were honours held in roughly equal esteem. The focus of popular memory on 1948 has done disservice to how dominant the team was in these years.

When Ireland retained the Triple Crown in 1949 with a rare victory on Welsh soil, they had won 'the most coveted honour of the rugby season' (*Irish Times*, 10 March 1949). After a disappointing campaign in 1950, Ireland again won the championship in 1951. The team's success was built on a strong, tenacious forward pack featuring a dynamic back-row of Billy McKay, Jim McCarthy and Des O'Brien. Kyle was the creative force in what contemporaries viewed as an otherwise workmanlike backline. During these years Ireland jostled for supremacy with a great Wales team: while Ireland took championship honours in 1951, Wales denied them a third Triple Crown in four years with a 3–3 draw in Cardiff, Kyle scoring Ireland's try.

By then, Kyle was at his peak and was rated internationally as one of the greatest players ever, having burnished his reputation with superb performances on the British Lions tour to New Zealand and Australia in 1950. The team, captained by Mullen, was on tour for nearly six months and played thirty matches. The Lions drew one and narrowly lost three tests against the All Blacks and comfortably defeated Australia in two further tests. New Zealand crowds and commentators, knowledgeable and difficult to impress, were enthralled by Kyle's performances. The Lions played a running style of rugby that not only suited Kyle but also endeared the tourists to the home crowds. The highlight of Kyle's tour was the drawn first test in Dunedin. He scored a characteristic try early in the second half, sprinting through a gap to score. While the Lions lost their remaining three tests in New Zealand, coming off a poor second best in the forward exchanges, they produced some dazzling back play, often orchestrated by Kyle. According to one local newspaper, 'Kyle, with much less of the ball than his opposites, has shown in two tests the contribution a player with genius can make' (*Bay of Plenty Beacon*, 26 June 1950).

After the championship win of 1951, Ireland's fortunes waned. In 1953 Kyle was appointed captain of Ireland and remained in the role for six tests. His run of thirty-two consecutive tests for Ireland was interrupted by injury in 1954, and he was dropped for the championship fixture against Scotland in 1955. His omission, albeit for just one test, nonplussed commentators for he remained capable of producing the magic of his earlier career. In 1956 Ireland's shock 11–3 win in Dublin over Wales included a forty-yard drop goal by the outstanding Kyle.

However, the general trajectory, both for Ireland and Kyle, was decline. Ireland came last in the championship in 1955 and again in 1958. During the latter campaign, it was clear to commentators that Kyle had lost the step of pace so essential to his play. After a victory over Scotland (1 March 1958), he lost his place on the team. The press correctly assumed that he would never regain it and paid him generous tributes, one paper recalling 'The superb technique of the Belfast boy's play, the quickness of his reactions, his hawk eye for openings, speedy thrusts, precision kicking … were a joy to watch' (*Irish Press*, 5 March 1958). Kyle finished his career with forty-six caps for Ireland, an immense number by the standards of the time. With the addition of his six test appearances for the Lions, Kyle earned fifty-two international rugby caps in all, setting a world record that was only broken in 1971. Kyle scored seven international tries, the last against France in 1957. He also appeared eight times for the Barbarians (1948–54), his off-the-cuff attacking instincts providing a perfect match with the club's ethos.

At club level he won two Ulster Senior Cup titles: one with Queen's in 1951 and another with North of Ireland Football Club in 1955. He was also a member of an Ulster team that dominated the inter-provincial series in the early 1950s, taking titles in 1951, 1952, 1954 and 1956. After his international retirement he continued to play club rugby for North of Ireland and, as late as 1960, was the captain of the third XV.

By then Kyle was eager to get his medical career off the ground. He had graduated MB, BCh and BAO in 1951 and, intent on pursuing surgery, took positions at the Royal Victoria Hospital and Belfast City Hospital. Keen to travel and intent on forging a career somewhere he was less known, Kyle took a post in Indonesia for two years. Shortly after returning to Belfast in 1964, he decided to emigrate again, this time to Zambia, where he worked as a consultant surgeon and stayed for nearly thirty-five years. Pursuing his medical career in a remote location brought a pleasing anonymity with it: 'I wanted to be seen as a surgeon first and foremost … it was very important to me that life was not defined by my rugby career' (*Conversations*, 148). In the mining town of Chingola, where the Kyle family settled in 1966, surgeons were few, expertise narrow and diagnostic equipment scarce. Kyle, of necessity, carried out operations across a wide range of surgical specialisms. He enjoyed the rhythm of life in Zambia where his family lived comfortably and were part of a vibrant expatriate community. After his retirement, Kyle returned to Northern Ireland permanently in 2000 and was a regular attendee at international rugby matches in Dublin, where he was always greeted with particular affection.

Though little is known about Kyle's political opinions, he stated in a letter to *The Irish Times* in July 1966 his abhorrence at what he viewed as Ian Paisley's melding of unionism with religious bigotry. He also took genuine pride in the all-island composition of the Ireland rugby team. Awarded an OBE in 1959 for services to rugby, he was named as the 'Greatest ever Irish rugby player' by the Irish Rugby Football Union (2002) and was an inductee to the International Rugby Board's Hall of Fame (2008). He received honorary degrees from QUB (1991) and University College Dublin (2009). Among his medical honours was a silver medal from the Royal College of Surgeons in Ireland, and in 2007 he was awarded a Lifetime Achievement Award by the *Irish Journal of Medical Science* and the Royal Academy of Medicine in Ireland.

In May 1957 Kyle married Shirley Anderson at Lambeg Parish church in Lisburn. The couple, who later divorced, had two children, Caleb and Justine. His close friend and Queen's, Ulster and Ireland teammate, Noel Henderson, married Kyle's sister, Betty. After a period of ill health, Jack Kyle died on 28 November 2014 at Bryansford, Co. Down. He was widely mourned, not just for his sublime rugby skills, but for his humanity, generosity and modesty.

Liam O'Callaghan

Sources

Belfast News Letter, 27 March, 27 December 1944; 10 February 1947; *The Irish Times*, 27 March 1944; 10 March 1949; 17 March 1951; 26 July 1966; 29 November 2014; *Irish Press*, 10 February 1947; 5 March 1958; *The Times* (London), 29 May 1950; *Bay of Plenty Beacon*, 26 June 1950; *Limerick Leader*, 3 March 1958; Justine Kyle McGrath, *Conversations with my father* (2014)

John Fortune Lawrence

1833–97

SPORTING MERCHANT AND PUBLISHER

John Fortune Lawrence was born 13 January 1833 in Dublin, the eldest of six sons and five daughters (three of each reaching adulthood) of William Lawrence (d. 1887), a clerk of works at the General Post Office, and his wife Elizabeth (née Mervyn; d. 1889), a shopkeeper. From 1854, after learning his trade in his mother's shop at 5–7 Upper Sackville Street (O'Connell Street), John Lawrence ran his own toy and sports warehouse, the Civit Cat Bazaar, at 39 Grafton Street, Dublin. Incorporating a photographic gallery and portrait studio from 1858, he sold cricket and archery equipment, fireworks and a variety of toys and jewellery. Lawrence expanded the Grafton Street premises (1864) to include a 'large ware-room, archery gallery for butt shooting and photographic gallery with waiting rooms' (Dictionary of architects, 'William George Murray'), and in 1874 occupied 38 Grafton Street too.

Exiting the photographic business, Lawrence sold his negatives to his younger brother William, and became the leading sports merchant in Dublin. As interest in archery and cricket (the latter, between the great famine and the land war, becoming perhaps the most popular sport in Ireland) rose and waned through the 1860s and early 1870s, Lawrence turned increasingly to promote athletics, rugby and association football. He organised Irish cricket selections (often under the Gentlemen of Ireland banner) to compete against visiting English teams (1857, 1860, 1861, 1865, 1868, 1869), playing at the Leinster Cricket Club (Rathmines) or Dublin University grounds (Trinity College Dublin).

Equipping teams and cataloguing their exploits during cricket's zenith in the 1870s, he commenced publication of *John Lawrence's handbook of cricket in Ireland* in 1865. The annual, the compilation of which was attributed to 'J. T. H.' (James T. Hurford (d. 1897), a judicial civil servant active in Dublin athletics circles and honorary secretary of Phoenix Cricket Club), remains an invaluable record of sport and leisure in Victorian Ireland. Advertising Lawrence's expanding range of goods (tennis, badminton, croquet, fives, fencing, gymnastics equipment and parlour games), the *Handbook* (sixteen editions, 1865/6 to 1880/81, the last a double number) carried club listings, fixture lists and sports reports, alongside occasional historical sporting accounts. Outlining the rules of cricket, archery, rugby and association football, it fulfilled an important instructional function in the absence of national organising structures. Growing interest in rugby and association football saw their expanding treatment in later editions of the handbook, gradually displacing cricket and archery. Lawrence also published *The Irish cricketers in the United States 1879 [by one of them]*; was the Irish agent for the English serial-journal *Athlete*; and promoted baseball and lacrosse exhibitions in the mid-1870s.

The *Handbook of cricket* remains the essential source in mapping the rapid growth of cricket in Ireland from the mid-1860s. By the early 1870s there was an active cricket club in every Irish county, before the sport went into decline later that decade. The newspaper *Sport* lamented the disappearance of the *Handbook*: 'Mr Lawrence kept publishing the guide with the most persistent pluck at a heavy loss for a long time, and cricketers have only themselves to thank for its suspension' (*Sport*, 26 June 1886).

Lawrence emphasised his patronage by successive lord lieutenants—especially the 7th earl of Carlisle, the marquess of Abercorn and the 5th Earl Spencer—for his events, wares and publications. Aristocratic support for (and occasional playing of) cricket, notably by Carlisle, was integral to cricket's growth and popularity, especially amongst the gentry and the aspirational middle class. Lawrence also promoted himself as a 'pyrotechnic artist' and manufacturer of fireworks, organising displays (often accompanied by musical levees featuring Royal Irish Constabulary, Dublin Metropolitan Police or regimental bands) in the Rotunda Gardens, in Dublin, the Marine Gardens in Kingstown (Dún Laoghaire), various cricket grounds, and at agricultural shows and aristocratic 'coming-of-age fêtes' around the country.

Selling cricket and tennis paraphernalia, scoring cards, archery targets, croquet and polo equipment, and books promulgating the rules of various sports to the Irish sporting public, Lawrence astutely advertised the use of his wares by the emergent 'official' sporting organisations at 'grand national' championships. He also promoted, presented prizes and sold tickets for sporting events and competitions. His Grafton Street premises (moving to 63 Grafton Street in 1878, then to 19 Grafton Street in 1886) became the nexus of sporting culture in Dublin and its committee rooms hosted various notable Irish sporting firsts. There the Irish Football Union (IFU) held discussions (December 1874–January 1875) leading to the organisation of the first Ireland–England rugby game. Lawrence also hosted IFU annual general meetings (1875–6), early meetings (1873–5) of the Irish Championship Athletic Club and Lansdowne FC (rugby), and the founding meeting of the Irish Cricket Union (3 May 1884). A key figure in the expansion of sport and leisure activities, Lawrence helped to lay the bedrock of associational sporting culture in Victorian Ireland.

On 12 February 1897, Lawrence collapsed in the Eastman shop, 25 South Great George's Street, Dublin, and was pronounced dead upon examination in the Adelaide hospital; his death was attributed to cardiac syncope. He married Rebecca (née Aikenhead) on 16 April 1863 in Kilkenny. They had three daughters and two sons and resided at addresses in Bray, Co. Wicklow; Blackrock, Co. Dublin; and Baggot Street, Dublin.

Turlough O'Riordan

Sources

General Register Office Dublin (death certificate, marriage certificate); National Archives of Ireland, Census of Ireland, 1901; National Library of Ireland, Accession 5,540, 'Ancestry of William Mervyn Lawrence'; *The Irish Times, passim*; esp.: 15 February 1897; *Saunders's News-letter, passim; Thom's Irish almanac and official directory* (1855–98), *passim; Freeman's Journal, passim; Dublin Evening Post,* 16 June 1869; *Irish Sportsman and Farmer,* 10 October, 19 December 1874; 2 January, 27 May, 4 December 1875; 30 September 1876; 6 October, 16 December 1877; *Sport,* 26 June 1886; William Patrick Hone, *Cricket in Ireland* (1955); Neal Garnham, 'The roles of cricket in Victorian and Edwardian Ireland', *Sporting Traditions,* vol. 19, no. 2 (May 2003), 27–48; Sean Reid, 'Identity and cricket in Ireland in the mid-nineteenth century', *Sport and Society,* vol. 15, no. 2 (March 2012), 147–64; Architectural Association of Ireland, Dictionary of Architects, 'Co. Dublin, Dublin, Grafton Street, No. 039 (Lawrence's Toy Shop & Civet Cat Bazaar)', ref. William George Murray, www.dia.ie/architects (internet material accessed August 2021)

This entry has been abridged for publication. The full version is available at www.dib.ie.

Elizabeth Le Blond

1860–1934

Mountaineer and author

Elizabeth ('Lizzie') Le Blond (née Hawkins-Whitshed; Burnaby; Main) was born 26 June 1860 in Dublin, the only child of Sir St Vincent Bentinck Hawkins-Whitshed, 3rd baronet of Killincarrick House, Greystones, Co. Wicklow, and his wife Anne Alicia (née Handcock). After her father died in 1871 'Lizzie', as she was known to intimates, continued to live with her mother, becoming a ward in chancery due to property he bequeathed to her in Ireland. As befitting the family's wealth and status Elizabeth was educated by a governess, retained a personal maid and was initiated into London society.

During her first London season she met maverick soldier and popular hero Colonel Frederick 'Fred' Gustavus Burnaby (1842–85). They married in 1879, and she gave birth to their first and her only child, Harry, in 1880. While Fred was preoccupied with soldiering, travel and ballooning, his taste for adventures and proclivity to write about them, indicate they were a good match. Of her three husbands Burnaby finds most mention in her memoir *Day in, day out* (1928), and her first two books were secured under his publisher. *The high Alps in winter* (1883) and *High life and towers of silence* (1886) recount her explorations in the western Alps.

Her first visit to Chamonix, France, in 1881 was essentially restorative. Sent by doctors to take the mountain air for persistent respiratory problems, she realised that expeditions above the snow line left her feeling physically fitter, igniting her interest in mountaineering and winter sports. She returned in the summer of 1882 (notably making two guided ascents of Mont Blanc), and again in the winter of 1882–83, hiring Edouard Cupelin as her mountain guide; she would dedicate her second book to him. By 1884 she had made a first ascent of the 4,135m-high (13,566ft) summit of the Bishorn with guide Josef Imboden, who named it 'Pointe Burnaby' in her honour.

After Fred's death at the Battle of Abu Klea, Sudan, in 1885, she married mathematician John Frederic Main (1854–92) in 1886, publishing her second book that year under the name 'Elizabeth Main'. Although her marital

status afforded her some protection from unwanted at-
tentions or suitors whilst abroad, the marriage apparently provided little else. In 1887 John permanently settled
in Denver, Colorado, while from 1886–90 Elizabeth retained a suite at the luxurious Kulm Hotel in St Moritz,
Switzerland, which was already renowned as the birthplace
of modern winter sports. She enjoyed tobogganing and
ice-skating, becoming the first woman to pass the men's
skating test, and also undertook bicycle tours through the
Alps and participated in hill-climbing competitions using
early motor cars. Personal wealth rendered her immune
from being 'cut off' from paternal, fraternal or spousal
support due to her radical sporting choices.

This financial and social independence allowed her ven-
tures to Norway over successive seasons 1897–1903. Until
1899 she focussed on summer and winter mountaineering
in the Norwegian Artic and completed pioneering work in
the company of trusted guide Josef Imboden and his son
Emil. Numerous first ascents (accounts suggest twenty-six
to twenty-eight) during this period mark her out as one of
the most successful mountaineers—man or woman—of
the day. In 1900 she married (Francis Bernard) Aubrey
Le Blond (1869–1951) at Kensington, London. She
enjoyed a more companionate marriage with Le Blond;
the dedication in *Mountaineering in the land of the midnight sun* (1908) reads 'To my husband whose love for
our northern playground fully equals my own.' She continued to explore Norway and the Alps, and in the latter
she made an unprecedented 'manless' traverse (*c.*1900) of
Piz Palü (Bernina Range) with Lady Evelyn McDonnell
(1860–1947). Away from the public gaze, isolated mountain locations were perfect for adventurous women like
Le Blond. She avoided offending public sensibilities by

cutting a sartorially elegant figure in London society, evidenced in photographs of her which accompanied the occasional features written by or about her in periodicals such as *Cosmopolitan Magazine* and *Pall Mall Magazine*.

The measured and informative tone of her many books secured Le Blond's reputation as the most authoritative woman mountaineer in Britain and Ireland. In 1907, with her active mountaineering days behind her, she recruited members for, and was elected president of, the newly formed Alpine Section of the Lyceum Club, a women's intellectual club in London. By 1909 she had steered a fully independent Ladies' Alpine Club into being—the first mountaineering club exclusively for women—remaining president until 1912. She was also a member of the Lyceum's Writer's Circle and its Council of Photographers, photography being her other great interest.

Indeed, she was a pioneer of mountain photography from the early 1880s. *The high Alps in winter* (1883) contains examples of her early work, and by 1895 her technical knowledge of process and composition had advanced significantly enough to enable authorship of *Hints on snow photography*, which belied her extensive photographic knowledge. Indeed, when mountaineering in Norway she took a bespoke tent for developing plates 'on the spot'. Acquiring a film camera, drawing on her photographic skills, around 1900 she filmed bobsleigh racing, tobogganing and ice skating in the Engadin Valley in the eastern Swiss Alps. Undoubtedly the first to film mountain pursuits, Le Blond was also one of the very first women filmmakers.

Mountaineering in the land of the midnight sun (1908) contains seventy-one photographic illustrations charting her explorations in Norway. Thereafter, advances in film and shutter speeds allowed Le Blond to turn her skills to the photography of 'action' sports in the resorts of St Moritz (famed for the development of the Cresta Run for tobogganing) and Davos (notable for skiing). E. F. Benson was impressed enough to include forty-seven reproductions of her black and white photographs to illustrate his book *Winter sports in Switzerland* (1913). Le Blond used her photographs in her own books and sold copies to raise money for philanthropic causes. She inaugurated the St Moritz Aid Fund to support those who could not otherwise afford to go to the Engadin in search of health, as she had in the early 1880s.

In common with all sportswomen and travellers of the Victorian and Edwardian periods Le Blond endured inconveniences on account of her sex; given her social status, she also had to be sensitive to public sentiment. Her grand-aunt, Lady Bentinck, pleaded with Le Blond's mother 'Stop her climbing mountains! She is scandalizing all London and looks like a Red Indian!' (*Day in, day out*, 90). Although she always took care to don a conventional skirt at the beginning and end of her mountain expeditions, away from the public gaze she changed into rational dress for safety and encouraged others to do so in her writings. She also used a cloth mask when climbing, deployed by ladies fearing damage to their complexion. Writing for *Cosmopolitan Magazine* in 1904, Le Blond reassured readers that 'proper judgement' was the antidote to the various dangers posed by the climbing of snow peaks. Reflecting on her expeditions in Norway she asserted that there had been 'no narrow escapes' because she had been 'too well guided'. In always readily acknowledging the importance of her professional guides, she was, perhaps, being too self-effacing. One obituarist observed:

'Her staying powers were quite outstanding, she was slight but very strongly built, with the finished stride of the first-class guide' ('In memoriam Mrs Aubrey Le Blond', 383).

Besides publishing books and articles on mountaineering, Le Blond authored historical accounts of her ancestors, historical and genealogical research, and travel guides to Italy and Spain alongside other travelogues. With the outbreak of the first world war in 1914 she served as a nurse in the Hôpital Militaire at Dieppe until late 1916. She led the Appeal Department of the British Ambulance Committee, which dispatched an Alpine Motor Kitchen (funded by a Ladies' Alpine Club appeal) to the Vosges, eastern France. At the request of the War Office, she gave lantern lectures, exhibiting her photography, to troops in Britain and France.

Elizabeth Le Blond used her talent with the pen, the camera, and as a speaker to familiarise the public with the wonders of mountaineering, simultaneously retaining an aura of social respectability in keeping with her aristocratic background. She adeptly navigated a period of transition in public attitudes, between overt censure and greater acceptance of women participating in physically demanding sporting pursuits. In the process she became a role model for daring to challenge gendered norms of behaviour. Her contribution to the development and promotion of women's mountaineering is well illustrated by her re-election to the presidency of the Ladies' Alpine Club in 1933. Following an operation, she died unexpectedly on 27 July 1934 at her brother-in-law's home in Mangalore, Llandrindod Wells, Radnorshire, Wales.

Carol A. Osborne

Sources

Mrs F. Burnaby, *The high Alps in winter or, mountaineering in search of health* (1883); Mrs Main, *High life and towers of silence* (1886); 'Obituary: John Frederic Main', *Minutes of the proceedings of the Institution of Civil Engineers,* vol. 110 (1892), 394–6; Mrs Main, *Hints on snow photography* (1895); Mrs Le Blond, 'Perils of the High Peaks', *Cosmopolitan Magazine,* vol. 37 (1904), 245–52; Mrs Le Blond, 'Wintering in the High Alps', *The Pall Mall Magazine,* vol. 38 (1906), 797–802; Mrs Le Blond, *Mountaineering in the land of the midnight sun* (1908); E. F Benson, *Winter sports in Switzerland* (1913); *Ladies' Alpine Club Report 1917,* 13–14; Mrs A. Le Blond, *Day in, day out* (1928); E. L. S., 'In memoriam Mrs Aubrey Le Blond', *Alpine Journal,* vol. 46 (1934), 283–384; Peter H. Hansen, 'Le Blond [née Hawkins-Whitshed], Elizabeth Alice Frances', *Oxford dictionary of national biography* (2010), doi. org/10.1093/ref:odnb/52565; Rosemary Raughter, 'Elizabeth (Lizzie) Le Blond', womensmuseumofireland.ie/articles/elizabeth-lizzie-le-blond--2; (2013); Stephen Bottomore, 'Elizabeth Alice F. Le Blond—British Mountain filmmaker', Who's who of Victorian cinema, www.victorian-cinema.net (all internet material accessed November 2021)

Beatrice Hill-Lowe

1869–1951

ARCHER

Beatrice Hill-Lowe (née Ruxton; Thompson) was born 26 January 1869 at Ardee House, Ardee, Co. Louth, the youngest of five daughters and three sons of William Ruxton (1823–95), landowner, justice of the peace, deputy lieutenant, and vice-lieutenant for Co. Louth, and his wife

Caroline Diana (née Vernon). On 15 July 1891, Beatrice married Arthur Hill-Lowe at St Mary's Abbey (Church of Ireland), Ardee. After honeymooning in London and Edinburgh, they settled at his family seat, Court of Hill, Nash, in south Shropshire, near Tenbury Wells in the west midlands, where he was a justice of the peace. Here they raised Ada, a daughter from his first marriage, alongside their own children, Arthur Noel Vernon (b. 1892) and Sibyl (b. 1897).

Assuming a genteel life of attending hunt balls, acting in summer fêtes, and competing in and judging arts-and-crafts fairs, Beatrice (as 'Mrs Hill-Lowe') participated from summer 1894 in local archery competitions, often in Cheltenham, which had a thriving club. Arthur was honorary secretary of the Archers of the Teme, based in Tenbury Wells, which held two meetings in July and two in August each year, at which the Hill-Lowes both competed (women often outnumbered men in archery competitions). In July 1897 Beatrice won the Crystal Palace meeting and was then awarded the 'first gross score prize' at both the 54th grand national archery meeting at Malvern (August 1897) and the 20th grand northern archery meeting at Birkdale (September 1899). She was consistently competitive in open and handicapped competitions that comprised a variety of scoring and prize formats, and frequently successful in the 'national round' and 'most golds' or 'most hits' competitions. Placing second in the scoring to the formidable Alice Legh (1855–1948), of the Cheltenham club, Beatrice Hill-Lowe was awarded the 'silver challenge belt for most hits' at the grand national archery meeting at Oxford (August 1906).

Archery was the only sporting event open to women at the 1908 London Olympic games, and Hill-Lowe was one of twenty-five competitors, all of whom represented Great

Britain. The competition was undertaken over two days (17–18 July) at the White City Stadium. In the 'double national round' format, each competitor shot 48 arrows at 60 yards and 24 arrows at 50 yards each day. The gold medal was won by Sybil Fenton 'Queenie' Newell, with Hill-Lowe winning the bronze. She thus became the first Irish woman to win an Olympic medal.

Legh, the predominant archer of the period had not competed at the Olympics, preferring to defend her national title at the grand national archery meeting the following week. She was again victorious, with Hill-Lowe in third. In September 1908 Legh and Beatrice competed together at the Archers of the Teme meeting to mark the jubilee of the club, at which the Hill-Lowes were presented with a silver goblet in recognition of their organising efforts on behalf of the club. Beatrice competed again in Archers of the Teme meetings in summer 1909, but thereafter seems to have ceased competing.

After Arthur Hill-Lowe's death on 17 April 1910 at Bayview, Tenby, Pembrokshire, Wales, Beatrice married secondly (29 June 1911) Lieutenant-Colonel Roland (Rowland) Wycliffe Thompson (1864–1940) at Pennaly, Pembrokshire. Roland served as a major with the Loyal North Lancashire Regiment during the Boer war (1899–1902) and was awarded the Distinguished Service Order (April 1901). After honeymooning at Ballyshannon, Co. Donegal, the couple lived mostly at Giltar Lodge, Penally, Pembrokeshire. They lived for periods (c.1922–8) at Newbridge Lodge, Celbridge, Co. Kildare, before moving to 12 Queen's Parade, Tenby, where Roland died 15 April 1940, and Beatrice remained till her death on 2 July 1951.

Turlough O'Riordan

Sources

General Register Office Dublin (parents' marriage certificate; subject's birth certificate, marriage certificate); National Archives UK, England and Wales census, 1891, 1901; General Register Office England and Wales (death certificate); *The Times* (London), *passim*; Fred T. Follett (ed.), *Archers' register 1893–94*, 56–8; *London Daily News*, 17 July 1897; *Morning Post*, 7 August 1897; *Manchester Guardian*, 1 September 1899; *Illustrated sporting and dramatic news*, 11 August 1906; *Sportsman*, 20 July 1908; *The Irish Times*, 18 September 1909; 16 February 1924; John Burke, *A genealogical and heraldic history of the landed gentry of Ireland* (1912 edition), 612; Bill Mallon and Ian Buchanan, *The 1908 Olympic games: results for all competitors in all events, with commentary* (2000), 42, 462–3; Jean Williams, *A contemporary history of women's sport, part one: sporting women, 1850–1960* (2014), 71–2; Jean Young, 'The big house in County Louth, 1912–23', in Donal Hall and Martin Maguire (eds), *County Louth and the Irish revolution 1912–1923* (2017); 'Archery at the 1908 London summer games: women's double national round', www.sportsreference.com/olympics/summer/1908/ARC/womens-double-national-round.html; 'Captain Arthur Noel Vernon Hill-Lowe', www.northirishhorse.com.au/NIH/Images/People/Full%20pictures/Hill-Lowe.html (all internet material accessed November 2017)

This entry and the related sources have been abridged for publication. The full version is available at www.dib.ie.

Bill McCracken

1883–1979

SOCCER PLAYER

Bill (William Robert; 'Offside') McCracken was born 29
January 1883 in Thames Street, Belfast, son of William
McCracken, tenter, and Eliza McCracken (née McDowell)
of Thames Street. He joined the Belfast club Distillery as
a part-time player while employed as an apprentice in
the building trade and played in IFA Cup finals in 1902
and 1903, winning the latter 3–1 against Dublin club

Bohemians. He was a Distillery player when he made his international debut (one of three caps he won in the left-full-back position; he usually played at right-full-back) in a 3–0 victory for Ireland against Wales in Cardiff (22 February 1902). He won six caps with the club before being signed by the English first-division side Newcastle United for a fee of £50 (May 1904). The transfer was the subject of an English Football Association (FA) investigation, with allegations both of secret payments and of his being illegally approached by Newcastle player Colin Veitch after an international against England.

He went on to become one of United's most famous and longest-serving players, making 377 league appearances for the club (443 in total) over nineteen years, winning three league championships and one FA Cup medal, and having two spells as captain of the side, until his retirement in 1923. He made his debut for the club in the first game of the 1904/5 season, a 3–0 home win against Arsenal (3 September 1904). Newcastle went on to dominate the English game for the next ten years, playing a short-passing brand of football.

In his first season they won the League Championship, although a bad injury in October 1904 meant that McCracken was restricted to thirteen games and missed the FA Cup final defeat to Aston Villa. The following year he played twenty league games as the club finished fourth, and he missed another cup final defeat, a 1–0 reversal to Everton. League Championship medals followed in 1906/7 and 1908/9, and McCracken finally played in an FA Cup final, losing the 1908 decider 3–1 to Wolves. His second FA Cup final was to be luckier, as Newcastle won 2–0 against Barnsley in 1910 after a replay. They went on to contest another final the following year, losing

1–0 to Bradford City, again after a replay. His career was interrupted by the first world war, but he played on until the 1922/3 season, when, with full-back partner Billy Hampson, who was also forty, he was part of what is probably the oldest full-back partnership ever seen in top-class soccer. His last match for Newcastle was a 5–0 defeat away against Cardiff City (10 February 1923).

An enthusiastic and extremely quick full-back, who had tremendous powers of recovery and anticipation and could kick with either foot, he was also an expert penalty taker and a superb motivator. For all his ability and achievements as a player, he is remembered as the man who, virtually single-handedly, forced a change in soccer's offside law in 1925, when the number of players needed to play a forward onside was reduced from three to two. Known as 'Offside' McCracken, he had a speed and anticipation that meant that, by stepping up at the right time, he would invariably catch an opposing forward offside. In an era when amateur Corinthian values were still felt to apply in football, his tactics were widely perceived as unsporting. He could, almost by himself, disrupt the flow of a game, and matches in which he played usually degenerated into stop-start affairs. Disliked by opposing spectators, he frequently had fruit, coins and other missiles thrown at him; he once had the shirt torn off his back by Chelsea supporters. As more teams adopted his tactic, the goals per game average fell from 3.00 per game to just 2.21 by the 1923/4 season, forcing the football authorities into action.

A gregarious and outgoing personality, who was tall and handsome, McCracken enjoyed the furore that surrounded him and often baited opposing players and supporters. His combative nature was a consistent feature of his character: once, after being sent off, he sent a referee a four-page letter explaining why his decision had been wrong and received a four-week suspension instead of the usual seven days.

At international level, he played a mere fifteen times for Ireland, because of a ten-year dispute with the Irish Football Association (IFA) over international match fees. He refused to play for Ireland in the 1907/8 season when he discovered that English players were getting £10 for each game while Irish players received only £2. 2s. The IFA suspended him from international football until he pleaded by letter for his suspension to be lifted during the war. By 1919 he was back in the fold and played a further five times for Ireland, his last appearance being against Scotland in 1923, when he captained the side at the age of forty. McCracken's stand meant that he missed out on international football at his peak.

Soon after retiring as a footballer in 1923, he became manager of second-division Hull City, and the highlight of his reign there was guiding them to an FA Cup semi-final in 1930. Working with limited resources he fashioned a useful side that challenged for promotion in 1926/7 but eventually was relegated to the old third division (north) in 1929/30. He resigned (May 1931) and moved to Gateshead as manager, and subsequently to Millwall (May 1933). In February 1937 he became manager of struggling Aldershot and remained there during the war years, when Aldershot's status as a major garrison town ensured that he had the cream of Britain's footballers under his control. He was dismissed as manager in November 1949 and subsequently became a talent scout, spending some years with Newcastle in that capacity during the 1950s. It was while scouting for Watford in the 1960s that he discovered future Northern Ireland legend Pat Jennings and persuaded him to sign for the club. He continued to scout enthusiastically until 1971, when he was in his late eighties, and was presented with a medal by the FA for long service to the game in 1978.

He died 21 January 1979 in Hull, just short of his ninety-sixth birthday. In 1907 he married Jeanie McArthur, who was also from Belfast. They had at least one child, a son.

Jim Shanahan

Sources

General Register Office Dublin (marriage certificate); Malcolm Brodie, *The history of Irish soccer* (1963); Malcolm Brodie, *100 years of Irish football* (1980); Chris Elton, *Hull City: a complete record 1904–1989* (1989); Paul Joannou, Bill Swann and Steve Cooke, *Newcastle United: a complete record 1882–1990* (1990); John Gleeson (ed.), *Fyffes dictionary of Irish sporting greats* (1993); Paul Joannou, *United: the first 100 years* (1995); Roger Hutchinson, *The Toon: a complete history of Newcastle United football club* (1997); Matthew Gillespie, *Soccer: the international line-ups and statistics series—Northern Ireland 1882–1997* (1998); Michael Walker, *Green shoots: Irish football histories* (2017)

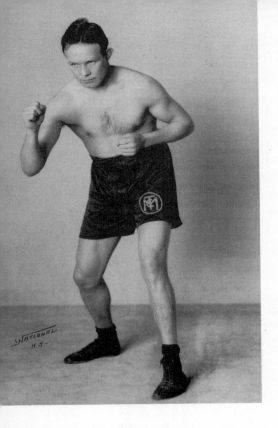

Mike McTigue

1892–1966

Boxer

Mike (Michael Francis) McTigue was born 26 November 1892 in Lickaune, Kilnamona, Co. Clare, one of eleven sons and a daughter of Pat McTigue, farmer of Kilnamona, and Ellen McTigue (née Neylon). He emigrated to New

York in 1912. While working as a beef handler, he defended his foreman from two assailants and was encouraged by his employer to go into boxing. He was taken on by respected trainer George 'Elbows' McFadden and began boxing in 1914. State law in New York at the time meant that many of his fights were technically ten-round 'no decision' exhibitions (unless one of the participants was knocked out), although these usually had 'popular' or 'press' decisions, to facilitate rankings and illegal gambling.

Described as boyish, softly spoken and dapper, he was initially a middleweight: he wavered between 155 and 175 pounds (70.3kg–79.4kg) and stood 5ft 9in. (1.75m). He was a clever and skilful boxer, masterful in defence and a good hitter but lacked a strong punch; especially in his earlier years, he relied heavily on his left hand. Spectators disliked his conservative tactics, which left promoters struggling to find good matches for him. For long he was consigned to fighting journeymen in small venues in the New York area. In 1920 he married Cecelia Cuniff, a New Yorker whose parents were from Cahersiveen, Co. Kerry. They had three daughters.

Trying his luck in Canada, he surprised his detractors by knocking out the undefeated Canadian middleweight champion Eugene Brosseau in April 1920 and established himself as a box-office draw in Montreal with a string of knockout victories over the next eighteen months. Following his impressive win over 'Panama' Joe Gans in Jersey City in September 1921, he was rewarded that December with a fight in Madison Square Garden, but his victory over Jeff Smith was such a tedious affair that it seemed to have done terminal damage to his career. After about 111 professional fights, he was nearing retirement with little to show for it in 1922 when he headed for Britain, aiming for some reasonable purses against the easier competition there.

He failed to land a big fight in Britain but was in the right place to benefit from the sensational victory of the colourful Senegalese 'Battling' Siki over the French world light-heavyweight champion George Carpentier. The French, British and American boxing authorities abhorred the prospect of blacks triumphing over whites in the ring and refused to sanction any further fights for Siki. The British Home Office took the further precaution of banning Siki from setting foot in Britain. This gave Irish promoter Tom Singleton his chance to stage a world title fight in Dublin: Ireland was newly independent from Britain while Siki, desperate for money, was willing to accept a small purse. Needing an Irish fighter, Singleton alighted on McTigue, who was to hand and, moreover, one of the few whites prepared to box across the 'colour line'.

A fight was arranged for St Patrick's Day 1923 in the La Scala Theatre, Dublin, regardless of the civil war in Ireland. The republican guerrillas sought to discredit the government's claim to be in control and issued death threats against both boxers. McTigue and Siki were brought to La Scala under armed guard, with Siki's convoy beating off an ambush en route. A landmine exploded nearby shortly before the fight began and a gun battle raged in the streets outside afterwards. Yet the protagonists had been received rapturously during their pre-bout public appearances and a huge crowd gathered outside La Scala on the night. On the defensive for the first ten rounds against his much larger opponent, McTigue attacked more as Siki tired but was hampered when he broke his thumb in the thirteenth round. In the last world title fight to be decided over more than fifteen rounds—it went the full twenty—McTigue won a points victory. The general view was that Siki had done at least enough to merit a draw.

McTigue returned to a sceptical America as the world light-heavyweight champion. He miscalculated in agreeing to risk his title against the formidable W. L. 'Young' Stribling in Columbus, Georgia, in October 1923 and attempted to withdraw before being forced into the ring at gunpoint. Although most accounts maintain that McTigue was comfortably beaten on points, the referee ruled the fight a draw, prompting a riot that only temporarily led to the decision being reversed.

Pleading a sore right hand, amid much wrangling over fight contracts, McTigue held on to his title until 1925 either by avoiding tough opponents or by agreeing to 'no-decision' contests in which he performed unimpressively while managing to avoid getting knocked out. These tactics, exasperating to boxing fans and to the boxing authorities, long prevented him from capitalising financially on his title. Eventually, he secured a $50,000 payday against the 'Astoria Assassin' Paul Berlenbach and fought valiantly in losing a points decision after fifteen rounds before a crowd of 45,000 in New York on 31 May 1925.

His mid-thirties saw him producing his best boxing under his new manager, Jimmy Johnson, who encouraged McTigue to box more aggressively. A successful operation on his troublesome right hand made him a real contender for the world heavyweight title. From July 1926 he was involved in a succession of thrilling fights; hailed as the 'Methuselah' of boxing, he became a major box office attraction. His return bout with Berlenbach in January 1927 was probably his greatest display. Despite being nine years older, McTigue had Berlenbach on the floor four times before having him counted out in just the fourth round.

This win set McTigue up for a contest with Jack Sharkey on 3 March, the winner of which would meet Jack Dempsey in a final eliminator for a shot at Gene Tunney's world heavyweight title. Despite conceding ten years, two stone (12.7kg) in weight, and four inches (10.16cm) in height to his opponent, McTigue outboxed Sharkey (a future world heavyweight champion) and was leading on points in the twelfth round when McTigue suffered a chipped tooth that burst an artery, stopping the fight. Like most contemporary boxers, McTigue did not wear a mouth guard, but mouth guards became prevalent in boxing after this famous defeat. In October 1927 he fought Tommy Loughran for the vacant light-heavyweight title, this time conceding ten years and fifteen pounds (6.8kg) to his opponent. He lost on a split decision in a classic contest.

Knocked out in the first round of his next fight, he went nine fights and eighteen months without winning but continued to box regularly until his retirement in 1930. The most comprehensive records available show that in 174 professional fights, he won 77 (52 inside the distance), drew 9 and lost 26; 2 were declared no-contests and the rest were officially 'no-decision' bouts. Some records credit him with 108 victories, taking 'popular' verdicts into account.

In the late 1920s he possessed a palatial home in Jackson Heights, Queens, along with some $250,000 worth of investments. He was robbed of this wealth, first by the 1929 financial crash, then a few years later by his business agent. Thereafter, he worked variously as a labourer, floor manager in a ballroom and a physical instructor in a naval base. He drank heavily, became increasingly accident-prone and was estranged from his wife and daughters. In later life he lived in poor circumstances. McTigue's final years were marked by an illness that forced him into a mental institution for a time, leaving him unable to recall much about his boxing career. He died 12 August 1966 in Jamaica, Queens, New York.

Jim Shanahan

Sources

Irish Independent, 15 August 1966; 10 February 1967; *Clare Champion*, 20 August 1966; *Irish Press*, 23 August 1966; Patrick Myler, *The fighting Irish: Ireland's role in world boxing history* (1987); John Gleeson (ed.), *Fyffes dictionary of Irish sporting greats* (1993); Ian Buchanan and Peter Matthews, *The all-time greats of British and Irish sport* (1995); Andrew Gallimore, *A bloody canvas* (2007); Mark Roettger (ed.), *Modern sports dentistry* (2018), 113; '"Bold" Mike McTigue', www.cyberboxing-zone.com/boxing/mctigue.htm; 'Mike McTigue', boxrec.com/en/proboxer/11287 (all internet material accessed September 2020)

Kay Mills

1923–96

Kay (Kathleen) Mills was born 8 October 1923 at 31 South Square, Inchicore, Dublin, to Thomas Mills, originally from Glanmire, Co. Cork, and his wife Winifred (née Wills) of Inchicore. Thomas Mills was employed by Great Southern Railways (later subsumed into CIÉ); he helped at the company's sports club, which was set up for the workers and their families. Kathleen had three siblings, Gertrude, Ada and Robert.

When Kathleen was eighteen months old, her mother died. Her maternal grandmother, Charlotte Wills, who had ten children of her own, raised the Mills children in her home across the square at 1 Abercorn Terrace, Inchicore. Kathleen was educated at the nearby Goldenbridge convent. She left school aged fourteen to work in Lamb's jam factory. An all-round athlete, she participated competitively in athletics, table tennis and gymnastics with the CIÉ sports club. Camogie, however, was her first love: she first held a hurley in her hand aged five and quickly mastered the game to a high degree. She donned the wine, green and white colours of the club camogie team at the age of fourteen, earning immediate promotion to the club's senior side.

She first played for Dublin in 1941. Throughout her twenty-year inter-county career, she played in one position, the left side of midfield. Her first attempt to win an all-Ireland medal was thwarted at the final hurdle by Cork in 1941. She had to fight hard to get her first all-Ireland medal, as Dublin were held to a draw by Cork in 1942 but won the replay. Her brilliant stickwork, fine goal and general play drew compliments from the match reporters. In the 1943 and 1944 all-Ireland victories, she evolved from a fine player to be one of the stars of the side. Her collection of all-Ireland medals was halted temporarily, as the Leinster counties withdrew from the all-Ireland championship from 1945 to 1947. The CIÉ club had a wonderful team and were given the honour of representing Dublin in 1948 when she collected her fourth all-Ireland medal.

Mills did not play in the 1949 championship following which Dublin enjoyed a run of six championship victories from 1950 to 1955. This was a golden era of Dublin camogie when she was surrounded by a galaxy of stars, including Idé O'Kiely, Peg Griffin, Doreen Rogers, Eileen O'Mahony, Una O'Connor and Annette Corrigan.

Antrim claimed the all-Ireland title in 1956, but from 1957 Dublin won an unequalled ten-in-a-row. Kathleen added five more to her collection from 1957 to 1961 and captained the Dublin team in 1958. As captain, she had great presence in a refined way and inspired those around her. On her thirty-eighth birthday, she won her fifteenth all-Ireland medal in 1961. She was carried shoulder high around Croke Park by her teammates, later receiving a replica of the O'Duffy Cup, the all-Ireland senior camogie championship trophy. The occasion marked her retirement from inter-county camogie. Her total of fifteen all-Ireland senior medals has not been matched by anyone else in Gaelic games field sports and is unlikely to be equalled.

A natural left-handed player, she approached the ball at speed, lifted it onto her stick, continued running, and struck the ball without taking it into her hand. Always pleasing to watch, she read the game brilliantly, distributed the ball intelligently and remained composed under pressure. She regularly scored long-range goals and from sideline cuts. Men frequently lined up to take off their hats and shake her hand after matches. Tall, slender and fair-haired, she was dedicated to camogie and modest about her achievements. She was dignified and soft-spoken, gentle with a droll sense of humour; popular with her teammates, she went out of her way to encourage and help newcomers to the team. Her collection of camogie medals is displayed in the Gaelic Athletic Association Museum at Croke Park. Included are medals from fifteen all-Ireland senior championships, twenty Leinster senior championships, four inter-provincial championships and six Dublin senior championships. She was the first camogie player to be named as the 'sports star of the week' in the *Irish Independent*. Her outstanding performances merited a Cúchulainn Hall of Fame award and a place on the team of the century.

In 1947 Kathleen married George Hill but was always known by her maiden name. They ran the Red Seal Handbag Company, which was located close to the North Circular Road, and later on Hill Street. George cut out the bags while Kathleen put on the frames and sewed the bags. With Kathleen's drive and entrepreneurship, the business grew. They were kind and caring employers. Years later, they switched to the vintner trade and ran the Seventh Lock public house on the Grand Canal in Ballyfermot. They had no children. Kathleen Mills died peacefully at her home on the Naas Road, Dublin, on 12 August 1996. She was buried in Palmerstown cemetery.

The all-Ireland camogie premier junior championship cup is named in her honour. The Kay Mills Cup, a replica of the O'Duffy Cup, is presented to the winning all-Ireland senior captain to keep in perpetuity, at the bequest of Kathleen's husband, George. She is commemorated by a plaque on the wall of her former home at 1 Abercorn Terrace in Inchicore, which carries the inscription: 'Lithe and graceful, a superb midfield player with neat wrist work, quick to lift and strike at full speed. She could score from any angle.'

Mary Moran

Sources

Mary Moran, *A game of our own: camogie's story 1904–2010* (2011); information from: Marian Carolan (niece); Eileen O'Mahony, Carmel Hanley and Brídín Uí Mhaolagáin (playing colleagues); and Phyllis Breslin (past president of the Camogie Association); 'A brief history of the CIÉ GAA Clubs Nationwide', web.archive.org/web/20110708154103/http://www.ciegaa.com/history.html#DublinGAAClubs (internet material accessed October 2021)

This entry has been abridged for publication. The full version is available at www.dib.ie.

Tony Mullane

1859–1944

BASEBALL PLAYER

Tony (Anthony John) Mullane was born either 30 January or 7 February 1859 in Co. Cork, eldest among three sons and one daughter of Dennis Mullane, a labourer, and his wife Elizabeth (née Behan). His family emigrated to the USA in the early 1860s, eventually settling in Erie, Pennsylvania. He became a multi-talented athlete, adept at boxing and at ice and roller skating, as well as a proficient musician, but found fame as a right-handed baseball pitcher at a time when Irish-Americans dominated this sport.

After playing from 1876 with amateur and semi-professional teams, he enjoyed a promising professional apprenticeship with an independent team in Akron, Ohio (1880–81), and then endured an injury-plagued major-league debut season with the Detroit Wolverines of the National League (NL) late in 1881, playing only five games. Joining the Louisville Eclipse of the newly launched American Association (AA), he won 30 games in 1882, with a personal-best 1.88 earned run average per 9 innings pitched (ERA), and a league-leading 170 strikeouts, and pitched the association's first no-hit game. One of his best seasons was 1883, when with the St Louis Browns he had a won–lost record of 35–15, a 2.19 ERA and 191 strikeouts. In 1884 he struck out a career-high 325 batters while winning 36 games (another personal best) for a Toledo Blue Stockings team that won only 46 games. The early seasons of Mullane's career were peripatetic, as he played rival leagues and teams against one another in pursuit of the most favourable contracts. This eventually backfired; accused by the AA of 'sharp practice almost equivalent to actual dishonesty' (*The Neyer/James guide to pitchers*, 66), he was declared ineligible for the 1885 season. Signing in 1886 with the Cincinnati Red Stockings (latterly the Cincinnati Reds), he remained with them for seven-and-a-half seasons.

The 1880s were the second decade of organised professional baseball, and the sport was in flux, with frequent rules changes, many of which involved pitching technique. Pitchers threw not from a raised mound, as in the modern game, but from a chalked box within which they could make a short run before releasing the ball at a point

50ft from home plate. Mullane was foremost among those pitchers who tested the underhand delivery rule, throwing pitches of marginal or dubious legality. The enthusiasm among the sport's public for higher velocity pitching induced rules changes allowing sidearm (1883) and overhand (1884) deliveries.

Mullane was ambidextrous and could pitch with either hand, having developed his left-handed facility as a fallback upon injuring his right arm in 1881. After his retirement myths arose regarding this. He probably pitched left-handed in regular-season games on a mere several occasions, largely reserving the skill for exhibition games and as a practice-session or warm-up stunt. His ambidexterity enhanced his exceptional fielding skills: competing bare-handed in a period when fielding gloves were uncommon and of rudimentary design, he could catch and throw equally effectively with either hand.

Remarkably handsome, a roguish charmer in demeanour and a dandy in grooming and dress, Mullane was nicknamed the 'Count' and the 'Apollo of the Box'. He was a great favourite with women, who flocked to the ballpark on days that he pitched. Exploiting this appeal, the Cincinnati management regularly designated a 'Ladies' Day', offering reduced admission prices to women (most of whom would be chaperoned by a full-paying gentleman) while guaranteeing that Mullane would pitch. The successful initiative was widely emulated, and 'Ladies' Day' promotions remained common throughout professional baseball well into the twentieth century.

A self-infatuated prima donna, overly enamoured by his own talent, charisma and celebrity, Mullane was a frequent focus of controversy. His career was punctuated by contract disputes, a game-throwing scandal (in which he was officially exonerated), public criticism of teammates and management, club-imposed sanctions for insubordination, and outbursts of temper and violence. He has attracted retrospective notoriety for his overt racism. The Toledo team of 1884 included the Walker brothers, the last two African-Americans to play major-league baseball before imposition of the unwritten 'colour line' that persisted until 1947. Mullane refused to take pitch signs from catcher Fleet Walker, which he regarded as taking 'orders' from a black man. On occasion he would attempt to befuddle or injure Walker by deliberately throwing a pitch into the dirt. Mullane later conceded that Walker was the best catcher with whom he had worked.

Akin to other pitchers of the period, Mullane often played at other positions, but with greater hitting and fielding ability than most. In addition to pitching in 555 major-league games, he played outfield in 154 and divided 111 games among all four infield positions. A switch hitter, he had a career batting average of .247, with 8 home runs and 223 runs batted in (RBIs), making him one of the best pitchers ever with the bat. His best season as a batter was 1889, when he batted a personal best .296, with 29 RBIs and 53 runs scored. Commanding the respect of rival pitchers, he drew 221 career walks. As was common in the 1880s, Mullane pitched in a high proportion of his teams' games. Through his first three full seasons he pitched over sixty per cent of the games, completing nearly all his starts, and as late as 1891 was appearing in over one-third. In 1884 he pitched a personal-best 567 innings and pitched over 500 innings again in 1886.

In 1892, having already won 21 games, Mullane refused to accept a mid-season salary cut imposed on the Cincinnati players (reducing his earnings from $4,200 to $3,500), and played out the season with Butte in the minor Montana State League. At thirty-four-years-old, he struggled to adjust to the increased pitching distance of 60ft 6in. introduced in 1893, was traded away from Cincinnati in mid-season and concluded his major-league career in brief NL stints with the Baltimore Orioles and Cleveland Spiders (1893–4). Thereafter, he competed in minor leagues for the duration of the 1890s and briefly in 1902, and worked as an umpire in several minor leagues (1898–1904).

Winning 30 or more games in each of five consecutive seasons (1882–4, 1886–7), Mullane had career major-league totals (across thirteen seasons) of 284 victories and 220 defeats, and a 3.05 ERA, despite playing with mediocre teams. His career won–lost average of .563 compares to a .477 average by his teams when he was not pitching. Though he was a forgotten figure for most of the twentieth century, his achievement has been belatedly recognised by baseball historians. The officially endorsed baseball encyclopaedia, *Total baseball*, ranks him eighth among all players and third among pitchers in the 1876–92 period. Mullane was the outstanding pitcher in the ten-year history of the American Association (1882–91). In his seven AA seasons before Cincinnati transferred to the NL in 1890, he had a won–lost record of 202–134 (a .601 average) and a 2.75 ERA. Regarded among the best several pitchers not to be enshrined in the Baseball Hall of Fame, he was inducted into the Cincinnati Reds Hall of Fame in 2010.

Mullane's marriage (1886) to Barbara Lawless, with whom he had one daughter, ended in an acrimonious divorce (1894), amid allegations of extreme cruelty and domestic violence. Joining the Chicago police department

(1903), he attained the rank of detective, and retired in 1924. Roman Catholic in religion, he died 25/6 April 1944 in Chicago and was buried in Holy Sepulchre cemetery, Alsip, Illinois. His gravestone features the outlines of a baseball and a shamrock.

Lawrence William White

Sources

Chicago Daily News, 26 April 1944; *Chicago Daily Tribune*, 27 April 1944; *New York Times*, 27 April 1944; Geoffrey C. Ward and Ken Burns, *Baseball: an illustrated history* (1994); J. A. Garrity and M. C. Carnes (eds), *American national biography* (1999); John Thorn, Peter Palmer and Michael Gershman (eds), *Total baseball: the official encyclopaedia of major league baseball* (2001 edition); Bill James, *The new Bill James historical baseball abstract* (2003 edition); Bill James and Rob Neyer, *The Neyer/James guide to pitchers: an historical compendium of pitching, pitchers and pitches* (2004), 3–5, 28, 65–71, 317; Ray Birch, 'Tony Mullane' (2017), Society for American Baseball Research (SABR): biography project, sabr.org/bioproj/person/tony-mullane; 'Tony Mullane statistics', www.baseball-reference.com; www.findagrave.com/memorial/23261/anthony-john-mullane#view-photo=158536534 (all internet accessed September 2020)

This entry has been abridged for publication. The full version is available at www.dib.ie.

Terry Mullen

1938–89

Terry (Teresa) Mullen (née Kelly) was born 27 April 1938 in Dublin, daughter of James Kelly and Lily Kelly (née Boles) of Ellenfield Road, Whitehall, Dublin. After attending school locally and working as a machinist, she married Christopher John ('Christy') Mullen in 1961. Initially, they lived in the North Strand area of Dublin but eventually moved to Coolock, Dublin. In her mid-thirties, following complications resulting from an epidural, Mullen was confined to a wheelchair.

Encouraged to attend the Clontarf day centre of the Irish Wheelchair Association, she was introduced to lawn bowls sometime in 1984 and proved a natural. Her career in both special bowls and lawn bowls was short but spectacular. In 1985 she won the national special bowls novice title; she went on to win the Irish senior titles in 1986 and 1987, becoming the first bowler from the Republic to do so. In 1986 and 1987 she also took part in the Stoke Mandeville Games (later renamed the IWAS World Games), winning bronze medals in both the singles and doubles events. In preparation for the 1988 Paralympic Games in Seoul, South Korea, she travelled regularly to Northern Ireland for competition and training, where she competed with—and often defeated—the top able-bodied players.

Shortly before the 1988 games she was diagnosed as terminally ill with a tumour. Against the advice of her doctors, but with the support of her family and medical supervision provided by the Paralympic Council of Ireland, she left her hospital bed and travelled to South Korea. Conditions in Seoul were difficult for her, and she spent much of her time in bed, leaving only to compete. She felt ill ten minutes into her first match, which lasted two hours, but concealed this from her opponent. Against all odds, she not only competed but won the gold medal in the Women's Bowls Singles category, with the reigning champion, Patriga Kihungi of Kenya, in second place. Her achievement made front-page news in Ireland, and her courage and determination were widely admired. A measure of her achievement in a sport that requires intense concentration, superb hand-eye coordination, and an ability to stay calm and relaxed, is the fact that the terminal cancer was to claim her life within a year. Her story is widely seen as a testament to her determination to overcome a double disability and to the value of sporting activity for the disabled. She died 23 August 1989 at her home in Coolock, leaving a husband, one son, two daughters, and grandchildren. She is buried in Fingal cemetery, Balgriffin, Co. Dublin.

Jim Shanahan

Sources

General Register Office Dublin (birth certificate); *Evening Press*, 25 October 1988; *Irish Press*, 24 August 1989; *Irish Independent*, 24 August 1989; *Evening Herald*, 24 August 1989; John Gleeson (ed.), *Fyffes dictionary of Irish sporting greats* (1993); Robert Steadward and Cynthia Peterson, *Paralympics: where heroes come* (1997); Joan Scruton, *Stoke Mandeville: the road to the Paralympics* (1998); information from Ann Ebbs (Paralympic Council of Ireland)

Anne O'Brien

1956–2016

SOCCER PLAYER

Anne Monica O'Brien was born 25 January 1956 at Holles Street hospital, Dublin, one of five daughters and five sons of John O'Brien, a distillery labourer, and Rosanna O'Brien (née Giles) from 13 Oblate Drive, Inchicore, Dublin. Her father died when she was five. Good at all sports, especially athletics and soccer, she was obsessed with soccer, which she played on the streets of Inchicore with the boys. Her relations included Irish soccer internationals Jimmy Conway and Johnny Giles. When Anne was twelve, her mother formed a girls' team for her called Inchicore Celtic. At age fourteen, she finished her education at the Model School in Inchicore to work locally in a sweet factory and then in a chicken factory.

In 1970 she joined Vards, a factory team playing in the Dublin league first division. She scored three goals, despite being the youngest and smallest player on the pitch, as Vards won the 1971 Drumcondra Cup beating Drimnagh Boscos 3–2 at Tolka Park. When Vards became one of three Dublin League teams to amalgamate into Ballyfermot All-Stars in 1972, she began participating in her first proper training sessions. In 1972 she excelled as Ballyfermot All-Stars came second in the Leinster League while winning various cup competitions. She received her first international cap when she played in the Republic of Ireland's second international women's match, a 4–1 victory over Northern Ireland in Dublin on 1 July 1973.

That August the celebrated French women's club side, Stade de Reims ('Reims'), visited Ireland for a two-week tour that consisted of playing an Irish selection and local selections in Dundalk, Limerick, Kilkenny, Waterford and Dublin (twice). O'Brien was among the seven or eight Dubliners picked in most of the 'local' selections and in the Irish selection. She lined out for Reims in the Limerick encounter (21 August). The Ireland versus Reims match occurred at Kilkenny on 26 August and is considered an international, which Ireland won 2–1 with O'Brien scoring a penalty. She also scored against Reims for a Dublin selection in a match held in Bray, Co. Wicklow, on 30 August, which was abandoned over a disputed penalty decision.

When Reims then offered O'Brien a contract, she grabbed the chance to escape an Irish women's soccer scene that she regarded as shambolic. Her Ireland team-mate, Carol Carr, who performed similarly well, missed out, possibly because she was considered too old at twenty years of age. O'Brien had to wait until she turned eighteen before her mother allowed her to leave home. In the interim she won her third international cap against France (10 October 1973) at the Parc des Princes, Paris, earning a player of the match award even as Ireland lost 4–0.

In January 1974 she joined Stade de Reims. As professionalism in women's soccer was not permitted in France, her three-year contract was technically with a local factory, where she worked part time with plenty of leeway allowed for training and matches. The club also arranged a free shared flat for her. Her Reims teammates were either students or (effectively) part-time professionals; most of them were teenagers, like her, with the rest being in their early twenties. She was not the first woman footballer in Ireland or Britain to sign what was effectively a professional contract—Sue Lopez of England had joined the Italian club Torino on a contract in 1969—but it was the first such signing to generate publicity in Ireland and Britain. This inspired O'Brien's Scottish contemporaries, Rose Reilly and Edna Neillis, to embark upon similarly pioneering careers on the European continent.

Initially a centre-forward, she shed half a stone upon arriving in France (leaving her at eight stone (50.8kg)) to play in midfield, becoming renowned for her relentless running. She had balance, technique and speed, and was an intelligent reader of the game, capable of routinely unpicking opposing teams with her passes. Although primarily a creator rather than a scorer, her fierce long-range shooting and heading ability posed a serious goal threat. Throughout her career, she generally took her team's corners, free kicks and penalties.

Upon the revival of the French women's football championships in 1974, she won two French national championships (1974/5 and 1975/6) with Reims, scoring a goal in the 1974/75 championship final. The Reims women acted as the curtain raiser to their men's team and so routinely played before crowds of 10,000–20,000. Reims toured abroad regularly, as there were not many women's teams in France, and she played in Haiti, Guadeloupe, Martinique, Morocco and Algeria.

In 1976 she joined the Rome-based club, Lazio, mainly because Italy was then the only country where there was enough money in women's football for her to become a full-time professional. The Federazione Italiana Calcio Femminile (FICF) was a mix of professional and semi-professional teams with funding coming from business rather than the Italian football federation. It was a summer league before switching to a conventional season from 1981/1982 onwards. Europe's best women footballers then gravitated towards Italy, where star imports like O'Brien raised standards. A strong character and a good team leader, she had a lively personality, which she used to encourage younger players. As had been the case in France, she took quickly to the Italian culture and language.

First appearing for Lazio in April 1976, she quickly established herself as the Italian league's top *trequartista*, the crucial playmaking role that links the midfield with the attack. She played for seven Italian clubs: Lazio (1976–81), Trani (1981–4), Lazio again (1984–6), Modena (1986–7), Napoli (1987–8), Prato (1988–9), Reggiana (1989–91) and Milan (1991–4), before retiring at the age of thirty-eight. Her travels indicate the febrile nature of a league where newly formed clubs could flourish through a wealthy backer, then just as abruptly fall away and even fold when the money dried up. In 1990 she was reported to be earning IR£15,000 a year. She won two league titles with Lazio (1979, 1980), one with Trani (1983/84), two with Reggiana (1989/90, 1990/91) and one with Milan (1991/92). Her team finished second on five occasions. She also won the Italian cup twice with Lazio (1977, 1984/85) and once with Trani (1982/83).

In the 1980s women's soccer became a reasonably big draw in Italy. The big-city clubs occasionally played their matches as a prelude to the men's match: as a result, she played before 50,000-strong crowds in places such as the San Siro Stadium in Milan. Home matches at provincial clubs, such as Trani, could draw up to 10,000 passionate fans who would embrace their successful women's teams as a source of local pride. In her first two seasons there, Trani narrowly lost out to Lecce for the league title. Both clubs hailed from Italy's deep south, and an intense rivalry developed between the teams and their respective fans.

She formed memorable partnerships with some of the league's most illustrious goal scorers, including Susanne Augustesen, Carolina Morace, Conchi Sánchez and Rose Reilly. During Trani's triumphant 1983/4 season, O'Brien, Morace and Reilly comprised one of the most potent attacking triumvirates in the league's history. She won four league titles (1983/4, 1989/90, 1990/91, 1991/92) playing behind Morace, who dominated Italian club soccer for much of the 1980s and 1990s. At the outset of her career, the younger Morace saw O'Brien as her role model. They became close, with Morace acting as godmother to O'Brien's only child, her son Andrea (b. 1987). O'Brien resumed playing competitive soccer just four weeks after giving birth, breastfeeding Andrea in the dressing room on match days.

Much to her regret, moving abroad all but prevented her from playing for her country again, as the Women's Football Association of Ireland (WFAI) could not cover her travel expenses. The WFAI did pay for her flight back for a crucial European Championship qualifier against the Netherlands, which ended scoreless in Dalymount Park, Dublin, on 29 April 1990. It was her fourth and final appearance for Ireland.

Following her mother's death in 1994, she retired from playing football and briefly lived in Ireland before pursuing a full-time coaching career in Italy. She had moved into coaching in 1990 by setting up a soccer school for children. In 1992 she obtained her coaching badges from the national football academy in Coverciano, Florence, and became involved in coaching at her club, Milan. Later, she coached Italian national underage teams and managed Lazio for a season (2005/06), but the club was in crisis, and she could not prevent its relegation. She also managed Civitavecchia for the 2007/08 season. The 2008 financial crash hit Italy hard with women's soccer suffering especially. Latterly, she worked as a childminder and cleaner. Retaining her infectious love of soccer and of Rome, she ran a soccer school for children on the beach near her apartment in Fregene, outside Rome.

Anne O'Brien died in Fregene on the 29 August 2016 following a short illness. Her ashes were brought back to Ireland where she gained recognition only after her death. The FAI paid tribute to her at the World Cup qualifier against Georgia on 6 October 2016. In 2019, she became the second woman to be inducted into the FAI Hall of Fame.

Helena Byrne

Sources

General Register Office Dublin (birth certificate); *Irish Independent*, 25 May, 15 July 1971; 25 February 1974; 3 June 1975; 15 April 1976; 8 September 1990; 8 June 1992; *Irish Press*, 8 March 1974; *Evening Herald*, 1, 9 June 1971; 20 May 1972; 25 January 1974; 27 April, 1 May 1990; *Cork Examiner*, 22 August 1973; *Kilkenny People*, 31 August 1973; *Sunday Independent*, 20, 27 January 1974; 17 February 1985; 19 October 2014; 4 September 2016; *Sunday Press*, 15, 22, 29 June, 6 July 1975; *Evening Press*, 1 August 1986; *The Irish Times*, 28 April 1990; 8 September 2016; Marco Sappino, *Dizionario del Calcio Italiano* (2000); Jean Williams, *Globalising women's football* (2013); *Irish Examiner*, 30 August 2016; 'Anne O'Brien', www.the42.ie/anne-obrien/news/; 'Anne O'Brien, footballer (1956–2016)', womensfootballarchive.org/2016/10/02/anne-obrien-footballer-1956-2016/; 'France—list of woman final tables', www.rsssf.com/tablesf/fran-womhist.html#75; 'Italy—list of woman final tables 1968–98', www.rsssf.com/tablesi/italwomhist.html; 'Anne O'Brien: the unknown legend of calcio', gentlemanultra.com/2015/08/18/anne-o-brien-the-unknown-legend-of-calcio/; 'From Inchicore to Italy—Irish soccer legend Anne O'Brien on Off the Ball', archive.vn/20150119003053/http:/www.newstalk.com/anne-obrien-on-off-the-ball; 'O'Brien—the flame that helped light a path...', www.echo.ie/sport/article/echo-sport-replay-o-brien-the-flame-that-helped-light-a-path-for-women-footballers-in-ireland; 'Calcio stories, Calcio stars: Anne O'Brien, parts i–iii', www.calciostories.com/ (all internet material accessed January–April 2021); information from Tony O'Brien (brother)

Vincent O'Brien

1917–2009

RACEHORSE TRAINER

(Michael) Vincent O'Brien was born 9 April 1917 at Clashganiff House near Churchtown, Co. Cork. His father, Dan O'Brien, a fox-hunting farmer who trained a few horses, lost his first wife, Helena, in childbirth while she was bearing their fifth child. Eighteen months later, he married his deceased wife's first cousin, Kathleen Toomey. This union yielded four children, of whom Vincent was the oldest. One of his two younger brothers, Phonsie, was an accomplished amateur jockey.

Vincent was devoted to horses from his earliest days and by the age of four could recite the pedigrees of the horses kept on his father's farm. He attended the national school in Churchtown before being sent at the age of ten to stay with his godfather, Dan O'Leary, in Bruff, Co. Limerick. There he attended the De La Salle Brothers' school. Three years later he transferred to the prestigious Jesuit College at Mungret, near Limerick. He was an intelligent pupil, but his main interest was horses and he left school at fifteen when he became apprenticed to the trainer Fred Clarke at Leopardstown, Co. Dublin. After a year he returned to assist his father at Clashganiff, taking unofficial charge of the horse training until his father's sudden death in summer 1943. The farm at Churchtown went to the family of Dan O'Brien's first marriage, and Vincent considered becoming a butcher until agreement was reached for him to rent the stables and for the younger family to remain at Clashganiff.

EARLY CAREER: NATIONAL HUNT, 1943–55

In 1944, his first year as a trainer, O'Brien pulled off the Irish autumn double at the Curragh: Good Days won the Cesarewitch and Drybob dead-heated for the Cambridgeshire; O'Brien had £2 each way on the double at 800–1, yielding £1,000. Cottage Rake then put him on the map. He overheard two vets discussing this fine horse, whose sale had twice fallen through because he suffered from a respiratory problem. 'But at his age, I don't think it will ever affect him', said one of the vets. O'Brien called wool merchant Frank Vickerman, 'the only man I knew with any money', and told him to buy the horse. Cottage Rake duly arrived at Churchtown and in autumn 1947 won the Irish Cesarewitch. The following year he won the Cheltenham Gold Cup. It was O'Brien's first time at an English racecourse.

On his second visit to Cheltenham's National Hunt Festival, in 1949, O'Brien achieved a remarkable double: the Champion Hurdle with Hatton's Grace (bought a year earlier for eighteen guineas) and a second consecutive Gold Cup with Cottage Rake. He completed a Gold Cup hat-trick with The Rake in 1950, also taking three consecutive Champion Hurdles with Hatton's Grace (1949–51). His fourth Gold Cup winner was Knock Hard (1953). Amid economic stagnation in Ireland, O'Brien's victories in major English races were a source of pride and inspiration for Irish people.

His record at the Cheltenham Festival from 1948 to 1959 was outstanding. At that time the Gloucestershire Hurdle (later the Supreme Novices Hurdle) was sometimes run in two divisions. O'Brien trained ten winners out of twelve runners during 1952–9 with his other two runners finishing second. In 1994 the Cheltenham Racecourse executive decided to change the name of one of the oldest festival races, the County Hurdle, to the Vincent O'Brien County Hurdle.

If Cheltenham was considered national hunt racing's premier festival, the Aintree Grand National was the most storied race, its four-and-a-quarter-mile distance over the most hazardous fences in steeplechasing making it the ultimate test for a trainer. And it was O'Brien's achievement in winning three consecutive Grand Nationals with three different horses between 1953 and 1955 that marked him out as truly exceptional. His first two Grand National winners, Early Mist and Royal Tan, had both been difficult horses to train; the third, Quare Times, defied interrupted preparations and unsuitably heavy conditions as O'Brien became the first trainer to claim three Grand Nationals in a row.

Betting was an all-important element of O'Brien's early success, notably on his annual visits to Cheltenham. He landed some legendary gambles. The English bookmaker William Hill, who had served in Ireland with the Black and Tans, remarked to O'Brien: 'It would have paid me to have had you shot years ago!' His success in betting, together with a bank loan, enabled him to buy Ballydoyle House, a 280-acre farm near Cashel in Co Tipperary, for £17,000, in 1950. It developed into the most sophisticated training establishment in Europe, increasing in size to over 600 acres.

In 1951 he met the young Jacqueline Wittenoom, an economics graduate from Western Australia, who was staying with a relative in Belfast. She and Vincent were married on 29 December 1951 in University Church, St Stephen's Green, Dublin. Jacqueline's parents were the Honorable Charles and Constance Patricia Wittenoom (née Hanrahan). Her father was the long-serving mayor of Albany Municipal Council and an elected member of the upper house of the Western Australian Legislative Council. An outstanding photographer, Jacqueline O'Brien authored and co-authored various books, including the official biography of her husband, and others dealing with his greatest horses, great Irish houses and castles, ancient Irish monuments, and the Irish Derby.

ON THE FLAT, 1953–72

O'Brien began concentrating on the flat, where the prize money was greater, and, as flat horses were not gelded, he could utilise more fully his knowledge of pedigrees and breeding. He had won the 1953 Irish Derby with Chamier;

then, in 1955 at Doncaster Sales, he met an American owner, John McShain, for whom he bought eight yearlings. Among them was Ballymoss, who, in 1957 came second in the English Derby and won the Irish Derby and the St Leger. The following year, Ballymoss won all the major middle-distance European races: Coronation Cup, Eclipse Stakes, King George VI and Queen Elizabeth II Stakes, and the Prix de l'Arc de Triomphe. By then McShain also owned O'Brien's brilliant staying mare, Gladness, who won the 1958 Ascot Gold Cup, Goodwood Cup and the Ebor Handicap carrying top weight.

During spring 1960, following the win of Chamier's son Chamour in a maiden race at the Curragh, the stewards of the Irish Turf Club informed O'Brien that the colt had proved positive for a minuscule amount of a substance 'resembling' an amphetamine derivative. Although it hardly made sense to dope a horse in a minor race with no betting involved, O'Brien's licence was withdrawn for eighteen months from 13 May. Many felt that O'Brien was targeted due to his success from outside the 'racing establishment' based around the Dublin and Kildare tracks. He was 'warned off' the turf and ordered to move away from his house and stables. O'Brien's brother Phonsie took over the licence at Ballydoyle, assisted by his other full brother, Dermot. When Chamour won the Irish Derby three months later, racegoers surrounded the weighing room chanting: 'We want Vincent'. O'Brien was fishing on the river Blackwater at the time; deeply patriotic, he felt like an exile in his own land.

Evidence was assembled from world authorities showing that the tests on Chamour purported to measure a substance that could not be isolated or measured in saliva and sweat samples. As a result of overwhelming scientific evidence and growing exasperation by the racing public, O'Brien's eighteen-month suspension was reduced to twelve months. Facing a libel action that they were certain to lose, the stewards of the Turf Club read out an apology to O'Brien on the steps of the supreme court and paid all legal costs. The trainer, who had asserted his innocence throughout, was vindicated though deeply scarred. He generously waived damages.

In 1962, Larkspur won O'Brien the first of his six Epsom Derbies. O'Brien won the Irish Oaks with Ancasta in 1964, following this the next year with the Oaks at Epsom with Long Look and the Irish Oaks with Aurabella. In 1966 he took the 1,000 Guineas at Newmarket with Glad Rags. O'Brien, who had first booked Lester Piggott as jockey for Gladness in 1958, was now using him whenever possible for his runners outside Ireland. After riding O'Brien's Valoris to victory in the 1966 Epsom Oaks, Piggott teamed up increasingly with O'Brien to form one of the most successful and enduring partnerships in racing history.

Since the 1950s O'Brien had cultivated rich American owners, becoming increasingly convinced of the virtues of American-bred horses. Many of the best European bloodlines had been sold to America during previous generations, and O'Brien's success with American-breds led to a renewal of European thoroughbred breeding strengths. In 1968 O'Brien sent out the handsome bay Sir Ivor (by Sir Gaylord), owned, like Larkspur, by the US ambassador to Ireland, Raymond Guest, to win the English 2,000 Guineas and the Epsom Derby. Bred at the famous Claiborne Farm stud in Kentucky, the horse went on to win the Champion Stakes at Newmarket and the Washington International.

That same year O'Brien inspected a colt at the Windfields Farm in Canada on behalf of the platinum magnate Charles

Engelhard. O'Brien advised against a purchase but recommended successfully that Engelhard instead buy another colt at the stud, a son of the then untried stallion Northern Dancer. This was the brilliant Nijinsky, regarded by many as the greatest racehorse of the twentieth century. Trained by O'Brien, the colt won races of the highest calibre over distances spanning six to fourteen furlongs during his two- and three-year-old career, including the Dewhurst Stakes in 1969 and the English triple crown (2,000 Guineas, Derby and St Leger) in 1970, when he also won the Irish Derby, and the King George VI and Queen Elizabeth Diamond Stakes.

Two years later O'Brien was back in the Derby winner's enclosure at Epsom with the enigmatic Roberto (by Hail to Reason). He won by a short head from the subsequent Prix de l'Arc de Triomphe winner, Rheingold. Roberto had fragile knees and required a left-handed track to show his best form. His performance in winning the inaugural Benson and Hedges Gold Cup (later the Juddmonte International) at York in 1972, beating the hitherto, and subsequently, unbeaten Brigadier Gerard by three-and-a-half lengths in course record time, was one of the greatest ever on a European racecourse.

OWNER AND BREEDER

Among O'Brien's owners was the Irish-American, Jack Mulcahy, who told him to invest in the horses he trained, thereby profiting from their prize money and, more importantly, their value at stud. O'Brien called this 'the best advice I ever got', and he subsequently owned shares in all the horses under his care. In 1973 he bought a majority share of a stud farm at Fethard near Ballydoyle called Coolmore. Later he was joined in this venture by the

British tycoon Robert Sangster and by John Magnier, who owned Castlehyde Stud at Fermoy. (Magnier later married O'Brien's daughter Susan.) The studs were merged, and the trio formed a syndicate to purchase yearlings with the pedigree and build to become champion racehorses and successful sires.

The O'Brien–Sangster–Magnier syndicate, which initially included wealthy American and European owners and was joined later by the Greek shipping magnate Stavros Niarchos, enjoyed over a decade of extraordinary success. They bought the finest yearling colts, mostly American bred and frequently by Northern Dancer. Trained at Ballydoyle to win major races, the successful horses would then breed at Coolmore, syndicated as stallions for millions of pounds. Thanks to a highly advantageous incentive introduced by the Irish government in 1969, none of the profits arising from Coolmore's stud fees were subject to tax.

O'Brien's role was crucial. There was no better judge of a yearling, and he had an unrivalled knowledge of pedigrees. He also had great business acumen, investing in Northern Dancer's progeny at a time when the stallion was unproved. His reputation encouraged wealthy investors; in 1975, just before the partnership became operational, O'Brien had sent seven horses to Royal Ascot, and six of them had won. The syndicate's first set of yearlings was bought in 1975 and included The Minstrel (by Northern Dancer), which won the Derby in 1977. That year, another of their purchases, Alleged (by Hoist the Flag), won the first of two consecutive victories in the Prix de l'Arc de Triomphe.

As a trainer, O'Brien was meticulous in his attention to detail and single-minded in his determination to bring out the best in his horses. When he thought that The Minstrel would be upset by the noise of the Epsom crowd, he had cotton wool stuffed in the horse's ears. He was the first trainer to weigh horses regularly and to install all-weather gallops. And while it became not unusual for a trainer to oversee more than 200 horses, O'Brien seldom had more than sixty, declaring that he could not have given enough individual attention to a larger number.

The success of the Ballydoyle syndicate was exemplified by two of its earliest purchases: the Minstrel, bought for $200,000 and later syndicated for $9 million, and Alleged, who cost $165,000 and was syndicated for $16 million. Almost overnight, the thoroughbred became a valuable international commodity. The sales at Keeneland, Kentucky, hitherto almost unknown territory for Europeans, with the exception of O'Brien, who had been a regular visitor from the 1960s, became an annual battleground for the wealthiest owners, with a growing interest from the Middle East. The bidding between the syndicate, leading American and European owners, and the Al Maktoum family of Dubai, raised the value of bloodstock to unimagined levels, climaxed by the sale of a yearling for $13.1 million to the Ballydoyle syndicate in 1985.

The syndicate also bought well-bred yearling fillies with the pedigrees to become successful brood mares when crossed with future Coolmore stallions. One such filly had the greatest impact on the early development of the Coolmore Stud brand. Fairy Bridge (by Bold Reason) was from a family that had yielded numerous champions for O'Brien. Purchased for just $40,000 at the Saratoga sales in 1976, she was trained by O'Brien to win her only two races as a two-year-old. At stud she produced the outstanding European sire of the twentieth century, Sadler's Wells (by Northern Dancer).

The winner of the Irish 2,000 Guineas, Eclipse Stakes and Irish Champion Stakes for O'Brien in 1984, Sadler's

Wells was champion sire in Britain fourteen times, three times in France and once in the United States, and also sired various future champion sires, including Galileo and Montjeu in Europe and El Prado (also trained by O'Brien) in the US. Sadler's Wells's dominance over nearly two decades helped Coolmore become the most powerful thoroughbred breeding operation in the world by the beginning of the twenty-first century.

O'Brien trained his sixth and final Epsom Derby winner, Golden Fleece (by Nijinsky), in 1982. He nearly attained a seventh two years later, when his brilliant Dewhurst Stakes and English 2,000 Guineas winner, El Gran Senor (by Northern Dancer), was narrowly beaten in a sensational finish by Secreto—trained by his son, David O'Brien. El Gran Senor went on to win the Irish Derby.

By the mid-1980s, Arab owners, particularly the Al Maktoum family, were investing apparently unlimited funds into flat racing. In response, O'Brien, Magnier, Sangster, Michael Smurfit and John Horgan launched Classic Thoroughbreds, a publicly listed company, to buy yearlings for Ballydoyle. The initial IR£12 million raised, however, proved no match for the Middle Eastern money. Shortly thereafter, bloodstock prices fell internationally, leaving little opportunity to recoup the initial outlay through stallion syndication.

Classic Thoroughbreds was wound up in 1991 but enjoyed some successes, most notably the victory of Royal Academy in the 1990 Breeders' Cup Mile at Belmont Park, New York. He was ridden by fifty-four-year-old Lester Piggott, whom O'Brien had persuaded to come out of retirement a few weeks earlier. Royal Academy (by Nijinsky) cost $3.5 million and was O'Brien's sole purchase at the 1988 Keeneland sales. He had the colt in peak condition for the New York race where Royal Academy came with a late run to secure a historic victory. Royal Academy became a successful Coolmore sire in Kentucky and Australia.

LATER LIFE

After his Breeders' Cup triumph, O'Brien gradually reduced his stable of horses and retired aged seventy-seven following the victory of Mysterious Ways at the Curragh in September 1994. During his career O'Brien had won 1,529 races in Ireland to the value of £5,789,460 and been champion Irish trainer thirteen times. He had twice been British champion trainer on the flat and twice over obstacles. Ballydoyle was incorporated into the Coolmore Stud holdings under the ownership of John Magnier, where it continued as one of the world's leading racehorse training centres.

A naturally shy and private individual, Vincent O'Brien was a devoted husband, parent and grandparent, who preferred to spend his free time with his family and close friends. Hugely intelligent, he had an engaging personality and an excellent sense of humour. In separate polls conducted by the *Racing Post* newspaper, O'Brien was voted the greatest national hunt trainer of the twentieth century, and the greatest flat trainer of the twentieth century. Furthermore, he helped to create the international surge in the value of bloodstock, which began in the 1970s and brought Ireland to the pinnacle of thoroughbred breeding.

His many honours included an honorary doctorate in law from the National University of Ireland; an honorary doctorate in science from the University of Ulster; honorary life membership of the Royal Dublin Society; a Cartier award for outstanding achievement in racing; and the George Ennor award for outstanding achievement from the UK Horserace Writers Guild.

Vincent and Jacqueline O'Brien had three daughters and two sons. Both sons became trainers. David trained the winners of the English, Irish and French derbies before the age of twenty-six. After retiring from racing, he became a successful winemaker at Vignelaure near Aix-en-Provence, France. Charles trained at Baronrath Stud near the Curragh; his father was one of his leading owners up to his death.

Latterly O'Brien and his wife purchased a house in Jacqueline's hometown of Perth, Western Australia, splitting their time between there and Ireland. Vincent died on 1 June 2009 at his Irish home in Straffan, Co. Kildare, aged ninety-two. Following a service at St Conleth's church, Newbridge, Co. Kildare, on 4 June 2009, his remains were cremated. His grave is in the Straffan churchyard. After his death in 2009, the National Stakes at the Curragh, the leading Irish race for two-year-olds and which O'Brien had won a record fifteen times, was renamed the Vincent O'Brien National Stakes. There is a life-size bronze statue of Vincent O'Brien in the village of Rosegreen, Co. Tipperary, and various memorabilia relating to his career are displayed in the museum at Coolmore Stud. His papers and other memorabilia are held by the O'Brien family.

P. Gerry McKenna

Sources

Ivor Herbert and Jacqueline O'Brien, *Vincent O'Brien's great horses* (1984); Raymond Smith, *Vincent O'Brien: the Master of Ballydoyle* (1990); Jacqueline O'Brien and Ivor Herbert, *Vincent O'Brien: the official biography* (2005); *Daily Telegraph*, 2 June 2009; *Independent* (London), 2 June 2009; *Guardian*, 2 June 2009; *The Irish Times*, 12 September 2009

This entry has been abridged for publication. The full version is available at www.dib.ie

Pat O'Callaghan

1906–91

Pat (Patrick) O'Callaghan was born 28 January 1906 at Knockanroe, Derrygallon, near Kanturk, Co. Cork, the second of three sons of Paddy O'Callaghan, farmer of Knockanroe, and his wife Jane (née Healy). After being educated locally, he won a scholarship, aged fifteen, to the Patrician Academy in Mallow, Co. Cork. A year later he passed the matriculation exam for the Royal College of Surgeons in Ireland in Dublin and in 1927 became Ireland's youngest medical graduate, aged twenty. Over the next four years, he pursued postgraduate studies in University College Cork (UCC) and held numerous temporary positions, including stints in the Royal Air Force medical corps at Halton, Buckinghamshire, and in hospitals in Dublin, in Cork and in Killarney, Co. Kerry.

His father, maternal uncle and brothers were noted sportsmen; his younger brother Con competed for Ireland at the 1928 Amsterdam Olympics in the decathlon and won that event at the 1932 Tailteann games. Pat played Gaelic football and hurling in his youth, rugby during his college years in Dublin. In adulthood he did some boxing and played senior rugby for UCC and Cork Constitution. But from an early age his main sporting focus lay in athletics, the weight throwing events particularly. He became interested in hammer throwing in 1925. At home in Cork for the summer, he did not have a hammer, then a costly piece of equipment, so he collected an old cannon ball from Macroom Castle, had it drilled at a foundry and fitted with a handle and wire, and used it to train at the family farm.

In 1927 he won the Irish hammer title with a throw of 142ft 3in. (43.36m) and improved to 162ft 6in. (49.53m) in retaining his title the next year. He qualified for the Olympics in Amsterdam, which he entered as an unknown with a previous best of 166ft 11in. (50.87m), as against three other contenders who had thrown well over 170ft (51.8m). His technique, moreover, was still rudimentary. The hammer event was staged on 30 July 1928 and, lying third after four rounds, with his penultimate attempt he threw 168ft 7in. (51.38m) to win by 10cm (4 in.). The first athlete representing an independent Ireland to be crowned Olympic champion, he declared 'the world has been shown that Ireland has a flag, that Ireland has a national anthem, and, in fact, we have a nationality' (*Irish Examiner*, 1 August 2018).

An outstanding all-round field athlete, over the following years he won events across Ireland and Europe, claiming six Irish titles in one afternoon in 1931. He won twenty-two Irish national titles, comprising three high jump titles (1930–2), five shot put titles (1930–32, 1934–5), one discus title (1931), six hammer titles (1927–8, 1930–2, 1935), four titles in the 56lb (25.4kg) hammer for distance (1928, 1930–2) and three titles in the 56lb for height (1927, 1930–31). Despite weighing sixteen stone (101.6kg)— he stood 6ft 1in. (1.85m)—he was an international-class high jumper, once clearing 6ft 4in. (1.93m) at a time when the world record was 6ft 7in. (2.01m). In the 1931 Swedish games at Stockholm, he broke the record for the hammer on European soil with a throw of 178ft 8.88in. (54.48m), before breaking it again a month later at Clonmel, Co. Tipperary, by throwing 183ft 11in. (56.06m).

He became assistant medical officer in St Luke's Mental Hospital, Clonmel, in January 1931. In 1932 he was granted three months paid leave to prepare for and compete in the Los Angeles Olympics, following which attempts were made by the Department of Local Government to have him pay his replacement's salary. The authorities relented after he successfully defended his Olympic title on 1 August 1932, despite struggling for the first four rounds because his spikes were too long for the concrete surface. With help from Bob Tisdall, who was hotfoot from winning gold for Ireland in the 400m hurdles, he filed down his spikes using a hacksaw before snatching victory with his last throw, which went 176ft 11in. (53.92m), 5ft (1.52m) beyond the mark. Declining an offer to star in the next *Tarzan* movie, he returned to Ireland where, as had been the case after his 1928 gold, he was hailed as a national hero.

Going on to win the American and British hammer throwing titles in 1933 and in 1934 respectively, he broke his European record with a throw in 1933 of 186ft 8.4in. (56.91m) at Enniscorthy, Co Wexford, and was the favourite for the 1936 Berlin Olympics. But in 1934 Ireland's National Athletic and Cycling Association (NACA) refused to accept the decision of the International Amateur Athletic Federation (IAAF) to recognise Northern Ireland as part of the UK for athletics purposes. NACA was suspended from international athletics, meaning no Irish team went to the 1936 Berlin Olympics. As an Irish nationalist, O'Callaghan endorsed NACA's decision, though it probably cost him a third gold medal. He watched from the stand while German hammer throwers took gold and silver at the Berlin Olympics by copying and further developing his technique of turning with the heel and toe.

Throughout his career, he continued to hone and experiment with his action, enabling him to execute his best hammer throws when he was past his physical prime. He effectively retired in 1937 after throwing 195ft 4.75in. (59.55m) at an event in Fermoy, Co. Cork, breaking the world record by more than 6ft (1.83m) with a hammer that turned out to be too heavy. As the IAAF still refused to sanction the NACA, the record was not internationally recognised. His unofficial world record was not surpassed until 1949.

He was dogged by an incident that occurred on 24 August 1930 when he participated in a Garda Síochána sports event in Mallow, Co. Cork. As he was throwing his hammer, the chain snapped, flinging the head into a crowd of spectators where it fractured a fifteen-year-old boy's skull. In June 1934 the boy's parents sued O'Callaghan and the event organisers in the high court. The Garda Síochána reached a settlement for £450 while O'Callaghan failed even to deny the claim of negligence, losing the case by default. In June 1936 a jury awarded damages of £2,500 against him. Married since 1934 to Kitty O'Reilly, a Clonmel woman, he had two young sons by then— another two sons and a daughter would follow—and was making about £300 a year as a dispensary doctor in Emly, Co. Tipperary, and from his general practice.

In May 1938 he left for America to take up what promised to be a lucrative professional wrestling contract. He engaged in over forty bouts in various US cities and acquitted himself well, excepting the occasion when an opponent went 'off script' and mauled him badly. Dissatisfied with his promoters' failure to make good on their financial promises, he returned to Ireland in October where he was adjudged bankrupt on 25 November 1938. His residence at Roseville, Western Road, Clonmel, was not in his name, and it is unclear whether he paid any of the £2,500 compensation. Resuming work as a dispensary doctor and general practitioner in the Clonmel area, he does not seem to have experienced financial hardship but remained in a state of technical bankruptcy for decades.

In 1960 he was the first person voted into the Texaco Hall of Fame. He managed the Clonmel Commerical senior Gaelic football team to three county championships (1965–7), later becoming the club's chairman and honorary president. Made a freeman of Clonmel in 1984, he was revered locally as a humble, jovial man, known for his kindness to his poorer patients. He kept active by fishing, shooting pheasant and training greyhounds. He died 1 December 1991 in Ardkeen regional hospital, Waterford, and was buried in Powerstown cemetery, Clonmel. A bronze statue of him was unveiled in Banteer, Co. Cork, in 2007. His son Hugh won twelve Irish national athletics titles (four shot put, four discus, two hammer, one javelin and one decathlon) and three Irish weightlifting titles, setting eight Irish shot put records and three Irish weightlifting records; he was also a successful weightlifting coach in the USA.

Paul Rouse

Sources

General Register Office Dublin (birth certificate); *Cork Examiner, passim*, esp.: 2 December 1991; *Irish Independent, passim; Irish Press*, 1 September 1932; 30 June, 15 November 1934; 24 August 1937; P. D. Mehigan ('Carbery'), *50 years of Irish athletics* (1944); William Dooley, *Champions of the athletic arena* (1946); David Guiney, *Ireland and the Olympics* (1976); *Nationalist (Tipperary)*, 17 January 1931; 7 December 1991; 10 November 2011; *The Irish Times*, 29 June 1993; Lindie Naughton and Johnny Waterson, *Irish Olympians* (1992); John Gleeson (ed.), *Fyffes dictionary of Irish sporting greats* (1993); Peter Matthews and Ian Buchanan, *The all-time greats of British and Irish sport* (1995); Henry Boylan, *A dictionary of Irish biography* (1998 edition); *Sunday Independent*, 1 August 1982; 31 August 2008; *Irish Examiner*, 1 August 2018; Margaret Molloy, *Martin Sheridan: Mayo's famous son, 1881–1918* (2018), 248, 250; 'Two Olympic Golds for Irish hammer thrower' [1966], www.rte.ie/archives/2017/0726/893067-pat-ocallaghan-olympic-hammer-thrower/; Tipp FM podcast, 'Hugh O'Callaghan, son of famous Olympian, Dr Pat O'Callaghan', soundcloud.com/tippfmradio/hugh-ocallaghan-podcast; 'Roll of Honour: Irish athletics champions: 1873–2014', www.athleticsireland.ie/downloads/statistics/Copy_of_ROH_Outdoor_1873-2014-Final_Version.pdf; 'Tipperary Athletics: the hammer corner', www.tipperaryathletics.com/forms/The%20Hammer%20Corner.html (all internet material accessed August 2021)

Nannie Power O'Donoghue

1843–1940

EQUESTRIAN AND AUTHOR

Nannie (Ann) Power O'Donoghue (née Lambert) was born 2 June 1843 and baptised as Ann Stewart Lyster Lambert in St Thomas Church of Ireland, Marlborough Street, Dublin. She was the youngest child of four daughters and one son of Charles Lambert, post office official, and his wife, Jane Catherine, daughter of Arthur J. Irwin, a landowner with estates in Connacht, and the widow of R. H. Mahon. Nannie had two half-brothers from her mother's first marriage. Charles Lambert came from an Anglo-Irish family with an estate at Castle Ellen, Co. Galway. The family had a large residence at 19 Upper Gloucester Street (latterly Sean MacDermott Street), Dublin. Nannie learned to ride aged fifteen, probably while visiting cousins in the country.

Her other interest was writing, and in 1868 she published her first novel, *The knave of clubs* (1868), which had a limited press run. The following year she married (2 November 1869) William Power O'Donoghue, member of a Cork merchant family, freemason and professor of music. They lived at 24 York Street, Dublin, a few doors up from Nannie's cousin Edward Carson. During the 1870s she published one book of poems, *Spring leaves* (1877), mostly sentimental verse, with one moving poem inspired by the suicide of her favourite sister, Lizzie.

She was in the first wave of British and Irish women to participate in hunting, which held a particular appeal for socially aspiring middle-class women. Among the most renowned equestrians of her day, she rode in the Phoenix Park, Dublin, and hunted with the Meath, Kildare and Ward Union packs. Her riding instructor and mentor was Allan MacDonogh (1800–81), a jockey who twice came second in the Grand National. Her best horse, Pleader, became famous through her writings. She was on Pleadar when she became the first woman to ride without mishap or refusal over the steeplechase courses of Punchestown, Fairyhouse and Baldoyle; this impressive feat, the more so for being done riding side saddle, involved navigating assorted hedges, hurdles, water-jumps, banks and stone walls.

When Elizabeth, empress of Austria, visited Ireland to pursue her love of hunting during February–March 1879, and again during February–March 1880, O'Donoghue rode with her, finding her to be a kindred spirit. At a large meet in Dublin (February 1880), attended by the empress, O'Donoghue noticed how badly dressed and badly seated many of the women were, and this led to her suggestion to the editor of the *Illustrated sporting and dramatic news* that she write a series of articles on etiquette for ladies on horseback (from October 1880). These were so immediately successful that they were collected into a book, *Ladies on horseback* (1881), which went through five editions and remained in print until 1904, selling strongly in New York, India and Australia; its success inspired a rash of imitators. She was asked to write a similar series for *Lady's Pictorial*, which was also gathered into a book. *Riding for ladies* (1887) sold 94,000 copies, was translated into five languages and remained in print until 1908.

Her two books on women's equestrianism were exhaustive, covering dress, tackle, mounting, seat, and all aspects of riding and care for horses. She interspersed her common-sense advice with stories of her adventures with the Meath, Kildare and Ward Union packs, until an accident in January 1881 cut short her riding career. Her articles were so influential that manufacturers and retailers of riding equipment would advertise their products as endorsed by Mrs. Power O'Donoghue. She helped pioneer the level side saddle and registered her disapprobation of bearing reins and other tackle that harmed horses.

In *Riding for ladies* she recounted her experiences of the growing conflict in Ireland between hunters and irate tenant farmers, and bemoaned the attendant proliferation of wire fencing, noting that this practice was designed at least partly to injure unwary riders. She dismissed the widespread opposition to hunting in Ireland in the 1880s as 'blind idiotcy' (*Riding for ladies*, 173), though she acknowledged that behind the sometimes-specious objections lay a deep-rooted animus towards landlordism. A staunch defender of landlords and of their favourite pastime, she argued that hunts stimulated economic activity in poor rural areas by drawing in wealthy outsiders. As for hunting itself: 'Who that has ever experienced these joys will be likely to forget them, or will fail to promote … so healthy and life-giving a sport?' (*Riding for ladies*, 173).

Ladies on horseback maintained that women riders needed pilots when hunting—pilots were men who would lead the woman rider over fences—though she did not practice what she preached; moreover, her second book declared experienced women riders had no such need. *Riding for ladies* also encouraged women to get involved in breeding, feeding and stable management, duties formerly left to men. Much of her advice was ahead of its time, the striking exception being her belief that women should ride side saddle rather than astride a horse: 'Nothing could be more ungraceful or unwomanly than for a woman to ride like a man' (*Nannie Lambert Power O'Donoghue*, 82). This long-held convention crumbled over the next generation, forcing her to concede in 1921 that riding astride was fine for young women with good figures. Her contradictory attitudes played a key role in making women's equestrianism socially acceptable by showing how women could become expert riders without forfeiting their femininity and respectability.

The success of her non-fiction helped sales of her novels. Her best work, *A beggar on horseback* (1884), sold 23,000 copies and is an amusing, sharply observed study of provincial society with intelligent and capable women characters. The O'Donoghues lost money with the crash of the Munster Bank in 1885, so Nannie's earnings contributed significantly to the household and, after her husband's death (22 September 1908), helped her support herself.

She moved then to Harold's Cross, Dublin, continuing to work as editor of the magazine *Irish Society*, and to write pieces for *The Irish Times* and *Lady's Pictorial*, amongst others. Her journalism shows her to be tory and unionist in her politics, censorious towards the latest high society fashions, supportive of social purity movements and a relentless campaigner for measures to alleviate poverty. She also opposed women's suffrage, despite being an enthusiastic advocate for women's right to work. Continuing to live in various parts of Dublin, she was a voluntary hospital worker during 1921–2. Her last home was the Standard Hotel on Harcourt Street where she died on 12 January 1940. She was buried in St Nicholas church, Galway.

Bridget Hourican

Sources

Irish Book Lover, vol. 2 (1910), 147; S. A. Allibone, *Critical dictionary of English literature and British and American authors living and deceased* (1959); *Burke's Irish family records* (1976); Hugh Oram, *The newspaper book* (1983); Anne Ulry Colman, *A dictionary of 19th century women poets* (1996); Olga E. Lockley, *Nannie Lambert Power O'Donoghue* (2001); Erica Munkwitz, 'Vixens of venery: women, sport and fox-hunting in Britain 1860–1914', *Critical survey*, vol. 24, no. 1, *Sporting Victorians* (2012), 74–87; Kate Wilkins, 'Mrs Anne (Nannie) Lambert Power O'Donoghue (1843–1940): Equestrian, Ascendancy writer and musician (1868–1916)', MA, University of Buckingham (2016); Stephanie Rains, 'Nannie Power O'Donoghue, 1843–1940', irishmediahistory.com/2016/08/23/nannie-power-odonoghue-1843-1940/ (internet material accessed September 2020)

This entry has been abridged for publication. The full version is available at www.dib.ie.

Kevin O'Flanagan

1919–2006

SPORTING ALL-ROUNDER

Kevin Patrick O'Flanagan was born 10 June 1919 in
Dublin, son of Timothy O'Flanagan, tobacconist, and
his wife Teresa (née McLaughlin). Raised in Terenure,
Dublin, he attended Christian Brothers School, Synge
Street, where he captained the school Gaelic football team

to the under-16 all-Ireland championship. Selected for the Dublin Gaelic football minor panel, he was dropped when the Gaelic Athletic Association (GAA) authorities discovered that he played soccer for Home Farm.

In soccer O'Flanagan played a senior season with Home Farm (1935/6), before joining Bohemians, making his first team debut aged sixteen. He remained with Bohemians, then an all-amateur team, for the following nine seasons, over which he scored ninety-four goals. A prolific scorer and crowd favourite, his blistering pace and terrific shot enabled him to play on the wing and at centre-forward. O'Flanagan's 1942/3 single-season scoring record for Bohemians of thirty-four goals in thirty-one games in all competitions stood until 2001. In the semi-final (May 1945) of the Inter-city cup against Distillery (Belfast), O'Flanagan scored two goals (one from the touchline) while his brother Michael (1922–2015) scored the winner. In the final Kevin captained Bohemians to victory over Belfast Celtic.

O'Flanagan scored on his senior international debut for Ireland (Football Association of Ireland (FAI)) in a 3–3 draw against Norway at Dalymount Park in his only World Cup qualifier (7 November 1937); aged 18 years, 150 days, he was Ireland's youngest international scorer until Robbie Keane in 1998. He scored two more goals in his best international performance away to Hungary on 18 May 1939 to rescue a 2–2 draw. Courted by English league clubs, he remained in Ireland to focus on his education, allowing him to compete in multiple sports.

While studying medicine at University College Dublin (UCD) from 1937 to 1945, he became vice-captain of the UCD Athletics Club (1940). After playing in two away soccer internationals, he returned to win the long jump title in the national student athletic championships in Dublin on 27 May 1939. He won numerous National Athletic and Cycling Association (NACA) national championships over the years: 60-yard dash (1939 and 1941), 100-yard dash (1941), and long jump (1938, 1939, and 1943); in the 1941 long jump competition he tied with David Guiney, to whom he generously conceded the medal. O'Flanagan's NACA athletics titles rendered him ineligible to compete for Ireland internationally, as only the Amateur Athletic Union of Éire was then recognised by the International Amateur Athletics Federation.

O'Flanagan took up rugby at UCD, appearing in two losing Leinster senior cup finals during the war. He also played for Lansdowne, partnering his brother Michael in the centre on his debut against Bective Rangers (21 September 1940). Selected mostly as wing-three-quarter, Kevin earned his first Leinster caps in 1940 against Ulster and Connacht. In January 1941, and again in 1943, he played for a 'Combined Universities' XV against a 'Rest of Ireland' selection, and appeared for an unofficial Irish XV against a British Army XV at Ravenhill, Belfast (February 1942). Although not a great defender, he combined searing pace with intelligent, creative running, dubbed the 'O'Flanagan waltz'. During 1944–5 the O'Flanagan brothers played together regularly both in soccer for Bohemians and in rugby for Lansdowne. But for the second world war, O'Flanagan would have accrued more soccer and rugby caps.

After qualifying from UCD as a doctor in 1945, he worked as a general practitioner in Ruislip, Middlesex. O'Flanagan contacted Arsenal and was invited to train. Offered professional terms, instead he signed with Arsenal as an amateur (May 1946), which allowed him to also pursue both his post-graduate medical training and his rugby career. In October 1945 he scored on his debut for Arsenal in a 2–6 loss to Charlton Athletic in the Football League South. Arsenal's manager, George Allison, held O'Flanagan to be the hardest kicker of a dead ball he had ever seen. A committed amateur, O'Flanagan would only accept his train fare to attend training and refused match day meal vouchers, noting he had to eat anyway. During the 1945/6 season he made eighteen appearances as centre-forward or right-winger for Arsenal, scoring eleven goals. With the resumption of the Football League proper in 1946/7, he played a further fourteen league games for Arsenal, scoring three goals, alongside two FA Cup appearances, scoring two goals. His natural fitness allowed him to compete at the highest level while missing training sessions; abstaining from smoking and alcohol also helped. From 1945 to 1949, while invariably playing soccer on Saturday, he played rugby on Sunday with London Irish, often as the team's star player and goal-kicker.

On consecutive weekends he played rugby in an unofficial international against France (26 January 1946) and soccer for an Irish Football Association (IFA) selection, effectively Northern Ireland, in an unofficial international against Scotland (2 February 1946). He earned three further FAI soccer caps while an Arsenal player, his last against Portugal (4 May 1947). In total, O'Flanagan won ten international soccer caps, two with the IFA (in 1946) and eight with the FAI (1937–47), scoring three goals. In the first ever soccer match between England and an FAI team representing an independent Ireland (30 September 1946), he and Michael were the only amateurs on the Irish team and the first brothers to appear together in soccer for Ireland.

The O'Flanagan brothers achieved the unique distinction of being awarded international caps in both rugby and soccer. Kevin won his only official rugby cap in Ireland's first meeting with Australia in a 3–16 loss in Dublin (6 December 1947); Michael's only rugby cap came against Scotland in a 6–0 victory in Dublin (28 February 1948) during the 1948 Grand Slam. Kevin could have earned more caps had he committed exclusively to rugby; the Irish rugby selectors frowned on his involvement with soccer.

O'Flanagan was appointed to the medical committee of the UK Olympic committee. Advising on medical services to national teams at the 1948 London Olympic Games, he also ran the injury clinic serving competitors at Wembley stadium. Specialising in orthopaedics, in July 1949 he went into practice in sports injuries with Bill Tucker, a former England rugby international. O'Flanagan's commitment to his medical career limited his Arsenal appearances, and after stints with non-league Corinthian Casuals (1947/8) and Barnet FC (1948/9), he played six times for second-division Brentford in 1949/50 before retiring (temporarily) from soccer owing to a recurring ankle injury.

He returned to Dublin and commenced his own practice on 1 March 1952 at 46 Merrion Square, later moving in May 1961 to 23 Upper Fitzwilliam Street, which was also his residence. During the 1951/52 season he played a further ten games for Bohemians, scoring another three goals, bringing his total for the club to 97 in 148 appearances. By the mid-1950s his sporting exploits were limited to charity football matches and golf. As a member of Portmarnock and Milltown golf clubs, he was a prominent amateur on the Irish club circuit over the next two decades. He also played competitive lawn tennis for

Templeogue Tennis Club and was a pavilion member of Fitzwilliam Lawn Tennis Club.

O'Flanagan built up a successful sports medicine practice while acting as honorary medical officer to various teams and sporting associations, including Bohemians and the Dublin GAA panel. The inaugural president of the Irish Sports Medicine Association (1970), he spent six years on the sports medicine committee of the Council of Europe. From 1967 he chaired the National Association for Rehabilitation, having been a director since 1960, and sought to improve facilities and programmes for those with mental and physical disabilities.

Serving as honorary medical officer to the Irish Olympic team for four Olympics (1960–72) and as a vice-president of the Olympic Council of Ireland (OCI), he was appointed in 1976 to the International Olympic Committee (IOC) as Ireland's representative. He served on the IOC's medical commission (1980–94) and on the Olympic programme (summer) commission (1993–4), before retiring from the IOC in 1995. His largely unpaid and generally exemplary service over five decades to the Olympic movement coincided with its fraught transition away from a voluntary, amateur ethos. In March 1999 a report commissioned by the New South Wales government into the awarding of the 2000 Olympic games to Sydney found that the Sydney bid committee had violated IOC guidelines by giving gifts to IOC members but concluded that no bribery or corruption had taken place. O'Flanagan was named as one of those IOC members who had benefited, receiving tickets, return flights and accommodation to attend the Wimbledon tennis finals in 1992.

One of the greatest Corinthians in the history of Irish sport and one of the best-known sporting figures in mid-twentieth century Ireland, O'Flanagan was voted into the Caltex (later Texaco) Hall of Fame (1965) and inducted into the Opel Sports Hall of Fame (1996). He retired from medicine and sports administration in 1993 and moved to Sutton, Co. Dublin. He died unmarried on 26 May 2006 in Dublin and was survived by his younger brothers Michael and Charlie (who also played soccer for Bohemians), and his sister Trixie.

Turlough O'Riordan

Sources

General Register Office Dublin (birth certificate); *Irish Independent, passim,* esp.: 4 June 2006; *The Irish Times, passim,* esp.: 26 August 2006; *Irish Press, passim*; *The official report of the organising committee for the XIV Olympiad* [*c*.1951]; Edmund Van Esbeck, *One hundred years of Irish rugby* (1974); Peter Bills, *Passion in exile: 100 years of London Irish RFC* (1988), 68; Stephen McGarrigle, *Green Gunners: Arsenal's Irish* (1991); Donal Cullen, *Ireland on the ball* (1993), 23–32; Bill Mahon, 'The Olympic bribery scandal', *Journal of Olympic History*, vol. 8, no. 2 (May 2000); *Sunday Times*, 28 May 2006; *Daily Telegraph*, 16 June 2006; *Independent* (London), 19 June 2006; *Guardian*, 22 June 2006; Gerard Farrell, 'The 1945 Inter-City Cup: War, goals, controversy and death by corner kicks', 1 October 2015, bohemianfc. com/?p=9377 (internet material accessed October 2021); Stephen Bourke, 'The Bohemian Gunner' [profile of O'Flanagan], *Bohemians Programme,* summer 2020, vol. 72, no. 5, 40–43

This entry and the related sources have been abridged for publication. The full version is available at www.dib.ie.

Joan O'Reilly

1924–2014

HOCKEY PLAYER

Joan O'Reilly was born 17 September 1924 in Dublin, one of three daughters and three sons of James O'Reilly, a prominent member of the Dublin Master Victuallers' Association, and his wife Mary (née Hall). Her father traded from 33 Sundrive, Crumlin, Dublin, where the family also lived until they moved (*c.*1942) to 125 Galtymore Road, Crumlin. Joan attended the private

Loreto junior school, 55 St Stephen's Green, Dublin, before gaining her secondary education at the linked (1936–43) Loreto College, where she played hockey. In the final of the 1942 Leinster Senior Schoolgirls' Hockey Cup, O'Reilly captained the Loreto St Stephen's Green side to victory against Dominican Convent, Sion Hill, Dublin, and scored the only goal, in extra time.

She competed in sprint events, mostly the 100-yards and 200-yards, at athletics meetings in the Dublin region from 1939 onwards. Playing camogie around this time, O'Reilly jointly won, with Doreen Rodgers, the Gaelic Athletic Association Dublin County Board Camogie Sports Championships, held at St James's Park, Crumlin, in May 1939. O'Reilly won the 100-yards race in 12.4 seconds. Winning the 100-yards race at the Civil Service Championships, 30 June 1940, in 12.6 seconds, accorded her the best time in Ireland that year. On 26 June 1943 she again claimed the best time, winning the 100-yards at the Kilkenny sports in 12.2 seconds.

Competing with the Crusaders Athletics Club short-lived 'women's section' (c.1947–51), she was good enough to have represented Ireland at the July 1948 Olympic Games in London. O'Reilly, however, was not considered for selection due to the prevailing widespread conservative antipathy to women participating in 'public' sports such as track and field events. Five women represented Ireland at the Olympics, one fencer and four artists. After the games, at a meet in Belfast against the Australian Olympic team on 16 August 1948, O'Reilly placed second in the 100-yards behind Shirley Strickland, who had won bronze in London. On 26 August, at the Clonliffe Harriers Sports, Lansdowne Road, Dublin, she placed third in the 100-yards, won by Fanny Blankers-Koen, who had taken gold in London. In July 1949 the newly formed Women's Athletic Association of Ireland held events alongside the Crusaders meet at Lansdowne Road stadium. O'Reilly won both the 100- and 200-yards events.

The opposition of the Roman Catholic hierarchy (especially Archbishop John Charles McQuaid) to women competing publicly in athletic sports led O'Reilly and many other women of her generation to turn to team sports. Playing club hockey from 1942 for Old College (later renamed Old Alexandra), she joined Muckross Hockey Club in 1945. On the Muckross first XI from 1946, captaining them from the mid-1950s, she featured regularly for Leinster in inter-provincial competition from 1949. Making her debut for Ireland in the 3–2 victory over Scotland (5 March 1949) in Belfast, O'Reilly became a stalwart of the international team over the next decade, accumulating 34 caps.

O'Reilly featured in all three 'home championship' matches in 1950, including a 5–3 victory over England in Belfast (who had not lost to Ireland since 1908), as Ireland clinched the Triple Crown. She scored in Ireland's 4–0 victory over Belgium in Dublin, 19 April, to close out Ireland's most successful season up to that point. Part of a dominant Muckross team, which competed with Pembroke Wanderers Hockey Club for league and cup honours through the 1950s, she captained Muckross to the rarely achieved triple of Leinster Senior League, the Leinster Senior Cup and the Irish Senior Cup in 1954. At her best on the right wing, where her positional intelligence, blistering pace and adept crossing was most impactful, her skilful shooting and stick-work allowed her on occasion to play centre-forward for Muckross, for whom she was a prolific scorer. Vera McWeeney, the doyen of

Irish hockey journalism, recalled O'Reilly 'bamboozling opposing defences with her astounding speed and setting up scoring chances for her inside forwards' (*Evening Herald*, 15 October 1959).

Playing at international hockey tournaments (Irish players paying their own costs) in South Africa (1950), England (1953) and the Netherlands (1959), O'Reilly revelled in such competitions, which brought teams together for prolonged periods. She captained the Irish team that toured the USA in October–November 1954, winning 22 of their 24 matches, drawing twice with the US national team.

Upon her retirement from playing for Muckross, Leinster and Ireland in 1959, O'Reilly turned to umpiring, gaining her 'A' badge in 1965. She officiated at international fixtures over the coming decades. Instrumental in the formation of the Irish Umpires' Association, she was deeply involved in the organisation and management of hockey in Ireland. Coaching Muckross for many years, she was also a Leinster selector and an Ireland selector from the 1960s onwards. She managed the Irish teams that competed in the International Federation of Women's Hockey Association (IFWA) tournament in Cologne, Germany (1967), and in the second IFWA world championships in Vancouver, Canada (1979). Frequently an official delegate of the Irish Ladies' Hockey Union (ILHU) at international fora, O'Reilly was chairperson of the Women's Hockey Board of Great Britain and Ireland in the late 1970s, which selected the joint Great Britain–Ireland Hockey team at that time, as well as organising the annual 'home nations' competition. She served as president of the Leinster branch of the ILHU (1973–78) and of the ILHU nationally (1977–78), and was awarded honorary life membership of the ILHU (1986). One of the inaugural inductees into the Irish Hockey Hall of Fame (2006), O'Reilly was a prominent figure in Irish hockey over four decades, regarded as one of the greatest hockey players of her generation.

A keen member of Grange Golf Club, Rathfarnham, Dublin, O'Reilly formed a formidable foursomes golfing partnership with her Ireland teammate and close friend, goalkeeper Johnnie Lambert. Elected Lady Captain (1964), she inaugurated the Ladies' Captain's show there.

From their shared butcher's premises in Crumlin, she focused on dispensing pig-meat, her brother James on selling beef. Their sister Angela ran an adjacent drapery shop. Joan was well known for gifting fine turkey and ham prizes for the Grange Golf Club's fundraising events and competitions. Active in Crumlin Civil Defence, she was a leading business and community figure in the Crumlin area, as likely to offer advice on taxation as to support community endeavours in the broadest sense. Later moving to live in Rathfarnham, she was a board member of Donnybrook Hospital, Dublin. She was also an avid bridge player and enjoyed travel. Modest and unassuming, she was widely respected and enjoyed the company of friends.

Joan O'Reilly died on 10 January 2014 at the Belmont Nursing Home, Stillorgan, Co. Dublin, where she had lived for some time. After a funeral mass in Terenure College Chapel, Terenure, Dublin, she was buried in Bohernabreena cemetery, Co. Dublin.

Turlough O'Riordan

Sources

General Register Office Dublin (birth certificate); *The Irish Times, passim,* esp.: 1 February 2014; *Evening Herald, passim; Irish Independent, passim; Irish Press, passim; Belfast News Letter,* 16 August 1948; *Thom's directory of Ireland for the year 1955* (1955), 911, 1501; *Belfast Telegraph,* 14 January 1967; Padraig Griffin, *The politics of Irish athletics, 1850–1990* (1990), 253–8; *Crusaders Golden Jubilee: celebrating 50 years of athletics* [*c.*1992]; Irish Ladies' Hockey Union, *The first hundred years 1894– 1994: a centenary history* (1996), *passim,* esp.: 54–5; John W. Brant, *Irish women's athletics 1891–1946: so there was none? The previously untold story* (*c.*2000); 'Death of Ireland hockey great Joan O'Reilly', www.rte.ie/sport/hockey/2014/0111/497190-death-of-ireland-hockey-great-oreilly/ (internet material accessed November 2020); information from Gladys Ruddock; information from IBVM (Loreto), Institute and Irish Province Archives

Paddy Perry

1909–83

HANDBALL PLAYER

Paddy (Patrick Joseph) Perry was born 19 March 1909 in Boyle, Co. Roscommon, one of four children of Henry Perry, labourer, and Kate Perry (née Harte) of St Joseph's Terrace, Boyle. Educated locally, he grew up playing hand-ball in Johnny Casey's ball-alley in Boyle and claimed his first national titles in 1929 when he won the national junior softball singles title, and the junior doubles title with fellow Boyleman Tom Gaughran. He was also a member of the Roscommon junior Gaelic football team that won the Connacht junior football championship that same year. He went on to dominate the softball variety of handball in Ireland in the 1930s, winning eight singles titles in a row (1930–37), a record unsurpassed until Michael 'Ducksie' Walsh in 1993. He also won two national doubles titles (1932–3), with fellow Roscommon man Alfie Mullaney, a teacher from Ballymore. In addition, he won a senior hardball doubles title in 1936, although he rarely played that form of the game.

Initially an insurance agent, he joined An Garda Síochána in 1931, serving in Kilkenny, Dublin and Wicklow for the rest of the decade. Garda commissioner General Eoin O'Duffy, who was also the first president of the Handball Council, identified sport as an important element in raising the public profile and morale of the new police force, and Perry was one of a number of garda players who helped to create a wider public interest in handball.

From 1929 to 1938 Perry remained undefeated in singles softball competition, and his victories included the Tailteann Games competition (1932). His only real rival in handball in this period emerged towards the end of his career, with the arrival of the great John Joe Gilmartin of Kilkenny. Perry narrowly defeated Gilmartin 3–2 in the 1937 singles final before losing the 1938 and 1939 finals to him, the latter game being regarded by many observers as one of the finest softball games of all time. He attributed his decline to the permanent damage done to his hands during the fiercely contested 1936 senior hardball final, when he discarded the protective strap around his hand and made no allowances for the harder pigskin in his ball striking.

Despite Perry's dominance of the singles game, he was not so successful in doubles competition, with just two senior titles to his name. It has been suggested that his all-action style of play did not lend itself to doubles. His partner in those victories, Alfie Mullaney, called him 'the greatest of all players in the softball code but the most difficult to partner' (*The story of handball*, 150). Perry was in many people's eyes the complete handball player: clever, fast, strong and always courteous to referees and opponents. His beautiful serve invariably ran only inches below the board at the top of the sidewalls, making it difficult to return.

A talented all-round sportsman, he played Gaelic football for the Garda club in Dublin, winning three Dublin senior football championships (1933–5), and for the Dublin senior team, winning a Leinster medal in 1933. Earlier he had played for the Sligo Rovers soccer team under an assumed name. Returning to the garda depot in the Phoenix Park, Dublin, in 1939, he spent the rest of his career there before retiring in 1972, after almost forty-one years with the force. In 1940 he married Margaret Roche, from Cork; they had five children. He died 22 April 1983 at his home in Palmerstown, Co. Dublin. In 1969 he was the inaugural member of the Roscommon Sports Stars Hall of Fame.

Jim Shanahan

Sources

Ray Doherty, *Handball* (1970); 'The handball champions', 49–51, *Jubilee: a souvenir of 50 historic years of sport in the Garda Siochana* (1972); Irish Handball Council, *Irish Handball* (1974); *Irish Independent*, 23 April 1983; *Roscommon Herald*, 29 April 1983; Tom Keroy (ed.), *Roscommon GAA Annual* (1984); Tom McElligott, *The story of handball* (1984); Owen McCann, *Greats of Gaelic games* (1984); Eoghan Corry (ed.), *Gaelsport GAA Youth Annual* (1985); Tony Conboy, 'Friday, February 19, 2010', tony-conboy.blogspot.com/2010/02/scor-in-boyle-boyle-was-active-club-in.html (internet material accessed November 2020)

Sean Purcell

1928–2005

Sean Purcell was born in Dublin Road, Tuam, Co. Galway, on 17 December 1928, the son of John Purcell, journalist and newsagent of Dublin Road, and his wife Norah (née Kilkenny). Successively educated in Tuam at the Presentation Convent, the Tuam Christian Brothers School and St Jarlath's College, he was a bright pupil who excelled at various sports, Gaelic football especially. He was selected for both the Galway minor team and the Connacht colleges team during 1946–7, winning an inter-provincial championship with Connacht in 1946. He played in midfield for the St Jarlath's side that reached consecutive all-Ireland colleges finals (1946–7), winning latterly.

With his club, Tuam Stars, he won a Galway county minor title in 1945 and was on the senior team by 1947. While studying at St Patrick's teacher training college in Drumcondra, Dublin (1947–9), he played club football with Erin's Hope. In autumn 1947 he made his senior debut for Galway in the league, emerging as one of the stars of the county team during the 1948 championship. He missed Galway's 1949 senior championship first-round defeat due to college exams, allowing him to win a Connacht provincial medal that year with the junior county team.

Having qualified in 1949, he worked as a primary school teacher, first in Co. Mayo and then from 1955 in Strawberry Hill school at Dunmore, Co. Galway, eight miles from his Tuam residence. From 1950 he was a part-time student at University College Galway (UCG), graduating BA in 1953. He picked up a Sigerson cup medal with the UCG football team in 1950, by which time he was considered one of the best footballers in the country. First selected to play for Connacht in the Railway Cup in 1949, he remained on the provincial team for thirteen years.

Contemporaries hailed him as the most complete and natural footballer they had seen, combining intelligence, strength, athleticism, courage and skill. He regularly switched positions during a match and could play anywhere down the middle of the pitch, except in goals, being most effective at centre-half-forward. Not especially tall at 5ft 11in. (1.8m), he was a superb fielder, while his flawless technique enabled him to solo the ball at speed and to jink past defenders. Slight and speedy as a youth, he weighed over 14st. (88.9kg) by his late twenties, his upper body strength compensating for the loss of mobility even as he remained quick over short distances. He was an accurate and powerful kicker off both feet, invariably the designated free taker, and could land points from sixty yards; goals were produced (directly or indirectly) by his fierce long-range shots.

He assumed the captaincy of his club and county in the early 1950s, but during this period the weakness of both obliged him to occupy himself during the summer by taking up golf. Tuam Stars revived in 1952, and he ended up accumulating ten county medals (1947, 1952, 1954–60, 1962) and three Connacht titles (1955–7) with his club. Tuam's dominance, however, intensified the inter-club factionalism within the county setup. Having begun as a midfielder or a half-forward for Galway, he switched first to centre-half-back and then to full-back.

When Galway faced Mayo in the first round of the 1954 championship, Purcell was enraged by the indifference of the county officials and of some of his teammates. He proceeded to give one of the great full-back displays, as Galway defeated a heavily favoured Mayo team that deployed three different forwards against him. Galway eventually lost that year's All-Ireland semi-final to Kerry, who had been winning comfortably until Purcell's move into midfield sparked his team's revival. This led to his re-emergence as a playmaker at centre-half-forward.

In 1955 Galway lost dismally to Roscommon in the first round of the championship, and Purcell became embroiled in a divisive controversy over the decision to order a replay of a match won by his club. He spoke forceful-ly at the annual county football convention in January

1956, attributing Galway's inconsistency to poor morale and an unwieldy management structure. A more sharply defined management hierarchy was established with the players allowed a greater say. When the Galway squad was given the right to elect its captain, however, it spurned Purcell, even though he was the incumbent. He swallowed his pride, as team spirit improved and the players trained assiduously for the 1956 championship.

Purcell's optimism reflected the blossoming partnership he had struck up in the Galway colours with his childhood friend Frank Stockwell. Tuam and Galway colleagues since the late 1940s, until autumn 1955 they never played together at inter-county level in the positions that made them famous: Stockwell as full-forward and Purcell as centre-half-forward. Their interplay, movement and positional switches baffled defenders and were largely improvised, relying on an understanding honed by years of playing together. Typically, Purcell would win possession, beat a defender, attract another and pass to the unmarked Stockwell in a scoring position.

Orchestrated by Purcell, the Galway forwards had by summer 1956 cohered into the devastating attacking unit that powered Galway to the 1956 all-Ireland and the 1957 National Football League titles. Purcell and Stockwell enshrined themselves in Gaelic football lore by ripping asunder a highly rated Cork defence in the first half of the 1956 all-Ireland final, giving a dazzling exhibition of fluid attacking play. The *Irish Press* journalist Mick Dunne dubbed Purcell and Stockwell the Terrible Twins of Tuam—the moniker stuck.

Galway failed to train properly for the ensuing two championships (1957–8), losing narrowly in consecutive all-Ireland semi-finals, as opponents learned how to neutralise an attack that was too reliant on the Terrible Twins. With Stockwell hampered by injury, Purcell could not quite carry his team to another all-Ireland. He captained Galway to the 1959 all-Ireland final, but the team had peaked and lost to Kerry.

In 1962 he retired from inter-county football with an all-Ireland (1956), a National League (1957) and six Connacht medals (1954, 1956–60). He also won Railway Cup medals with Connacht in 1951, 1957 and 1958 (in 1958 as captain). He was selected as centre-half-forward for the Gaelic football teams of the century (1984) and millennium (1999). For the former, in which the *Sunday Independent* invited the public to submit their choices, he received ninety per cent of the votes for centre-half-forward, the highest individual vote for any player in any position.

Pursuing a political career with Fine Gael, he was co-opted onto the Tuam town council, running unsuccessfully in the 1961 and 1965 general elections for the Galway East constituency. From the mid-1950s he became involved in the administration of the Gaelic Athletic Association, being prominent in the late 1960s among those members who argued successfully for repealing the rule banning members from playing 'foreign games'. He served as chairman of the Galway football board (1971–5), as selector for the Galway football team (early 1980s and mid-1990s), and as president of the Galway football board (1991–2000, 2002–04).

Personable and unassuming, he was a popular figure in Tuam, where he was universally addressed as 'Master'. A road in Tuam was named after him (1999), and he received an honorary doctorate from National University of Ireland Galway (2001). Spending most of his teaching career as principal at Strawberry Hill, he retired in 1988 to manage his mother's newsagent's in Tuam before selling the leasehold in 1999. He owned and trained greyhounds, and enjoyed socialising, singing and gambling.

In 1961 he married Rita Shannon. They had four daughters and two sons before the marriage ended. His son John played for the Galway senior football team in the mid-1980s. Sean Purcell died 27 August 2005 after a short illness, in the Blackrock Clinic, Co. Dublin, and was buried in the Tuam cemetery.

Terry Clavin

Sources

General Register Office Dublin (birth certificate); *Connacht Tribune, passim,* esp.: 2 September 2005; *The Irish Times, passim,* esp.: 3 September 2005; *Irish Press, passim; Irish Independent, passim; Connacht Sentinel, passim; Sunday Independent, passim;* Raymond Smith, *The football immortals* (1968 edition), 191–2, 227–39; (1995 edition), 10; Pádraig Puirséal, *The GAA in its time* (1982), 328–32; Brian Carthy, *The football captains* (1993), 240–5; John Gleeson (ed.), *Fyffes dictionary of Irish sporting greats* (1993); Owen McCann, *The AIB book of the record makers of Gaelic games* (1996), 98; Micheál Ó Muircheartaigh, *From Dún Síon to Croke Park: the autobiography* (2004), 37–42; Seamus McRory, *The All-Ireland dream* (2005), 39–51; *Connacht Telegraph,* 31 August 2005; Sean Óg Ó Ceallacháin, *Giants of Gaelic football* (2007), 208–12; John Scully, *The best of the west* (2008), 2–9, 132–3

This entry and the related sources have been abridged for publication. The full version is available at www.dib.ie.

Nicky Rackard

1922–76

HURLER

Nicky (Nicholas) Rackard was born 28 April 1922 in Killann, Rathnure, Enniscorthy, Co. Wexford, third child and eldest son among five sons and four daughters of Robert Rackard, farmer, publican and grocer, and Anastasia Rackard (née Doran). The family had a 120-acre mixed farm with licensed retail business in Killann and a similar business at nearby Caim.

Nicky was educated at Rathnure national school and boarded at St Kieran's College, Kilkenny city, where he showed great promise on hurling teams that won provincial and all-Ireland colleges titles, and on a Leinster selection that won an inter-provincial colleges title (1940). Powerfully built and phenomenally strong, he won high jump and long jump competitions, including a county youth title in the latter, and won junior and minor hurling medals with club (Rathnure) and county. While studying (from 1941) in Dublin at the Veterinary College, Ballsbridge, he won a Co. Dublin senior club hurling title with Young Irelands (1943). Qualifying as a veterinary surgeon in 1949, he practised first in Carnew, Co. Wicklow, and from 1953 in Bunclody, Co. Wexford, where he also farmed.

Beginning his senior inter-county hurling career in 1942, throughout the 1940s Rackard excelled at midfield and centre-forward on generally mediocre Wexford teams, losing the one Leinster final that they contested (1944). Displaying a range of hurling artistry, he was a skilful over-head and ground striker, and a powerful shooter. About 1950 he shifted position to full-forward and changed his style of play. A heavy drinker from his teens, he was putting on weight, losing pace and declining in all-round skills, but became expert at close-range shooting, resulting in prodigious feats of scoring. Tall and burly, he fearlessly challenged defenders with his Herculean strength, striking split-second shots of immense power and deadly accuracy. Especially renowned were his pile-driving twenty-one-yard frees aimed at goal, dubbed 'Rackard specials' by broadcaster Michael O'Hehir.

Rackard's individual prowess and charisma inspired a revival of hurling in Wexford, culminating in the great county teams of the 1950s, which won four provincial championships (1951, 1954–6), two oireachtas tournaments (1951, 1953), one National Hurling League title (1956), and two all-Ireland championships (1955–6; the county's first since 1910). During the first half of the decade, as Wexford hovered on the threshold of greatness, they suffered numerous heart-breaking near misses, defeated in the finals of many competitions, often in thrilling matches. Over the last eight years of Rackard's inter-county career, Wexford contested every Leinster final (1950–57), seven consecutive oireachtas finals (1950–56) and five league finals. These Wexford teams also included Rackard's brothers Bobbie and Billy, both backs. The 1951 side (captained by Nicky), which won the county's first Leinster title in thirty-three years, but lost the all-Ireland final to Tipperary, also included a fourth brother, Jimmy.

After scoring five goals and three points in the 1954 Leinster final against Dublin, Nicky scored an astonishing twenty-eight points (7–7, a championship individual record) against Antrim in the all-Ireland semi-final. In the all-Ireland final, however—one of the most celebrated ever, before a record attendance for a hurling final of 84,856—he was held to only a point from play by a cagey Cork defence, as Wexford lost by the low score of 1–9 to 1–6. During the next two seasons, Wexford won 33 out of 34 consecutive inter-county matches, the lone defeat coming in the 1955 league final, when all three Rackard brothers were absent owing to their father's death one week earlier. Nicky was the top-scoring inter-county hurler in both seasons, with 155 points (35–50) in nineteen matches in 1956 (a record subsequently broken in 1972). Two of his most acclaimed performances occurred in 1956, as Wexford swept all major inter-county honours.

In the league final, with Wexford held to one point in the first half and trailing by fifteen to Tipperary, he rallied the side with a rousing dressing-room speech and led a remarkable second-half comeback to a four-point victory. In the all-Ireland final against Cork, he secured Wexford's victory (by 2–14 to 2–8) with a thundering last-minute goal, moments after Wexford goalkeeper Art Foley had hand-saved a point-blank shot by the legendary Christy Ring. Rackard was named sports star of the year for 1956.

Picked regularly for Leinster in the inter-provincial Railway cup competition, he received his only winner's medal in 1956, having previously played on losing sides in six finals. He won three Co. Wexford senior club championships with Rathnure. Throughout his career, he scored 60 goals in 35 championship matches. He was renowned for exemplary sportsmanship, a quality emulated by the Wexford teams, contributing to their wide and enduring popularity. He retired in August 1957 after Wexford lost heavily to Kilkenny in the Leinster final. Thereafter, he represented Wexford on both the Gaelic Athletic Association (GAA) Leinster council and central council, and was a county hurling selector.

Also adept at Gaelic football, he played inter-county football from 1943 to the mid-1950s. A high-scoring full-forward, he won a Leinster senior title (1945, six years before his first comparable hurling title), and won county junior and senior club titles. He was the first man to represent Leinster in the Railway cup finals in both football and hurling in the same year (1950), being on the losing side in both codes. An accomplished horseman, he rode in point-to-points and attained some success as a breeder, trainer and owner of racehorses, both over jumps and on the flat.

Rackard married (1952) Ailish Pierce of Tinahely, Co. Wicklow; they had two daughters and one son. Convivial, big-hearted and expansive, elegant in dress and generous to a fault, he had a reckless, roguish edge. In the early 1950s, in his single-minded pursuit of all-Ireland honours, he joined the Pioneer Total Abstinence Association and successfully renounced alcohol for several years. On retiring from sport, he resumed drinking heavily, to the serious detriment of his health, and personal and professional lives. Hospitalised on several occasions, his career and finances in ruins, he eventually attained sobriety about 1970 through membership of Alcoholics Anonymous (AA). He spoke publicly about his alcoholism and became an energetic AA activist, personally assisting many alcoholics throughout the country. Ill for two years with cancer, he died 10 April 1976 in St Vincent's hospital, Dublin, and was buried in Bunclody.

The premier hurling full-forward of his era, arguably ever, he was chosen on the hurling team of the century in 1984, to mark the centenary of the GAA. His omission from the team of the millennium, selected in 1999, was controversial. The Nicky Rackard cup was launched by the GAA in 2005 as an annual competition for Division Three teams.

His brother Robert ('Bobbie') Rackard (1927–96) played senior inter-county hurling for Wexford for thirteen seasons (1945–57) as either centre-back or, latterly, right-corner-back, winning four Leinster championships, two all-Ireland medals, one league title and one oireachtas title. He was selected for the hurling teams of the century (1984) and of the millennium (1999). The youngest brother, William ('Billy') Rackard (1930–2009), appeared regularly for Wexford at wing-back, corner-back and centre-back from 1950 to 1964. He won six Leinster championships, two league titles, three all-Ireland medals and captained the Wexford side that lost the 1962 all-Ireland final (in which he continued playing after suffering a broken hand).

Lawrence William White

Sources

The Irish Times, 12 April 1976; *Wexford People*, 16 April 1976; Brendan Fullam, *Giants of the ash* (1991); Nicholas Furlong, *The greatest hurling decade: Wexford and the epic teams of the '50s* (1993); Brendan Fullam, *Hurling giants* (1994); *Wexford People*, 23 October 1996; *Sunday Tribune*, 27 October 1996; Billy Rackard, *No hurling at the dairy door* (1996); Colm Keane, *Hurling's top 20* (2002); Martin Codd, *The way I saw it: Nicky Rackard leads Wexford to hurling glory* (2005)

This entry has been abridged for publication. The full version is available at www.dib.ie.

Christy Ring

1920–79

Hurler

Christy (Nicholas Christopher) Ring was born 30 October 1920 in Kilboy, near Cloyne, Co. Cork, second youngest among three sons and two daughters of Nicholas Ring, gardener, and his wife Mary. In his childhood the family moved to Spittal Street in Cloyne village. After attending Cloyne national school until age fourteen, Christy worked for a few years as an apprentice mechanic. Thereafter, he earned his living as a tanker driver with the Irish Shell Oil Company, but hurling was his life. He played at juvenile, minor and junior levels with Cloyne, winning a county minor championship with Cloyne's associated club, St Enda's of Midleton (1938), and a county junior championship with Cloyne (1939). He joined the successful northside Cork city club Glen Rovers in 1941, the year in which the club won a record eighth consecutive county senior championship. Ring won fourteen county senior hurling championship medals with 'the Glen', the last in 1967. He also played some Gaelic football at club level, winning a county senior championship with St Nicholas in 1954 (and a football–hurling double), but is reputed to have said there was 'no skill' in that code.

Competing in inter-county minor and senior hurling for twenty-seven years (1937–63), he won all-Ireland minor championship medals as a substitute in 1937, and at the unusual position of left-half-back in 1938 (but coming forward to score a goal from a twenty-one-yard free). He made his senior inter-county debut in a league match against Kilkenny in October 1939, and his first senior championship appearances in the drawn and replayed 1940 Munster final against Limerick. In a brilliant senior inter-county career, he starred for Cork in all six forward positions, winning eight all-Ireland medals (1941–4, 1946, 1952–4). He won nine Munster championship medals (1942–4, 1946–7, 1952–4, 1956), and played twice on Cork teams that were beaten in the all-Ireland final (1947, 1956). He played on the Cork side that lost the 1941 Munster final, postponed to October owing to an outbreak of foot-and-mouth disease, one month after winning all-Ireland honours. The third man to captain three all-Ireland winners (1946, 1953–4), he remains the only man to do so since the inauguration of the Liam MacCarthy Cup in the early 1920s. He played on Cork teams that won four National

Hurling League championships (1940–41, 1948, 1953). Appearing for Munster in a record twenty-two consecutive Railway Cup finals (1942–63), he was on winning sides a record eighteen times, losing only in 1947, 1954, 1956 and 1962. Playing in forty-four Railway Cup matches, he scored 231 points (42–105), for a match average of 5.25, and failed to score in only three matches. His prowess did much to retain public interest in this inter-provincial competition; huge crowds, including tens of thousands from Northern Ireland, would attend the annual St Patrick's Day final, drawn largely by the opportunity to see Ring's genius on display.

'Ringy', as he was known to his legions of admirers, made the game of hurling a living art form. Generally considered the greatest hurler in the history of the Gaelic Athletic Association (GAA), he displayed an abundant range of skill and technical virtuosity, allied with speed, courage, intense mental concentration, ardent determination and immense physical strength. Though not a tall man—'middling small', as one ballad line has it—he weighed some 13 stone (82.5kg) with a powerful physique and was especially strong in the legs, arms and wrists. He commanded an enormous repertoire of strokes with the camán, which he could execute with either hand, and was supremely adept at scoring from first touch. A perfectionist, he practised long hours daily, alone or with teammates, to develop and maintain his skills. He always carried a camán and sliotar in the cab of his lorry and would practise in fields and against walls at intervals throughout his working day. A non-smoker and non-drinker, he revelled in hard training and maintained himself in peak fitness throughout the many years of his career. Confident in his ability, he did not suffer from false modesty in his estimation of his own genius. He once remarked that modesty was not to deny the ability that one knew oneself to have, but to know one's own ability while also knowing one's weaknesses. A pre-television superstar, though shy and reticent in social situations, he had tremendous charisma on the sporting pitch, a presence that drew and fired the crowds.

It is reckoned that Ring played some 1,200 hurling games. Among his countless superb performances, several stand out as supreme and defining examples of the greatness of his art. He came of age as one star among many (including Jack Lynch, who was also a Glen Rovers colleague) on the richly talented Cork teams that won a famed wartime four-in-a-row all-Irelands (1941–4). Ring's emergence into pre-eminence in the mid-1940s was epitomised by two celebrated solo runs, each ending in a goal, in critical matches. In the last moments of the 1944 Munster final replay against a Limerick side that included Mick Mackey, Ring soloed from deep in his own half of the pitch to score with a mighty shot from forty yards out, as Cork squeezed to victory by 4–6 to 3–6. As captain in the 1946 all-Ireland final against Kilkenny, he made a spectacular seventy-yard run from midfield just before half-time, eluding numerous defenders and scoring Cork's second goal. Some of his most memorable accomplishments were in the titanic clashes of the 1950s against Tipperary in the Munster championship and Wexford in the all-Ireland. Switching to midfield for the 1951 Munster final, he gave in defeat what many connoisseurs rate his most masterful all-round display. In the 1954 Munster final he beat three defenders to set up Cork's winning goal in added time. Probably his most famous match was the 1956 Munster final against Limerick;

having been closely and effectively marked all afternoon, and with Cork down two goals in the last quarter, Ring suddenly scored three explosive goals in a four-minute spell, resulting in victory by 5–5 to 3–5. Later in 1956 he was denied a ninth all-Ireland medal when his point-blank shot in the closing minutes was brilliantly saved by Wexford goalkeeper Art Foley.

Even in his last years Ring was capable of feats of prodigious scoring. In 1959 he scored 4–5 against Connacht in the Railway Cup final, and 6–4 in a league match against Wexford. In three years he was leading scorer in the country, all in the twilight of his inter-county career (1959, 1961–2). With 22–35 in 1959 he became the only player ever to average over ten points per game, and in 1961 he scored 104 points in thirteen games. Dropped from the Cork senior panel in 1964, he continued in senior club competition, winning his last two county championship medals (1964, 1967) and a Munster senior club championship (1965). After retiring in 1967, he became a selector with Glen Rovers and Cork, helping to select and train Cork's three-in-a-row all-Ireland winners of 1976–8. As a recreation he took up the game of squash, at which he became highly adept.

Ring married (1962) Rita Taylor, of Victoria Avenue, Cork city; they had a son, Christy, and a daughter, Mary. Strongly Catholic and nationalist, he was totally loyal and dedicated to the game of hurling, and to his club and county, while having a strong independent spirit and being very much his own man. He was involved in charitable causes and had the reputation of being helpful to individuals in need or trouble. He died suddenly 2 March 1979 after collapsing on the street in Cork city. His funeral took place at Our Lady of Lourdes church, Ballinlough, Cork

City. Thirty books of condolences were filled, some fifty to sixty thousand people attended and the oration was given by Taoiseach Jack Lynch, his former hurling confrère. He was buried in St Colman's cemetery, Cloyne.

Ring's iconic place in Cork tradition is reflected in photographic and verse displays in private and public houses. Partly because of the antiquity of the game, he has the folk status of a pre-historic hurling *gaiscíoch* (warrior, champion), typified by the many legendary occasions when, in heroic Cú-Chulainn style, he would snatch victory in the face of defeat. He was selected at right-half-forward on the hurling team of the century (1984) and on the team of the millennium (1999). He is the subject of a fine Louis Marcus film (1964) and of a striking sculpture by Seán MacCarthy in Cork airport. A nine-foot bronze statue stands in his native Cloyne, where also an ash grove (Ros Uí Rinn) is dedicated to him. In his adopted city a bridge over the River Lee and a GAA ground are named after him. Of the numerous ballads composed in his honour, the best is Bryan MacMahon's 'Song for Christy Ring'. The last verse recalls Cork's legendary rivalry with Tipperary, where the cup of summer happiness overflows when the hay is saved and victory achieved over the traditional enemy:

> How oft I've watched him from the hill, move here and there in grace,
> In Cork, Killarney, Thurles town, or by the Shannon's race.
> 'Now Cork is bet, the hay is saved!' the thousands wildly sing.
> They speak too soon, my sweet *garsún*, for here comes Christy Ring.

John A. Murphy

Sources

Cork Examiner, 3–5 March 1979; *Irish Independent*, 3–5 March 1979; Val Dorgan, *Christy Ring: a personal portrait* (1980); Brendan Fullam, *Hurling giants* (1994); Raymond Smith (ed.), *Complete handbook of Gaelic games* (1999 edition); Brendan Fullam, *Captains of the ash* (2002); Colm Keane, *Hurling's top twenty* (2002); Tim Horgan, *Christy Ring: hurling's greatest* (2007)

John Ryan

1871–1954

H U N T S M A N

John Joseph Ryan was born in Edermine House, Enniscorthy, Co. Wexford, on 25 March 1871, the eldest of nine children of Major-General Thaddeus Richard Ryan (1837–1905) of Scarteen House, Knocklong, Co. Limerick, and his wife Gwendaline (née Power), daughter of the whiskey magnate Sir James Power of Edermine House. John's father had inherited the family lease holdings in counties Limerick and Tipperary but, as he was a British army officer, generally posted abroad, responsibility for the estate fell to his widowed mother and other family members. In 1864 Clem Ryan (John's uncle) took over the family's pack of hounds, which the Ryans had kept since at least the early eighteenth century.

The Scarteen pack, distinguished by their black and tan coating, have always been Kerry beagles, which are a type of hound, akin to a harrier. This breed derived from an ancient Irish hound, with a continental strain introduced in the early modern period coming to predominate. The English foxhound supplanted the Kerry beagle among the Anglo-Irish gentry during the nineteenth century, but the Ryans, being well-to-do Catholic tenant farmers with Jacobite antecedents, stuck with the more indigenous article. By 1881 Scarteen hosted the only kennelled pack of Kerry beagles in Ireland, though Kerry beagles were scattered in ones and twos across different holdings in west Munster and used for hunts on foot. The Scarteen hounds were known as the Black and Tans, an appellation given to the black- and khaki-clad British auxiliary forces dispatched to Ireland during 1920–21.

Spending much of his childhood at Scarteen, John participated in the family hunt from an early age. He was educated at Oscott College, near Birmingham, England, before attending Glasnevin Agricultural College near Dublin (1890–2). In 1893 Thaddeus retired from the army and returned with his family to Scarteen, allowing John to act more regularly as the whipper-in (assistant) to Clem out hunting. The Scarteen hunt was then an unheralded affair, albeit one capable of drawing large crowds of local spectators. Fields rarely exceeded twenty, usually the Ryans and other affluent tenant farmers, though officers in the nearby British garrisons were keen participants. They hunted mainly the carted stag, but also the hare and the fox, both of which were scarce. An outstanding horseman, John honed his skills on a landscape dissected by ditches, flanked by towering banks. He won various point-to-point races, notably the 1896 Munster Plate at Kilmallock, and inaugurated the annual Scarteen point-to-point meeting in 1909. For the 1899–1900 season, he was master of the prestigious County Limerick hunt. Later, he was a long-serving judge at the Dublin Horse Show.

After working in the Power's distillery in Dublin during the late 1890s, he went to England to gain further experience in distilling, but the outbreak of the Boer War led him to volunteer for military duty instead. During 1900–01 he served in South Africa as a scout outrider in the Imperial Yeomanry. Thereafter, he ran the family estate at Scarteen. Upon his father's death in 1905, he inherited a sizeable estate, which peaked at 788 acres in 1908 following the buying out of the relevant landlords. In 1904 he became master of the Black and Tans, succeeding Clem who returned the pack to Scarteen after their fourteen years kennelled at Emly House, Co. Tipperary.

An astute breeder, John disregarded the prestige English foxhound strains in favour of unfashionable Irish bloodlines, scouring Clare, Kerry and Cork for suitable infusions. He resisted introducing foxhound blood in his hounds, stressing that the Black and Tans were a breed apart. In contrast to the submissive and subdued foxhound, Kerry beagles were affectionate, excitable, independent and disheartened by excessive discipline. Not as fast as foxhounds in the open, they were better adapted to the bank-strewn countryside, boasting superiority in nose and nimbleness. Their most celebrated trait was their long, melodious cry. Ryan handled his pack subtly, largely permitting them to hunt and cast for themselves; when they did look to him, he had an intuitive knack for casting them in the right direction.

The pack hunted foxes and deer on alternate days. From early in his mastership, Ryan set about increasing fox numbers in Scarteen by planting coverts (areas of scrub, brush or woods), enticing foxes down from the overhanging Galtee Mountains. Spectacular chases of over twenty miles were common, as the mountain foxes were very wild and, unlike the more parochial lowland foxes, travelled straight and far, the terrain being almost bereft of cover. At a time when much of the Irish countryside was becoming thickly fenced, Scarteen country increasingly stood out as the finest hunting ground in Ireland, comprising rich pasture with little wire, no forestry, and clear ditches and banks. Yet the pack often got clean away. During the 1912/13 season Ryan once returned home without his hounds after they disappeared over the Galtees. They were still hunting when he found them the next morning. A series of outstanding hunting seasons to 1914 raised the social profile of the Scarteen hunt, even drawing visitors from abroad.

Serving in the first world war with the 16th Lancers, Ryan was captured near Ypres on 21 February 1915 (he was trapped after his trench was mined) and held in various camps in Germany and the Netherlands until the war's end. In his absence his siblings Janey, Tha and Willy kept the farm and the hunt going. In 1919 he married Anita Purcell of Burton Park, Churchtown, Co. Cork; they had two daughters and two sons. As his efforts in establishing coverts bore fruit, fox numbers rose, allowing the hunt to stop chasing deer in the late 1920s. Ryan, however, could no longer afford to maintain the hunt independently: he was frequently under financial pressure, mainly due to the distractions and expenses arising from his love of hunting. In 1926 the newly established Scarteen hunt committee imposed an annual subscription on hunt members; the annual Scarteen hunt ball was also instituted to raise funds, becoming an occasion of wild revelry.

Following the collapse in agricultural prices in 1929, the hounds were briefly removed from Scarteen for fear that creditors might seize them. His uncle Sir Thomas Power provided the necessary financial assistance in return for Ryan agreeing to concentrate on managing his estate, which was later much reduced when subjected to a compulsory purchase order from the Land Commission. In 1929 Ryan resigned as master and loaned the pack to the Scarteen hunt committee, which appointed a series of caretaker masters. He followed the hunt occasionally but tended to leave early, as some of his successors were unaccustomed to Kerry beagles, and this could show in their handling of them. By then his decades of careful breeding had brought the pack to such a standard that few foxes could stay ahead of them for more than twenty minutes.

In 1938 he exercised his right to reclaim the mastership and arranged for Claude Thompson, later his son-in-law, to share this position with him and shoulder much of the expense and workload. Thompson, however, felt duty-bound to volunteer for the British Army in 1939, leaving the elderly Ryan to carry the horn for the duration of the war. He benefited from the support of his daughters Gwenda and Jean, who whipped in to him, despite both being initially under the age of twenty. On 11 February 1941 he participated in a twenty-five-mile chase, lasting two hours and fifty minutes from Glenefy to within a mile and a half of Knocklong, with only five riders finishing (John, Gwenda and Jean among them).

Suffering from heart trouble, Ryan retired in 1947, handing responsibility for the oldest private hunting pack in Ireland, and for Ireland's most celebrated hunt, to his son Thady. John Ryan died at Scarteen House on 16 December 1954 and was buried in the family vault at Emly, Co. Tipperary.

Terry Clavin

Sources

General Register Office Dublin (birth certificate); *Freeman's Journal*, 28 December 1881; *The Irish Times*, 4–6 March, 17 April 1915; 19 November 1928; 4 February 1929; Windham Henry Wyndham-Quin, *The fox-hound in County Limerick* (1919), 86–90; *Irish Field*, 10 November 1928; 25 December 1954; Joseph B. Thomas, *Hounds and hunting through the ages* (1928); *Limerick Leader*, 25 December 1954; Muriel Bowen, *Irish hunting* (1954), 145–51; Michael O'Dwyer, *The parish of Emly* (1987), 40–3; Michael MacEwan, *The Ryan family and the Scarteen hounds* (1989); Juliette Cunliffe, *The encyclopaedia of dog breeds* (1999), 329; Thady Ryan, *My privileged life with the Scarteen Black and Tans* (2002); Claudia M. Reidy, 'Marriage settlements of the Ryans of Ballyvista and Scarteen', MA dissertation, University of Limerick (2010); information from Claudia Reidy (granddaughter)

Elisha Scott

1893–1959

SOCCER PLAYER

Elisha ('Leesh', 'Lee') Scott was born 24 August 1893 off the Donegall Road in the Shankill area of Belfast, one of the younger sons in a Church of Ireland family of ten (five girls and five boys) of William E. Scott, a yarn bundler, and his wife, Jane (née Carruth). He attended St Simon's school on the Donegall Road. Starting league football playing as a centre-forward with the 4th Belfast Company Boy's Brigade team *c.*1906, he switched to goalkeeper as a fourteen-year-old, impatient with the inefficient performance of his team-mate in that position. Signing a professional contract with Broadway United in 1910, he played for two seasons before he was purchased by Liverpool in autumn 1912, having been recommended to the club by his brother, William Scott, goalkeeper for Everton and Ireland. Soon after recovering from a wrist injury, he made his debut on the senior club side in an away match against Newcastle on New Year's Day 1913, holding a strong striking force at bay in a 0–0 draw. His debut at Anfield occurred in October 1914 when he profited by a severe injury incurred by the first-choice goalkeeper, Scottish international Kenneth Campbell.

The English football league suspended games during the first world war. It is known that Scott played for some time on loan to Belfast Celtic during the war, but it seems that he also served in the British army on the western front, probably in the 36th (Ulster) Division. In 1917 he married Alice Maud Morrow, a Belfast woman; they had a son. He won an Irish Cup winner's medal in 1918 with Belfast Celtic. Suffering a period of discontent directly after the war, when Campbell continued to be the preferred choice in Liverpool, Scott made his way back to the first team by the 1919/20 season. It was during this season that he was first picked for Ireland in a match against Scotland (0–3). Though his international debut proved inauspicious, his first few seasons with Liverpool established him as one of the best goalkeepers in the English league. In winning the league championship in two consecutive seasons (1921/2, 1922/3), Scott's exceptionally low number of goals conceded per season was the critical difference for the emerging Liverpool team. He became the most consistent player and leading personality on the team during the 1920s. He was so closely identified with the club that the official Liverpool telegraphic address (equivalent to the modern website address) was 'Goalkeeper, Liverpool'. Though only of average height (5ft 9in. (1.75m)), he compensated with intense alertness and elastic reflexes. Unusually for the period, he put in considerable practice to refine his skills and made a habit of warming up mentally and physically for at least an hour before each match by bouncing balls on his own off a wall. Of masterful temperament, he made his presence felt during the match by an unceasing flow of caustic, often scurrilous, banter, directed at the opposition and at his own defence.

Playing in 31 of the 46 home internationals in which Ireland participated between 1920 and 1935, he stood between predatory opposition and humiliating defeat on numerous occasions, though it must be said that the Irish record (27 losses and 8 victories in the series) was discouragingly poor. The goalless draw between Ireland and England in Belfast in 1925, in which Scott was outstanding, was one of the Irish high points in the 1920s. He had the comfort of playing with superior team-mates in the league. His greatest rivalry (and one of his best friendships outside the game) was with the legendary striker Bill ('Dixie') Dean of Everton. It was joked that if the pair met on the street Scott would dive through the air when Dean greeted him with a nod.

After making 468 first team appearances, Scott was released from Liverpool in 1934 when he was appointed player-manager to Belfast Celtic, Belfast's 'Catholic' soccer club. Becoming full-time manager in early 1937, he succeeded in winning the Irish league six times with Celtic (1936–40, 1945). Under his management the club also won six Irish cups, eight gold cups, three city cups and other lesser honours. His transition from player to manager was seamless and indicates a natural mix of command and discernment in his makeup. Belfast Celtic players respected and feared his fierce enthusiasm and rasping comment: 'we weren't allowed to think negatively ... he wasn't interested in second-best' (*Lurgan Mail*, 10 October 1985).

He continued to collect post and draw wages as manager of the Belfast Celtic stadium for nearly eight years after the infamous riot at the Belfast Celtic–Linfield derby on 26 December 1948 which shut down the club. His greatest achievement as manager took place, however, some months later, when during the American invitation summer tournament of 1949 Belfast Celtic defeated a strong Scotland side 2–0 at the Triboro stadium, New York. Though he retired as 'the only boss in soccer who doesn't worry about next Saturday' (*Irish Soccer News*, 28 July 1956), he was remembered by 'Dixie' Dean in 1980 as the best goalkeeper he had ever seen. He died 16 May 1959 in Belfast after a two-year illness and was buried in Belfast City cemetery.

Des McCabe

Sources

General Register Office Dublin (marriage certificate); *Irish Soccer News*, 28 July 1956; *KOP*, 18 January 1966; *Belfast Telegraph*, 14 November 1969; 16 March 1996; 7 August 1999; *The game: an encyclopaedia of sport* (*c.*1972), 2,413; Mark Tuohy, *Belfast Celtic* (1978); Malcolm Brodie, *100 years of Irish football* (1980); *Lurgan Mail*, 10 October 1985; John Gleeson (ed.), *Fyffes dictionary of Irish sporting greats* (1993); Padraig Coyle, *Paradise lost and found: the story of Belfast Celtic* (1999)

Molly Seaton

1905–1974

SOCCER PLAYER

Molly (Mary Anne) Seaton was born 2 September 1905 in the family residence at Greencastle in the docks area of Belfast. She was the second youngest of the four surviving children (three daughters and a son) of Henry Seaton, brick layer, and his wife Mary Jane ('Anney') Seaton (née Quinn). Her father died when she was nine years old. Living on Dandy Street, she worked as a doffer at the Whitehouse Flax Spinning Mill and the Upper Corgery Road Spinning Mill. In time she became a doffing mistress.

By the 1920s women's football matches had become a popular way of raising money for charity in the UK. These matches were often organised by factory owners who put together teams drawn from their workers. Whereas the English Football Association (FA) had crippled this development by banning women from affiliated pitches in 1921 (the Scottish and Welsh FAs imposed partial bans), no such restrictions were imposed in Northern Ireland, though there was little organised women's football there for most of the 1920s. Seaton's first reputed high-profile appearance came in 1923 as one of three Northern Ireland women on the Scottish team Rutherglen that shocked the famed Dick Kerr Ladies 2–0 near Glasgow.

Seaton next appeared in 1927, when she participated in Rutherglen's ground-breaking tour of Britain and Ireland. To overcome the bias against women's football, women's teams provided their own opposition by travelling and playing as one large squad or two loosely affiliated squads. From 9 May teams styled Rutherglen and Edinburgh played matches in Belfast, Larne, Ballymena and Larne again. Seaton was Edinburgh's free-scoring centre-forward and captain, notching three of her team's goals in a 4–5 loss at Ballymena. On 21 May she participated in the first organised women's football match held in the Irish Free State. (The two most well-known women's football teams of that era, the Dick Kerr Ladies of Preston and Femina Sport of Paris, made numerous attempts to tour the Irish Free State but were thwarted by the opposition of the Catholic church.) She scored seven goals before a crowd of 12,000, the largest then seen at the venue in Milltown, Dublin, as Rutherglen routed the local Irish team 8–1.

The tour returned to Northern Ireland with matches in Derry and Portadown between sides billed as Ireland versus Scotland, even though the 'Irish' team, captained by Seaton, was overwhelmingly Scottish. In the Derry match she scored both goals for Ireland in a 2–2 draw in front of a capacity crowd of 5,000 at Bonds Field Park. A Derry journalist committed to print his outrage at the sight of women disporting themselves in shorts before prurient attendees, contrasting their attire with the long skirts worn by women hockey players. Ireland then lost further matches played in Manchester, England (August), and in Bellshill, Scotland (September), with Seaton scoring all of Ireland's goals in the 5–9 loss at Bellshill.

In 1928 a similar tour took place with Seaton again leading the 'Ireland' team and again featuring as star player and chief goal scorer. Ireland and Scotland played each other across Scotland from April to July followed by a shorter return tour to Northern Ireland in September. She scored five goals at least twice: in Ireland's 6–5 win over Scotland at Scone, Scotland, on 9 April and in the 5–5 draw at Larne in September. Belfast folklore has it that she played regularly in men's football games, and she may well have done so in informal kickabouts and perhaps also incognito in organised matches. Contrary to legend, she never signed for Linfield but did line out in a pre-season friendly for the Forth River men's team at Eldenderry in south Belfast on 12 September 1928.

From 1929 she featured as the main attraction in women's charity matches held in and around Belfast. She had a long association with the local Crusaders Football Club, which encouraged the use of their ground for women's football. As her fame grew, her local Greencastle team Castle Rovers became the Molly Seaton XI. Local boxing agent Josie Farrell was her manager and agent, and she often picked up 'gate money' of 10 shillings per game. During 1931–2 there was an unusually large number of women's matches involving prominent Belfast factories such as Ropeworks, York Street Mill, Owen O'Corks, Jennymount Mill and Milewater Mill as well as teams from outlying towns. She played for different mill teams including York Street Mill and Jennymount Mill, also refereeing many women's matches. Her Catholic faith was never an issue in a lively women's football scene that cut across Northern Ireland's religious divide.

Newspaper reports gave a mixed picture of the standard of play, with some suggesting that the predominantly male crowds turned up to be amused (or titillated). But even the most scornful of dispatches wrote glowingly of Seaton: 'at times [Seaton] literally walked through her opponents from one end of the field to the other, just to let the spectators see that ladies with training and experience can play good football' (*Larne Times*, 25 July 1931). By then she was playing in defence, presumably to give her opponents some chance of stopping her. Powerfully built, she towered over the other players at 5ft 10in. (1.78m); the Dick Kerr Ladies (Preston Ladies), who were known as a tough, strapping side, averaged about 5ft 5in. (1.65m). Yet her dominance cannot be attributed purely to her physicality, as match reports praised her clever play and skill, particularly her powerful and accurate shooting.

Her finest hour came on 27 July 1931 when a strong Dick Kerr Ladies team including Lily Parr, Jenny Harris and Lizzy Ashcroft played a genuine Irish selection in Windsor Park, Belfast. (The Ireland teams of the 1930s were more specifically Northern Ireland selections, often exclusively from the Belfast region.) Ireland lost 2–3 as the crowd of 4,500 saw Seaton nearly beat the English single-handedly: 'Nominally she was playing centre-half, but she took the corners, scored the goals, cleared dangerous rushes in the full back position and led the forward line' (*Northern Whig*, 28 July 1931). The three English players who marked her 'tried to sandwich her, to bamboozle her with three-cornered passing, to kick the ball over her head, to charge her, and to dribble past her, but she got the ball almost every time'.

The arrival of Femina Sport of Paris in summer 1932 generated great excitement in Belfast. The Femina players were mostly upper middle class and went about in the latest Parisian fashions; they also played in more revealing shorts. On 4 August they drew 15,000 paying spectators to Grosvenor Park where Seaton scored twice for Ireland in a ferociously contested 3–4 defeat. As before she was the outstanding player on the pitch; as before she was closely shadowed, eventually being one of several players to retire injured. After spending the night in hospital, she missed the second, similarly combative encounter between Ireland and France. She recovered by 19 August to appear at Grosvenor Park for Molly Seaton's XI in the inaugural and only Irish Ladies' Football Cup final; she scored twice as the Ropeworks Ladies were defeated 5–0.

From 1933 the number of women's football matches staged in the Belfast region fell markedly, probably due to renewed sectarian unrest in Northern Ireland. Seaton's last big match came on 10 August 1936 when Femina Sport, under the captaincy of Carmen Pomies, returned to Belfast to take on Ireland. The 2,000-strong attendance relished the rough-and-tumble nature of the proceedings, which abated somewhat after Pomies briefly led her team off the pitch over a bad infringement by Seaton. This marred a customary barnstorming performance by Seaton capped by her goal from an unstoppable twenty-five-yard free kick. The 1–4 score flattered the victorious French.

She continued to appear in those women's matches that were played until the second world war effectively ended women's football in Northern Ireland for the best part of a decade.

A formidable woman who liked a smoke and a pint of Guinness, Molly Seaton was sometimes mocked for her hulking, masculine appearance, but she was in the main cherished as a great Belfast character. Tales of her footballing exploits were preserved in local folklore for decades after her death in a Belfast hospital on 12 January 1974. Her remains were buried in St Mary's church cemetery, Greencastle.

Steve Bolton

Sources

General Register Office Dublin (birth certificate); National Archives of Ireland, Census of Ireland, 1911; *Belfast Telegraph, passim,* esp.: 10, 16 May 1927; 23, 25 July, 5 August 1931; 6, 20 August 1932; *Ballymena Observer,* 20 May 1927; 14 September 1928; *Ballymena Weekly Telegraph,* 21 May 1927; *The Irish Times,* 23 May 1927; *Northern Whig,* 24 May 1927; 13 September 1928; 6, 28 July 1931; 11 August 1936; *Derry Standard,* 27 May 1927; *Derry Journal,* 30 May 1927; *Daily Record,* 1 June 1927; 19 February 2018; *Bellshill Speaker,* 9 September 1927; *Dundee Courier,* 10 April 1928; *Isle of Man Examiner,* 10, 14 July 1931; *Larne Times,* 25 July 1931; *Belfast News Letter,* 5 August 1932; BBC Radio Ulster, 26 December 2020, 'Girls with goals: a history of women's football in Northern Ireland'; Steve Bolton, 'Molly Seaton—Ireland's Best. My tribute to the legendary Irish woman footballer', www.playingpasts.co.uk; Fiona Skillen and Steve Bolton, 'Women's football in interwar Scotland: Sadie Smith and the legendary Rutherglen Ladies FC'; Steve Bolton, 'Carmen Pomies: the most important woman footballer in history', www.playingpasts.co.uk, (all internet material accessed May 2021); interview with Valerie Beattie (daughter of footballer Betsy Briton); interview with Dorothy Connor (granddaughter of James Hislop Kelly (founder and manager of Rutherglen FC))

Martin Sheridan

1881–1918

Olympic athlete

Martin Joseph Sheridan was born 28 March 1881 in Bohola, Co. Mayo, the second youngest of five sons and one surviving daughter of Martin Sheridan, a farmer of Bohola and a rural district councillor, and his wife Jane (née Durkan). His uncle, P. J. Sheridan, was a member of the Invincibles, a militant splinter group of the Irish Republican Brotherhood; P. J. fled to the USA in 1882 after the Invincibles assassinated two senior government officials in the Phoenix Park, Dublin.

Martin attended Bohola national school and helped on the family farm. In 1897 he joined two of his brothers, Richard and Patrick, in New York City, where he worked as a streetcar driver. His brother Richard was a leading discus and weight thrower in New York, inspiring Martin to follow him; both brothers competed for the Pastime Athletic Club. A group of Irish athletes, known as the 'Irish Whales' on account of their impressive physique, then dominated US weight-throwing events, with Martin emerging as their finest exponent. He was renowned for his gargantuan appetite and, when in serious training, his dinner would consist of two plates of soup, one whole chicken, one steak, hash brown potatoes, three cups of tea, two pieces of pie and cheese, one loaf of bread, and an order of celery. Standing 6ft 3in. (1.9m) and weighing 13st. 6lb (85.275kg), his combination of power, speed and agility made him the leading all-round athlete of his generation.

Within a month of his first appearance at an athletics event, he broke the world discus record in September 1901 with a throw of 120ft 7.75in. (37.77m) at a meet in Paterson, New Jersey. He would improve on this with regularity over the next ten years, breaking the world record with three consecutive throws at an event in October 1902. By the end of 1911, his last year as a serious athlete, he had advanced the discus record to 141ft. 8.5in. (43.19m). The chaotic state of athletics officiating meant that many of these records were not officially recognised. He is credited with up to sixteen world bests, mostly for the discus throw and the all-round event (an early version of the decathlon). He won eleven US titles, including four in the discus (1904, 1906–07, 1911), three in the all-round event (1905, 1907, 1909), two in the pole vault for distance (1906–07), and one each in the shot (1904) and Greek style discus (1907).

In 1904 he and Richard joined the Irish-American Athletic Club (IAAC), as it became the powerhouse of US athletics. Founded in 1897 in opposition to the elitist and strictly amateur New York Athletic Club, the IAAC was more welcoming towards athletes of immigrant origins. (Sheridan would exemplify his club's tolerant attitude in 1907 by successfully proposing an African-American runner, John Baxter Taylor, for membership.) In 1904 he began working at the Pelham Bay Park athletics ground, prompting a formal protest from the New York Athletic Club, which claimed that he was being paid as a fitness instructor. He maintained that he was a foreman at Pelham Bay Park and had nothing to do with the athletics track. The protest was eventually found to be groundless, though his job did allow him to train as he worked. In 1906 he joined the New York Police Department (NYPD). One of many successful Irish-American athletes then employed by the NYPD, he was transferred to the licence squad— considered the easiest detail in the NYPD—for a period from 1908. He continued to be dogged by suspicions of covert professionalism and was accused in 1909 of accepting $500 plus expenses for competing in an athletics meet.

He represented the USA in three Olympic games. At the Olympic games in St Louis, Missouri, in 1904 he came fourth in the shot-put and claimed gold in the discus after tying for first and winning a throw-off. Due to the charges of professionalism hanging over him, he was not chosen at first for the US team sent to compete in the 1906 Intercalated Olympic Games at Athens, but his omission provoked such criticism that the selectors relented. (Although the 1906 Athens games were treated contemporaneously as a full-fledged Olympics, these games retroactively lost that status.) He entered seven events, winning gold in the discus and the shot-put, and silver in the stone throw, the standing high jump and the standing long jump. A knee injury prevented him from claiming the pentathlon championship. King George of Greece was so impressed that he gave Sheridan a gold goblet and ordered that a statue of a discus thrower be put up outside the Olympic stadium in his honour.

At the 1908 games in London, he won gold medals in the discus throw and the Greek-style discus throw, and a bronze in the standing long jump. An outspoken Irish nationalist, he publicly criticised Irish athletes who competed for Britain and was primarily responsible for the bad blood that developed between the US and British athletes at the 1908 games. He almost certainly influenced the refusal of the American flag-bearer at the opening ceremony, Ralph Rose, to dip the US flag to King Edward VII, though accounts that have Sheridan telling Rose 'This flag dips to no earthly king' are probably apocryphal. He stirred the pot further by accusing the British team of sharp practice after their victory over the US in the tug-of-war.

Following the 1908 Olympics, he spent six weeks in Ireland, where he was hailed as a conquering hero, associated closely with the Gaelic Athletic Association (GAA) and Sinn Féin, and gave exhibitions in Dublin, Dungarvan, Dundalk and Ballina. Alone among the prominent Irish-American athletes then visiting Ireland, Sheridan refused to partake in the athletic competition staged by the Irish Amateur Athletic Association (IAAA) in Ballsbridge,

Dublin, in August 1908. The IAAA was then vying ac-
rimoniously with the GAA for the right to regulate Irish
athletics.

After nearly dying from contracting blood poisoning
and mastoiditis in 1912, he retired from athletics but
remained involved as a coach. He showed conspicuous
courage in performing his duties with the NYPD and was
promoted from patrolman to first-grade detective in 1913.
Latterly he lived on 141 West 97th Street. His health was
never the same after 1912, and he died 27 March 1918 in
St Vincent's hospital, New York City, having contracted
pneumonia.

Members of the police department and the Irish-
American community erected a memorial Celtic cross
in Calvary cemetery, where he is buried, and the Martin
Sheridan Award for Valour was awarded yearly to members
of the police department for acts of bravery. At Bohola, a
bronze bust of him was unveiled in 1966, and the Martin
Sheridan Memorial Community Centre, which includes a
museum to his memory, was opened in 1994. In December
1988 Sheridan was inducted into the Track and Field Hall
of Fame in Indiana. His total of nine Olympic medals—
five gold, three silver, one bronze—makes him the leading
Irish Olympian to date, though those won in 1906 are not
recognised by the International Olympic Committee.

Paul Rouse

Sources

General Register Office Dublin (birth certificate); F. B. Dinneen, *Irish athletic record*
(1906); P. D. Mehigan ('Carbery'), *Fifty years of Irish athletics* (1943); P. D. Mehigan
('Carbery'), *Seventy years of Irish athletics* (1946); William Dooley, *Champions of the
athletic arena* (1946); David Guiney, *Ireland and the Olympic games* (1976); *The Irish
Times*, 27 September 1986; Bohola Community Centre Committee (ed.), *Bohola: its*

history and people (1992); Lindie Naughton and Johnny Watterson, *Irish Olympians* (1995); John Gleeson (ed.), *Fyffes dictionary of Irish sporting greats* (1993); David Guiney, *The Olympic Games* (1996); Henry Boylan, *A dictionary of Irish biography* (1998 edition); *American national biography* (1999); Kevin McCarthy, *Gold, silver and green* (2010); Margaret Molloy, *Martin Sheridan: Mayo's famous son 1881–1918* (2018); 'United States Championships (Men 1976–1942)', www.gbrathletics.com/ nc/usa.htm (internet material accessed November 2021)

Jim Smith

1901–70

GAELIC FOOTBALLER

Jim (James) Smith was born 7 April 1901 in Gola, Killinkere, Co. Cavan, the third of nine surviving children of James Smith, a small farmer of Gola, and Susan Smith (née Tully), from the adjoining townland of Derryhum. He was educated locally before being sent to Ballyjamesduff, Co. Cavan, to attend a Latin school in readiness for joining the priesthood. In 1915 he entered St Patrick's College, Cavan, where he became fluent in Irish and excelled at athletics, handball, hurling and Gaelic football. Playing senior club football for the Virginia Blues, he won his only Cavan county championship medal in 1919. In 1920 he entered the seminary of All Hallows College, Dublin, and studied at University College Dublin (UCD), graduating BA in 1924. He played for the UCD football and hurling teams and was selected for the UCD athletics team in middle distance running. In 1923 he won a Sigerson Cup medal with the UCD footballers.

Abandoning his religious vocation, he joined the Civic Guards (latterly An Garda Síochána) in 1924. He was based in garda headquarters in Dublin and played hurling and football for the Garda club, winning five Dublin hurling championships (1925–9) and two Dublin football championships (1927, 1929). During 1929–33 he served in various stations in counties Meath and Louth; in Meath he played club football and hurling with Erin's Own, winning three Meath hurling titles (1930–2). While based in Kells, Co. Meath, he met a local woman, Nancy McEntee. They married in 1932 and had two sons. He was transferred back to Dublin headquarters in 1933 and resumed playing for the Garda club.

Having been selected for the Cavan senior hurlers as early as 1917, he was first picked for the Cavan senior footballers in 1920. He would play senior football for Cavan for almost eighteen years, winning eight Ulster championship medals and two all-Irelands. A forward in his early years for Cavan, he was normally selected at midfield from 1924. In the 1930s he drifted back to the centre-half-back slot before ending his career at full-back. He was an automatic selection for Ulster for a decade and played on the Ireland team that participated in the Tailteann Games of 1924, 1928 and 1932. At 6ft (1.83m) tall, he was powerfully built, possessing tremendous stamina and a massive kick; it was said that no one could outfield him at his peak. All regarded him as a gentleman on the field of play. He was loyal to Cavan, spurning approaches from other counties.

An emerging Cavan side first came to national prominence when they lost the all-Ireland semi-finals of 1923 and 1925 to Kerry, both times by a single point and latterly to a highly questionable one. The objections and counter-objections arising from Cavan's 1925 defeat led to both counties being ejected from that year's all-Ireland championship, which was eventually declared void. A substitute championship involving the four provincial champions was held that winter, but Kerry's boycott destroyed its credibility; Smith played as Cavan lost the 'final' to Galway in January 1926. Cavan did reach the all-Ireland final proper in 1928, losing to Kildare thanks to a disputed goal.

During the 1929 Ulster semi-final held in Belturbet, Co. Cavan, Smith collided with Armagh's James Kernan, who suffered a perforation to his intestine and died two days later in Armagh Infirmary. While most witnesses at the ensuing inquest maintained that there was nothing untoward about the incident, statements were read out from some Armagh supporters accusing Smith of raising his knee dangerously. The jury at the inquest did not take a view on whether Kernan's injuries were accidental, which fuelled wild rumours. To scotch any suggestion of a cover up, Garda Commissioner General Eoin O'Duffy ordered that Smith be prosecuted for murder. Smith was charged at Cavan District Court (11 July) and cleared upon the hearing of preliminary evidence.

Cavan then lost the Ulster final to Monaghan in a replay held at Carrickmacross, Co. Monaghan, mainly because Smith, who was roundly barracked by the opposing fans, performed poorly. When the 1930 Ulster final, also involving Cavan and Monaghan, was scheduled for Carrickmacross, Smith declared he would not play there again. Cavan objected unsuccessfully to the venue before withdrawing, though in the end a weakened selection played and lost. Kernan's death poisoned relations between Cavan and Armagh for the next decade. Following the end of the 1931 Ulster final between the two counties, an Armagh supporter with a gun approached Smith on the field but was tackled and disarmed.

In 1933, in what was regarded as Ulster's greatest footballing day up to that time, Cavan beat a highly fancied Kerry side in the all-Ireland semi-final. In the final, Smith scored a goal direct from a forty-yard free kick as Cavan won its first all-Ireland senior football title by defeating Galway 2–5 to 1–4, making him the first man to captain an Ulster side to all-Ireland success. That same year, however, the former Garda Commissioner Eoin O'Duffy became leader of the quasi-fascist Blueshirt movement, following which Smith's presumed association with his old boss disastrously politicised Cavan football. Matters were not helped in 1934 by separate speeches made by O'Duffy and a prominent Cavan Blueshirt, claiming that their movement had the support of members of Cavan's football team. Smith refused to play in the 1934 Ulster final against Armagh after being heckled by a section of the crowd during the pre-match parade. He was then surprisingly dropped for the all-Ireland semi-final, which Cavan lost to Galway; overcrowding had brought large numbers of spectators onto the pitch in the second half, turning the match into a farce, but the result stood—an inexplicable decision in purely sporting terms. Thereafter, the political controversies swirling around Smith and the Cavan team subsided, as O'Duffy and his Blueshirts faded into irrelevance.

Smith sat out the 1935 Ulster championship before returning for the all-Ireland semi-final and starring at full-back in the all-Ireland final victory over Kildare. There had been questions about his eligibility to play in that year's championship, as he had been suspended by the GAA for barracking a referee while spectating at a Dublin club football match; it had required a special meeting of the Dublin county board held on the day of the 1935 all-Ireland semi-final to lift his suspension. Smith played his last championship game in the all-Ireland final replay against Kerry in 1937, retiring with a facial injury in the first half, as Cavan lost to a disputed goal.

His injury caused acrimony between the respective county boards, and Kerry refused to travel to the USA with Cavan on the 1938 tour. This tour was Smith's swansong as a player, and his third American tour—he had been a member of the 1934 and 1936 touring Cavan sides. Jim Smith was one of the great Gaelic footballers of the 1920s and 1930s and undoubtedly the most versatile.

Promoted to the rank of sergeant in March 1927, he served in Tipperary, Dublin, Meath, Louth, Wexford, Sligo, Leitrim, Monaghan and Roscommon in a garda career lasting twenty-eight years. In 1945 he separated from his wife, who moved away; he raised their two sons. Fed up with the deplorable living and work accommodation endured by members of An Garda Síochána, he resigned in 1952. He worked for a year in a factory in London before getting a job in the Department of Agriculture as a shipping inspector at Dublin Port. He died 20 July 1970 in St Kevin's hospital (later St James's hospital), Dublin, and was buried in Gallon graveyard, Killinkere, Co. Cavan. The Gaelic Athletic Association ground at Killinkere was named in his memory. Both of his sons played minor football for Cavan. Jim junior graduated to the Cavan seniors while Gearóid was on the Meath senior panel that won the 1954 all-Ireland title.

Jim Shanahan and Terry Clavin

Sources

General Register Office Dublin (birth certificate); *Anglo-Celt*, 29 September 1934; 24 July 1970; *Irish Press*, 20 September 1935; Raymond Smith, *The football immortals* (1968 edition); *Irish Independent*, 21 July 1970; John Gleeson (ed.), *Fyffes dictionary of Irish sporting greats* (1993); Raymond Smith (ed.), *Complete handbook of Gaelic games* (1999 edition); Marcus de Burca, *The GAA: a history* (1999); Jack Mahon, *A history of Gaelic football* (2000); Peter Kerr, 'Death of James Kernan, Armagh county footballer 2 July 1929', *Seanchas Ardmacha: Journal of the Armagh Diocesan Historical Society*, vol. 19, no. 2, Golden Jubilee Issue (2003), 263–79; Gearóid Mac Gabhann, *Big Jim Smith: man of Breifne* (2012); Garda museum and archive, Dublin

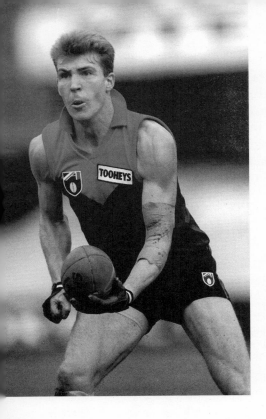

Jim Stynes

1966–2012

Jim (James Peter) Stynes was born 23 April 1966 in Rathfarnham, Dublin, the eldest of three boys and three girls of Brian Stynes and his wife Teresa (née Davey). Stynes attended Ballyroan Boys' national school and, aged nine, played under-11s Gaelic football with the local

Ballyboden St Enda's club. In 1979 he started secondary school at De La Salle in Churchtown. A talented all-round sportsman, he played rugby for De La Salle, Gaelic football for Ballyboden St Enda's and ran with the Brothers Pearse Athletic Club. He won an all-Ireland minor football championship medal with Dublin in 1984. Already taller than most of his contemporaries, he dominated midfield with his superb high fielding, and stood out for his athleticism and determination.

That year Stynes answered a newspaper advertisement from Melbourne Football Club, an Australian rules side, seeking talented Gaelic footballers taller than 183cm (6ft). Aged eighteen, he moved to Australia where he trained intensively and adapted well. In 1985 he played for Melbourne's under-19s and finished runner-up as their 'best and fairest' player for the season. The following year Melbourne loaned him to Prahran of the Victorian Football Association (second tier), where he played twelve games as a ruckman and was named best player in the end-of-season finals. Possessing the athleticism to range all over the field and the kicking skills to score goals, Stynes would help redefine the position of ruckman, usually a big player of limited mobility whose main task was to secure possession.

He returned to Melbourne in 1987 to make his full debut, aged twenty, in the Victorian Football League (renamed the Australian Football League (AFL) in 1990), against Geelong. He played in Melbourne's 1987 pre-season premiership winning team. In round eighteen, when another player retired, Stynes replaced him and kicked four goals, his joint-highest tally for a single game. This started a streak of 244 consecutive games played (1987–98), which remains an AFL record as of 2022, accomplished while playing with injuries such as broken ribs and torn knee ligaments. In 1987 Melbourne qualified for its first final series since 1964, but a mistake by Stynes in the dying minutes against Hawthorn cost them a spot in the grand final. Although devastated, Stynes used the incident to spur himself on. He represented Australia against Ireland in the 1987 international rules series held in Croke Park, Dublin, playing in all three games, as Australia won the series 2–1.

In 1988 Melbourne reached its first grand final since 1964; Stynes was Melbourne's best player in a losing team. He also represented Victoria in state of origin football against Western Australia, the first of ten appearances at state level. The same year he earned his bachelor of education degree. In 1989 he played in Melbourne's second pre-season premiership winning team and was the team's best player in its finals campaign, which ended in a semi-final loss. The following year he became Melbourne's deputy vice-captain, featuring strongly in the finals campaign, coming third in his team's best and fairest award. In the 1990 international rules series, held in Australia, Stynes played for Ireland against Australia in all three games, helping Ireland to win the series 2–1. In 1991 he starred as Melbourne vice-captain. His all-round skills and fighting spirit caught the public imagination, and he became the first, and as of 2022 still only, non-Australian to win the game's highest individual honour, the Brownlow Medal, for player of the season. He was also named in the all-Australian team of that season and again in 1993. He retired in 1998, having played 264 matches for Melbourne, scored 130 goals, and won his team's best and fairest award four times (1991, 1995–7).

While recognised as one of the finest players ever to play in the AFL, it was his work off the field that endeared him to the Australian public. In 1994, with film director Paul

Currie, he started the not-for-profit organisation Reach For The Stars (later Reach), which ran programmes for young people between the ages of ten and eighteen to promote their mental health and wellbeing. Stynes developed the idea from memories of how outdoor activities in summer college in the Gaeltacht in Ireland had helped him as a teenager. The organisation became an enormous success, running programmes in over 500 schools and communities across Australia, and working with an estimated 500,000 young people. Stynes contributed massively to its growth, giving up to 200 motivational talks a year, and was its chief executive until 2011. He wrote two inspirational autobiographies, *Whatever it takes* (1996) and *My journey* (2012), and co-wrote two children's self-help books with Dr Jon Carnegie, *Heroes* (2003) and *Finding heroes* (2006). His empathy with young people led to his appointment as a member of the Victorian premier's youth suicide task force in 1997. Those who worked with him in sport or charity found him a committed, enthusiastic and engaging figure, with a marked ability to invigorate the people around him. Having long been concerned at the persistence of racism in sport, he was appointed anti-racism officer for the AFL (1998) and AFL racial vilification officer (1999).

After his retirement from playing, he was a selector and coach for the Australian international rules teams up to 2006. In 1998 the Jim Stynes Medal was inaugurated, awarded to the best Australian player in the international rules series. His career encouraged his two brothers to take up Australian rules: Brian Stynes played in the AFL for Melbourne in 1992, won an all-Ireland senior Gaelic football championship medal with Dublin (1995) and represented Ireland in the international rules series against Australia in 1998 and 1999. David Stynes, who also represented Dublin in Gaelic football, played Australian rules at amateur level, helping Ireland win the Australian Football International Cup in 2002 and 2011.

Jim Stynes married (2000) Samantha Ludbey; they had two children, daughter Matisse (b. 2001) and son Tiernan (b. 2005). In 2000 he was selected in the Melbourne team of the century and awarded the prestigious Australian Sports Medal by the governor general for his contribution to the nation's sporting success. That year he became Melbourne assistant coach (until 2002). Named Victorian of the year in 2001 and 2003, he was inducted into the AFL Hall of Fame (2003) and the Melbourne Football Club Hall of Fame (2006). In 2007 he was awarded the Medal of the Order of Australia for his youth work and contribution to Australian rules football. He was appointed president of Melbourne Football Club in June 2008 and launched a successful campaign to remove the club from debt.

In 2009 he was diagnosed with metastatic melanoma, which required the removal of several cancerous brain tumours the following year. The courage, humour and dignity with which he fought his illness further enhanced the esteem in which he was held, and he was named Melburnian of the year in 2010. A television documentary, *Every heart beats true: the Jim Stynes story* (2010), detailing his struggle against cancer, was directed by his friend Paul Currie. In 2011 Stynes was awarded Australian Catholic University's highest honour, doctor of the university, for service to the community in the areas of youth depression, homelessness and suicide.

Surgery (and a range of alternative therapies) failed to arrest the spread of his cancer and, as his health declined, Stynes stepped down as president of Melbourne Football

Club in February 2012. He died at his home in St Kilda, Melbourne, on 20 March 2012, aged forty-five. He was honoured by a televised state funeral at St Paul's cathedral, Melbourne, on 27 March. His ashes were scattered at Sally Gap in the Wicklow mountains, where he ran as a youth.

After his death, the Jim Stynes achievement scholarships were announced, a partnership between the Australian government, the Reach Foundation and the AFL, for children of disadvantaged backgrounds. He was posthumously awarded the presidential distinguished service award for the Irish abroad by the president of Ireland, Michael D. Higgins, in 2012. That year the AFL introduced the Jim Stynes community leadership award, presented annually to a player demonstrating Stynes's sporting and personal values. In 2014 the Jim Stynes Bridge was opened over the Yarra river in Melbourne and a statue of Stynes was unveiled on the Melbourne Cricket Ground's Avenue of Legends in the Yarra Park.

Derek Barry

Sources

Jim Stynes, *Whatever it takes* (1996); *Herald Sun* (Melbourne), 29 August 2010; 28 March 2012; 'Jim Stynes awarded University's highest honour', ACU Alumni e-News Bulletin, issue 2 (July 2011), web.archive.org/web/20120424060812/http://www.acu.edu.au/alumni/news_and_events/newsletters/2011_issues/issue_2/jim_stynes_awarded_universitys_highest_honour/; Jim Stynes, *My journey* (2012); Matt Burgan, 'The life and times of Jim Stynes' (19 March 2012), www.melbournefc.com.au/news/2012-03-20/the-life-and-times-of-jim-stynes; *The Irish Times*, 21, 24 March 2012; *Irish Echo* (Australia), 23 March 2012; *Irish Independent*, 12 September 2012 (all internet material accessed December 2021)

This entry has been abridged for publication. The full version is available at www.dib.ie.

Pat Taaffe

1930–92

JUMP JOCKEY

Pat Taaffe was born 9 March 1930 in Rathcoole, Co. Dublin, a son of Tom Taaffe, breeder and trainer of Rathcoole, and his wife Catherine (née Nugent). Sending out flat and national hunt horses from his Rathcoole stables, Tom Taaffe won an Aintree Grand National with Mr What in 1958. Pat's younger brother Thomas 'Toss' Taaffe (1933–2019) was twice Ireland's champion jump jockey (1956–7) and rode Olympia to victory in the 1960 Irish Grand National.

In the saddle from childhood, Pat accomplished his first win in 1947 on Ballincorona at the Phoenix Park racecourse, Dublin. In 1950 he contracted to ride as a professional in the Co. Dublin stables of Thomas (Tom) Dreaper, remaining until the end of his racing career in December 1970. The introspective head jockey and equable trainer were well matched; Taaffe especially valued Dreaper's tact and judgment in a business not noted for sympathetic work relations. Taaffe first came to the fore as a jockey with a slew of wins and placings on Teapot II (trained by Clem Magnier) during 1953. In July 1954 he won the Irish Grand National on Royal Approach. The following year he achieved the double, in the Irish Grand National and the Grand National at Aintree, mounted on Umm and Quare Times respectively.

The aesthetics of his efficient but gawky horsemanship attracted dubious comment. Unusually tall for a jump jockey, he had to ride short, particularly in a finishing burst, giving the impression—according to one journalist—of carrying out an indecent manoeuvre 'on a box of red hot tin tacks' (*The Times*, 8 July 1992). He excelled at the task of facing horses into the jump, taking them over the most formidable barriers without risk or fuss. His races were won less by frenzied work in the straight than by sensible tactics well before the finish, together with clean, reliable jumping. He suffered comparatively few serious falls in his career, but one at Kilbeggan in August 1956 fractured his skull, nearly killing him. Even though he resumed riding that November he suffered recurring bouts of concussion and amnesia, and his personality changed for five years.

Winning the Irish Grand National again in 1959 and 1961, he came into his prime between 1962 and 1968. This coincided with the triumphant maturity of the remarkable Irish-born and Irish-trained Arkle (1957–70). Taaffe first rode Arkle in a hurdle race at Naas in March 1962 and was the only jockey to ride him in steeplechases (races over fences). He trained Arkle in steeplechasing during the off-season in 1962–3, bringing the horse to a high pitch of confidence and skill. Together, they went on to win twenty-two out of twenty-six steeplechases from 1962 to 1966; they also won the two hurdles they contested.

While fortunate to have such an extraordinary mount, Taaffe was also one of the few riders capable of bringing out his full potential. In the clash between Arkle and Mill House at Newbury in early 1963, a skid on landing at one of the later fences cost Arkle the race, one of the rare lapses by rider or horse in either career. In their next encounter in the 1964 Cheltenham Gold Cup, Taaffe struck at the second last fence to sweep irresistibly past Mill House, winning by more than five lengths and vindicating for good the rumours of his prowess. During the next two years only the contrivances of the handicapper could put a stop to their gallop: in Ireland a dual handicap system was put into operation, one to take effect only when Arkle ran. Despite the burden of extra weights, Arkle under Taaffe almost invariably won, taking the Cheltenham Gold Cup three times in succession (1964–6), winning two Hennessy Gold Cups, and once succeeding in the King George VI Chase at Kempton Park. Taaffe also won the Irish Grand National in 1966 on Flyingbolt, also from the Dreaper stables.

After Arkle was forced into retirement by an injury sustained in December 1966, Taaffe won another Cheltenham Gold Cup (1968) with Fort Leney in a break-neck finish. In 1970, as a magnificent finale, he captured the National

Hunt Two-Mile Champions Chase at Cheltenham on Straight Fort followed by the Aintree Grand National on Gay Trip. Upon his retirement, he was by consensus the finest Irish national hunt jockey in memory. He finished with four Cheltenham Gold Cups (1964–66, 1968), two Aintree Grand Nationals (1955, 1970) and six Irish Grand Nationals (1954, 1955, 1959, 1961, 1964, 1966). He had twenty-five wins at the Cheltenham Festival, his notable victories there including five wins in the National Hunt Two-Mile Champions Chase (later the Queen Mother Champion Chase), five in the Broadway Novices' Chase, three in the Cathcart Challenge Cup (later the Ryanair Chase), two in the Gloucester Hurdle (later the Supreme Novices' Hurdle) and two in the National Hunt Handicap Chase (later the Festival Hurdle). At Leopardstown he won the Leopardstown Chase twice and the Hennessy Cup twice. He won every national hunt race of consequence and was Ireland's champion jump jockey nine times (1952–5, 1961–4, 1966; he shared the title in 1962 and in 1963).

Retiring in December 1970, he set up a training stables in Straffan, Co. Kildare, raising Captain Christy to win the Cheltenham Gold Cup (1974) and two King George VI Chases (1974–5). Pat Taffe died in Dublin on 7 July 1992, a year after a heart transplant operation. In 1955 he married Molly Lyons from Navan, Co. Meath; they had three daughters and two sons. His eldest son, Tom Taaffe (b. 1963), was a leading Irish national hunt jockey and trainer, saddling Kicking King to win a Cheltenham Gold Cup in 2005.

Des McCabe

Sources

General Register Office Dublin (birth certificate); S. J. Watson, *Between the flags: a history of Irish steeplechasing* (1969); *The game: an encyclopaedia of sport* (*c*.1972), 93–4, 741, 2727; John Welcome, *Irish horse-racing: an illustrated history* (1982); John Gleeson (ed.), *Fyffes dictionary of Irish sporting greats* (1993); *Irish Independent*, 11 November 1991; *The Times* (London), 8 July 1992; *Irish Field*, 11 July 1992; Sean Magee, *Arkle: the life and legacy of 'himself'* (2005); Anne Holland, *Arkle: the legend of 'himself'* (2013)

Fay Taylour

1904–83

MOTORCYCLIST

Fay (Frances Helen) Taylour was born 5 April 1904 at 11 Oxmanton Mall, Birr, King's County (Co. Offaly), the second of three daughters of Herbert Fetherstonhaugh Taylour, county inspector in the Royal Irish Constabulary (RIC), and his wife Helen Allardice (née Webb). In addition to her having a conventional education, first at Miss Fletcher's boarding school in Fitzwilliam Square, Dublin, and then at Alexandra College, Earlsfort Terrace, Dublin, her father also taught her to shoot, fish and ride horses. She was reportedly able to drive by the age of twelve.

Following the war of independence and the disbandment of the RIC, her father moved his family to England in 1922. After graduating from Alexandra College that year, Fay lived in Berkshire, running her parents' house, Burghfield Bridge Lodge, as her mother had been diagnosed with liver cancer. Following her mother's death 18 November 1925, she bought a motorcycle—a small, light Levis 220cc which she soon swapped for a more powerful 348cc AJS.

Throughout 1926 Taylour learned how to assemble and disassemble her bike. At a repair shop in Reading, she spoke with the owner, Carlton Harmon, who encouraged her to enter the Camberley Club's 'Southern Scott scramble' to be held in March 1927. The race, run in the morning and again in the afternoon, was a circuit of twenty-two miles and was considered one of the toughest events for rough riders. After three months practicing with Harmon, Taylour was victorious, taking not only the Novice Cup but also the women's Venus Cup.

Noticing that some of the women competitors were sponsored, she wrote to AJS Motorcycles in Coventry, and they offered to take her on. In late summer 1927 she took a job with Rudge-Whitworth, nominally as part of their secretarial backroom staff. By winter 1927 she was racing as part of their trials team, riding a Rudge 500cc. Between March 1927 and May 1928 Taylour won victories against men as well as women in different classes—grass track, cross country, hill climbs and trials—taking gold and silver at events such as the Leeds £200, the National Alan, the Travers Trophy, the Colmore Cotswold and Victory Trophy trials, and the Auto-Cycle Union (ACU) 750-mile (1,207km) six-day trial.

Taylour was earning enough prize money to make a living. Between races she kept house for her father until he remarried in 1928, freeing her from domestic duties. She was determined to compete at the highest level, but her initial approaches to speedway promoters were rejected by virtue of her gender. The ACU forbade women from competing in speedway leagues, although they could compete as individuals in non-league races. Freddie Mockford, the manager of the track at Crystal Palace, London, agreed to allow her seven days' practice with a race at the end. On 9 June 1928 Taylour took part in a speedway race, the first woman in England to do so, and although she did not win, she proved her worth. Before long she was attracting huge crowds and winning significant amounts of prize money.

Throughout 1928 and 1929 Taylour raced in Australia and New Zealand, becoming the first dirt-bike racer from Europe or the USA to compete there. She was hailed in the Australian press as 'the most daring and speedy feminine motor cyclist' (*Register news pictorial*, 23 November 1929). At her first race in Perth, she beat the home champion Sig Schlam, equalling the track record, and then travelled to Melbourne where she continued her winning streak. She gained a significant following, as much for her daredevil style as for her ability, and often competed in front of crowds of more than 30,000, the Irish flag emblazoned on a scarlet leather jacket. She excelled at self-publicity, appearing on cigarette cards and taking part in radio broadcasts whenever possible.

In 1930, when she was at the height of her success, a UK-wide ban on women riding speedway was imposed. Taylour spent the rest of the 1930 season in Europe, especially in Germany. In 1931 she switched to four wheels, taking part in the Calcutta (Kolkata) to Ranchi run.

Driving a Chevrolet, Taylour broke the record for the event by forty minutes. Later that year she competed in the ladies' handicap at Brooklands Automobile Racing Club, England, winning the race and coming second overall, reaching a speed of 98.37mph (158.31kph). In 1934 she took part in a 4,000-mile race (6,437km) around Italy against more than 220 competitors, while in August she won the first ever Leinster Trophy, held at Skerries, Co. Dublin, as the only woman driver in a field of twenty-nine. That year she set a women's track record at Crystal Palace and won the British Ladies Championship.

She competed in few races after 1934, which led to problems finding sponsorship. In the late 1930s Taylour raced more in Germany and South Africa, and she only left Hamburg for Britain on 26 August 1939, a week before the second world war broke out. This placed her under suspicion, especially because she had met with Nazi officials and had broadcast to South Africa with Radio Berlin. Upon her return, neighbours complained that she listened to English-language broadcasts from Germany and publicly argued against the war. In October she was questioned by special branch officers, who asked if she was a member of Oswald Mosley's British Union (formerly the British Union of Fascists). Taylour had never heard of the British Union but was intrigued; she read their literature and 'quite frankly [found] their views were similar to mine' (KV 2/2143). Becoming deeply involved in British Union political activities, she attended meetings, wore the British Union badge on her coat collar and distributed propaganda material. In February 1940 she returned to Ireland briefly, and an intercepted letter showed that she met with a 'Father F', almost certainly Denis Fahey, a Catholic priest and renowned anti-Semite.

On 1 June Taylour was arrested at her father's home at Lucerne Cottage, Kensington, London, and interned in nearby Holloway prison as a suspected Nazi sympathiser. In an appeal hearing held on 28 August 1940, she denied engaging in anti-British activities and holding pro-German views but was confronted with a letter she had written in which she declared, 'I love Nazi Germany and the German people and their leader' (KV 2-2144). Her appeal was rejected, and she remained in Holloway until autumn 1942 when she was transferred to Port Erin internment camp on the Isle of Man. The prison warden described her as 'one of the worst pro-Nazis … [who] is in the habit of hoarding pictures of Hitler and [has] in her possession a hymn in which his name was substituted for God's' (KV 2-2144). She was released on 5 October 1943 on condition that she reside in Dublin for the remainder of the war. In Ireland she reconnected with Denis Fahey, as well as associating with the Irish Republican Army and other anti-British elements. She remained under British intelligence surveillance until 1976.

Taylour's uncompromising Nazi sympathies and lack of remorse dogged her for the rest of her life. She attempted to revive her racing career, travelling to Los Angeles in 1949 to resume midget and stock car racing. In 1952 she was refused re-entry to the United States after returning to England for her father's funeral. For the next three years she raced in Europe and Australia while she appealed the decision. She was allowed back into the United States in 1955, but arthritis forced her to retire from racing the following year. Remaining in the US until 1971, she took a series of jobs, including 'resident advisor' at a college and salesperson for General Tires.

Her last years were spent in England, living at Dairy House in Blandford, Dorset. She died in Weymouth hospital on 2 August 1983 before she could complete her autobiography; she donated her body to medical research. Fay Taylour dominated motorcycle racing in both Europe and Australia for a period, gaining fame by competing and winning at all levels on three continents against both men and women. She is remembered, however, more for her politics.

Niav Gallagher

Sources

National Archives of Ireland, Census of Ireland, 1911; The National Archives UK KV (Records of the Security Service) 2/2143-2144; KV 2/2144 (1941–53); *The Irish Times*, 27 August, 2 September 1929; 26 May 1934; 2 September 1953; 18 April 2007; Brian Belton, *Fay Taylour: queen of speedway* (2006); Martin Pugh, *'Hurrah for the Blackshirts': fascists and fascism in Britain between the wars* (2006); Stephen M. Cullen, 'Fay Taylour: a dangerous woman in sport and politics', *Women's History Review*, vol. 21 (2012), 211–32; Stephen M. Cullen, 'Taylour, Helen Frances [Fay]', *Oxford dictionary of national biography* (2013), doi.org/10.1093/ref:odnb/97894 (accessed December 2021); Stephen M. Cullen, *Fanatical Fay Taylour; her sporting and political life at speed, 1904–1983* (2015); Pádraig Turley, 'Offaly's queen of speedway: the career of Birr's Fay Taylour', *Offaly Heritage*, vol. 10 (2018), 303–28

This entry has been abridged for publication. The full version is available at www.dib.ie.

Sim Walton

1880–1966

Sim (Simon Francis) Walton was born 4 September 1880 in Reimeen, Tullaroan, Co. Kilkenny, one of four children (three girls and one boy) of John Walton, farmer, and Johanna Walton (née Bannon) of Reimeen. His father had been a pioneer of hurling in Kilkenny in the years prior to the formation of the Gaelic Athletic Association (GAA), and the parish of Tullaroan was to the forefront of hurling activity at county level. Walton was educated at Tullaroan national school, where he also learned the rudiments of hurling. At the age of seventeen he began to play junior hurling for his club but soon progressed to the senior side. In an inter-county career that lasted from 1900 to 1919, 'Little Sim'—as he was always known to distinguish him from a cousin of the same name—won seven all-Ireland medals for Kilkenny in the 1904–13 period. It was a time that not only saw the transition from seventeen-a-side to fifteen-a-side, but also saw the rise of Kilkenny as a hurling power, challenging the supremacy of the Munster counties. Walton, along with other great Kilkenny players such as fellow Tullaroan men, Pat 'Fox' Maher and Dick Grace, and other Kilkenny legends such as Jack Rochford from Three Castles, and Richard 'Droog' Walsh and Dick Doyle from Mooncoin, finally laid the bogey of four previous all-Ireland final losses for Kilkenny teams when they beat Cork by 1–9 to 1–8 in the 1904 all-Ireland final on 24 June 1906. Walton, playing behind the full-forward that day, scored Kilkenny's third point.

As club secretary of the county champions at the time, he also had had a major part to play in the selection of the winning Kilkenny team. His decision to ensure the strongest possible selection by picking the best players from rival Kilkenny clubs was unpopular in Tullaroan but contributed to the county's first all-Ireland win. He won further all-Ireland medals for 1905, 1907, 1909, 1911, 1912 and 1913, captaining the side in the 1912 victory over Cork, the last seventeen-a-side final. He was also captain of the side in 1911, when Kilkenny was awarded the title after Limerick refused to turn up because of a dispute over the choice of venue. The six victories in contested finals consisted of four wins over Cork opposition and two over teams from Tipperary. One of the highlights of the period was Walton's regular duel with Cork full-back James Kelleher, particularly in the 1907 and 1912 finals. He could well have won an eighth winner's medal when he again captained Kilkenny in the 1916 final against Tipperary, but an argument with Jack Rochford over the team selection resulted in the latter's refusal to play. After a tremendous comeback, Kilkenny led with less than ten minutes to go, but were undone by an injury to centre-back Dick Grace. Walton said later that the continued impact of club rivalries on the selection process cost Kilkenny another two all-Irelands during 1903–13.

Walton played his last match for Kilkenny in a Leinster championship defeat to Dublin in 1919 but continued to play for Tullaroan into the early 1920s. He won nine Leinster championship medals, and many sources credit him with fourteen county championship medals, although this is difficult to verify due to the fractious nature of Kilkenny hurling at the time. At one stage, Tullaroan parish had four different teams. Walton lined out for Kilkenny for twenty seasons and played fifty-two senior hurling championship games; only Mattie Power, who played in fifty-four matches, had more championship appearances in the first half of the twentieth century, and Walton was at number six in the all-time appearance listings as late as 2006. Although Walton was of only medium stature, he was a dynamic and clever hurler, playing mainly in the full-forward or centre-forward positions. Those who saw him play, including P. D. 'Carbery' Mehigan, the legendary sports journalist who played against him in the 1905 final, regarded him as one of the greatest forwards ever to play the game (*Clash of the ash*, 192).

During the war of independence (1919–21), he was captain of the Tullaroan company of the Irish Republican Army, though in practice this seems to have mainly involved assisting and sheltering the local flying columns. A farmer, he also had a keen interest in greyhounds and coursing, and one of his dogs—called 'Captain Sim'—ran in the Waterloo Cup. Modest and pleasant by nature, Walton (like many players from his era) preferred the more direct hurling of the past to the modern game. At the time of his death, he was one of four Kilkenny players whose total of seven all-Ireland medals each was eclipsed only by Cork's Christy Ring and John Doyle of Tipperary (with eight apiece). Patrick Purcell, the Irish Press GAA correspondent for many years, described him as second only to 'Fox' Maher, as the most legendary figure in Kilkenny hurling (*Irish Press*, 30 December 1966). He died 27 December 1966 at Aut Even hospital, Kilkenny city, after a short illness. After his funeral in Tullaroan church, he was buried in the adjoining cemetery. He was unmarried.

Jim Shanahan

Sources

General Register Office Dublin (birth certificate); Raymond Smith, *Decades of glory* (1966), 56–61; *Kilkenny People*, 29 July, 6 August, 30 December 1966; *Irish Independent*, 29 December 1966; *Irish Press* 29, 30 December 1966, 4 January 1967; *Gaelic Weekly*, 7 January 1967; Raymond Smith, *The clash of the ash* (1972); James J. Comerford, *My Kilkenny IRA days* (1980); Antóin Ó Dúill (ed.), *Famous Tullaroans 1884–1984* (1984); Brendan Fullam, *Legends of the ash* (1997); *The Irish Times*, 11 August 2003; *Sunday Tribune*, 28 May 2006

Image credits

Every effort has been made to trace the copyright holders of the images reproduced and to ensure the accuracy of their captions.

Brede Arkless; photograph courtesy of John Cleare.

George Baillie; photograph courtesy of Royal Belfast Golf Club.

George Best, appearing for Northern Ireland against the Netherlands, 13 October 1976, in Rotterdam; photograph by Hans Peters, Nationaal Archief Fotocollectie Anefo, 928-8290, reproduced under Creative Commons CC0 1.0 Universal License.

Harry Bradshaw; photograph courtesy of Portmarnock Golf Club.

Mabel Cahill (left); image originally published in Valentine G. Hall (ed.), *Wright & Ditson's lawn tennis guide for 1892* (1892; Wright and Ditson, Boston), p. 173.

Johnny Carey, Manchester United, in Football League Division One match versus Arsenal, 28 August 1948; photograph by PA Images/Alamy, G9JRAP.

Steve ('Crusher') Casey, World Heavyweight wrestling champion, 29th August 1946; photograph by Walter Bellamy/Express, © Getty Images.

Jack Charlton, European Championship Finals, Stuttgart, 12 June 1988; National Photographic Archive, Independent Newspapers Archive, courtesy of the National Library of Ireland.

Nina Coote; image originally published in *The Bystander* 6 August 1906.

Clara ('Ma') Copley; image originally published in Brian Madden, *Yesterday's glovemen* (2006), p. 92, reproduced by permission of Brian Madden.

Michael Cusack; image cropped from a mounted black-and-white group photograph of members of The Trinity College rugby team *c.*1870s; courtesy of Michael Cusack Archive, NUI Galway Library Archives.

Beauchamp Day; photograph originally published in William Dooley, *Champions of the athletic arena* (1946; General Publicity Service, Dublin), p. 80–1.

Jack Dempsey, 2 November 1895; image in public domain, reproduced under Creative Commons CC0 License.

Dan Donnelly; image from Pierce Egan, *Boxiana* (1829 edn; George Virtue, London), p. 70, courtesy of the National Library of Ireland.

Jack Doyle, *c.*1936; image in private ownership; reproduced by permission.

John Doyle, photographed between two Kilkenny defenders at the All-Ireland final, Croke Park, 3 September 1967. Image courtesy of the GAA Museum and Archive at Croke Park, Dublin.

Henry Dunlop; photograph courtesy of Lansdowne FC, Dublin.

Joey Dunlop; photograph by the late Brian Foley, reproduced courtesy of Harry Havelin.

Shay Elliott, on the left, World Cycling Championships in Ronse, 11 August 1963; image via Dutch National Archives, in public domain.

Dick Fitzgerald, demonstrating how to pass the football; image originally published in Dick Fitzgerald, *How to play Gaelic football* (1914; Guy Publishers, Cork).

Dave Gallaher; image from D. Gallaher and W. J. Stead, *The complete rugby footballer* (1906; Methuen, London).

Philomena Garvey; photograph courtesy of County Louth (formerly Baltray) Golf Club.

Mollie Gill, with Camogie Cup; image from Loretta Clarke Murray Collection (MS2016.016, Box 16, Folder 7), reproduced courtesy of John J. Burns Library, Boston College.

Ken Goodall, Five Nations Championship, England v Ireland, at Twickenham, 10 February 1968; photograph by PA Images/Alamy, G90CMC.

Vere Goold, 1884; image © All England Lawn Tennis Club, reproduced by permission.

Lady Mary Heath, Croydon Airport, London, 17 May 1928; image courtesy of Ashfield Press.

Kevin Heffernan, 18 September 1983, All-Ireland Senior Football Final, Dublin v Galway, Croke Park; photograph by Ray McManus/Sportsfile, 1552730.

May Hezlet, playing in the Ladies' Championship at Royal County Down, 1899; photograph courtesy of the Women's Golfers' Museum.

Alex ('Hurricane') Higgins, 23 March 1988, playing against Dennis Taylor in the Benson and Hedges Irish Masters Snooker Tournament; National Photographic Archive, Independent Newspapers Collection, courtesy of the National Library of Ireland.

Tom Horan, back row second from left, photographed as a member of the 1878 Australian cricket squad; photograph courtesy of Alamy, 2DGAMMW.

Moss Keane, photograph courtesy of Lansdowne FC, Dublin.

Iris Kellett and **Rusty**, competing at Blackpool, England, 1947; photograph courtesy of RDS Library and Archives.

Jack Kyle, photographed as a member of the Lions representative rugby union team, 1950; photograph from Crown Studies Ltd Negatives and Prints Collection, 1/2-190791-F, Alexander Turnbull Library, Wellington, New Zealand, reproduced courtesy of National Library of New Zealand.

John Fortune Lawrence, *c.*1865; image from Kieran Hickey (ed.), *The light of other days—Irish life at the turn of the century in the photographs of Robert French* (1973; Allen Lane, London), reproduced with permission.

Elizabeth Le Blond; image originally published in Mrs Aubrey Le Blond, *True tales of mountain adventure for non-climbers young and old* (1903, New York).

Beatrice Hill-Lowe competing at the 1908 Olympics; image in public domain.

Bill McCracken, *c.*1912; photograph in private ownership, reproduced with permission.

Mike McTigue; image courtesy of the H. J. Lutcher Stark Center for Physical Culture and Sports; reproduced with permission.

Kay Mills, holding the 1961 All-Ireland Senior Camogie Final trophy; photograph courtesy of the GAA Museum and Archive at Croke Park.

Tony Mullane, Cincinnati Red Stockings, baseball card portrait, *c.*1887–90; Library of Congress Prints and Photographs Collection, LOT 13163-05, no. 340, LC-DIG-bbc-0412f.

Terry Mullen, with the gold medal she won at the Seoul Paralympic Games in October 1988; photograph courtesy of the Mullen Family, reproduced with permission.

Anne O'Brien, playing for Stade de Reims in the French Championship of Women's Football final versus Arago Orléans, at stadium Auguste-Delaune in Reims on 31 May 1975; photograph by AFP, AFP_1CN0JV; © Getty Images.

Vincent O'Brien, 24 October 1959; photograph by PA Images/ Alamy, GBNTA5.

Pat O'Callaghan; photograph courtesy of the *Irish Examiner*, reproduced with permission.

Nannie Power O'Donoghue; photograph originally published in Mrs Power O'Donoghue, *Riding for ladies: the common sense of riding* (1887; Roberts Brothers, Boston).

Kevin O'Flanagan, in his Bohemian FC kit *c.*1944; photograph courtesy of Bohemians FC, Dublin.

Joan O'Reily, on 1950 tour of South Africa; photograph reproduced courtesy of Irish Hockey Archive and Dublin City Library and Archive.

Paddy Perry, pictured in the late 1930s; photograph reproduced courtesy of Tony Conboy.

Sean Purcell, in action for the Universities against Dublin; photograph courtesy of the GAA Museum and Archive at Croke Park.

Nicky Rackard, *c.*1955–56; photograph courtesy of the GAA Museum and Archive at Croke Park.

Christy Ring, holding aloft the Liam MacCarthy Cup in 1946; photograph courtesy of the GAA Museum and Archive at Croke Park.

John Ryan, approaching the meet at Mooresfort Gates, *c.*1928; photograph courtesy of Scarteen Hunt.

Elisha Scott, *c.*1922; image in private ownership; reproduced by permission.

Molly Seaton, from 1930s team photograph; reproduced courtesy of Valeria Beattie.

Martin Sheridan at the 1904 Olympic Games; photograph from the Missouri Historical Society Photographs and Prints Collections, N15578.

Jim Smith, leading the Cavan team out before the 1933 All Ireland Football final; photograph originally published in Gearóid Mac Gabhann, *Big Jim Smith: man of Breifne* (2012; Gearóid Mac Gabhann), reproduced courtesy of Gearóid Mac Gabhann.

Jim Stynes, playing for Melbourne, 16 June 1997, v Brisbane; photograph by George Salpigtidis, published in *Daily Herald Sun*, second edition, 2 July 2009, p. 7, courtesy of Newspix, Australia, NPX1160506.

Pat Taaffe on **Arkle**, 10 March 1962, winning the Rathconnell Handicap Hurdle, Naas, Co. Kildare; National Photographic Archive, Independent Newspapers Collection, IND7683, courtesy of the National Library of Ireland.

Fay Taylour on a Douglas motorcycle, Kilbirnie Speedway, Wellington, 1929; photograph from the Photographic negatives and prints collection of the *Evening Post* newspaper, 1/4-032445-G. Alexander Turnbull Library, Wellington, New Zealand, reproduced courtesy of National Library of New Zealand.

Sim Walton, photographed as a member of the 1911–12 All-Ireland Hurling Championship winning team; image courtesy of the GAA Museum and Archive at Croke Park.

Acknowledgements

The editors would like to express their gratitude to Professor Paul Rouse, School of History, UCD, for his help in selecting the sporting lives featured and for writing the introduction to this volume along with the entry on Jack Charlton. Dr William Murphy, School of History and Geography, DCU, gave sage advice during the initial development of the project and wrote our entry on Mollie Gill. Both original contributors to the *Dictionary of Irish Biography* (*DIB*), Professor Rouse and Dr Murphy were generous with their time and gave valuable support and encouragement for the production of this volume.

Dr James Quinn, managing editor of the *DIB*, tasked the editors with selecting sporting lives from the corpus, and remained hugely supportive of our endeavours; so too was the *DIB* interim managing editor (2019–2021), Dr Kate O'Malley.

Many contributors to this volume were incredibly obliging in revising their entries, including Harry Havelin, Bridget Hourican, Jim Shanahan and our former DIB colleagues Linde Lunney and Lawrence William White. Special thanks to Steve Bolton, Helena Byrne, William Murphy, Carol A. Osborne, Paul Rouse and Miles Templeton, who were commissioned to write new entries specifically for this volume. For all their efforts we are very grateful. Thanks are due also to contributors Helen Andrews, Derek Barry, Marie Coleman, Mark Duncan, Niav Gallagher, Patrick Geoghegan, Tom Higgins, Des McCabe, P. Gerry McKenna, Mary Moran, John A. Murphy, Liam O'Callaghan, James Quinn and John Rouse.

It has been a pleasure to work with the RIA Publications Office, whose managing editor Ruth Hegarty provided support and encouragement, and whose senior editor Helena King remains a rare breed in publishing—rigorous *and* compassionate. The designer, Fidelma Slattery, has ensured the elegant visual presentation of this volume. Thanks too to the Royal Irish Academy Library staff for help with access to research material during the COVID-19 closures, and in particular to Dave McKeown for assistance with imagery.

We wish to express our thanks to all those—far too numerous to mention—who assisted in our quest for portraits and images of the sixty lives collected here. We think they add significantly to the volume. The editors are truly grateful for the incredible assistance we received from archivists, club officials, family members, local historians, librarians, researchers and various institutions around the globe.

In collecting lives from the *DIB*—and indeed identifying new lives for addition to the corpus—this volume rests on the foundational work of James McGuire and James Quinn. We drew inspiration from their endeavours in bringing the *DIB* to publication in 2009. Finally, we would like to express our appreciation for the support provided by Professor Patrick Geoghegan, School of History and Humanities, TCD, chair of the DIB advisory board, and the former Executive Director of the RIA, Dr Tony Gaynor.

Terry would like to thank Michael, Pauline, Paul and David.

Turlough would like to thank Anne, Derry and Dorry, and most of all, Joanne and Eve.

TERRY CLAVIN AND TURLOUGH O'RIORDAN

Index